THE CONTEMPORARY DISCUSSION SERIES

THE MANY FACES OF RELIGION AND SOCIETY

The Many Faces of Religion and Society

EDITED BY
M. DARROL BRYANT
AND RITA H. MATARAGNON

A NEW ERA BOOK

PARAGON HOUSE PUBLISHERS
NEW YORK

Published in the United States by
Paragon House Publishers
2 Hammarskjold Plaza
New York, NY 10017

A New Ecumenical Research
  Association Book

"Civic Altruism and the Resacralization of
  the Political Order" by Richard L. Rubenstein
    © Richard L. Rubenstein, 1985

Library of Congress Cataloging in Publication Data
Main entry under title:

The Many faces of religion and society.

  (God, The Contemporary Discussion Series)
  includes index.
    1. Religion and sociology—Addresses, essays,
lectures. I. Bryant, M. Darrol. II. Mataragnon,
Rita H., 1947–   . III. Series.
BL60.M32   1984   291.1′71   84-26539
ISBN 0-913757-20-9 (hardbound)
ISBN 0-913757-21-7 (softbound)

Contents

INTRODUCTION

M. DARROL BRYANT
AND RITA H. MATARAGNON

The essays in this volume contribute to the growing discussion of the multiform relationships of religious faiths, institutions, ideas, and traditions to social life. When these topics are approached globally, it is not possible to speak in the singular about the relationship between religion and society. Rather, as these essays make clear, the relationships between religions and different societies are understood in different ways in different religions and different societies. This fact considerably complicates the task of the editors in writing an introduction to this volume, but it should also alert us to a very important feature of our current situation. At precisely the moment that we are recognizing the presence of different religions and societies on our planet we are also becoming more aware of our mutual interdependence and the fact that we increasingly share a common planetary future. Thus, the universal and the particular now come into a new configuration. This new configuration will be evident to the discriminating reader of these essays.

   Although the essays in this volume range widely—from philosophical analyses of modern Western culture to Buddhist social philosphy—it is possible to set them against a common backdrop. They can all be seen in relation to a pervasive global situation. We are currently in the midst of a deep, widespread, and perhaps epochal transition. The scope of this transition is not limited to a few nations, it is global. In varying ways and to varying degrees, it touches all peoples, religions, societies, and cultures. Many believe it is a period of epochal transition. Located, as we are, within this period of transition, it is not yet possible to discern fully its shape, nor to fully know its consequences. But we are all aware—regardless of our judgments of the significance of this transition—that long-standing relationships between religion and society are undergoing enormous change. These essays reflect, in various ways, the impact of this time of transition.

This situation has given rise to a growing concern in the general public and renewed interest in scholarly circles to explore anew the theme of religion and society. Despite the often repeated assertion that religion would "wither away" in an increasingly technological civilization, religions persist and even reassert their presence—often in disconcerting ways. Why is this the case? What roles do different religions play in their respective social settings? Do all religions understand their social significance in the same way? Are there crucial contributions that religion can make to processes of social change? Can religiously inspired viewpoints help us to understand social dynamics and processes? These questions are explored in the essays in this volume and, we believe, some light is shed on them.

A distinctive feature of this collection is that the authors are not drawn from a single discipline, nor from a single philosophical perspective, nor even from a single continent. This may prove disconcerting, but it should be instructive. Although disciplinary, religious, philosophical, or geographical commonality might add a certain uniformity to the volume, it could also distort the reality of our global situation. Instead, the reader is invited to enter into different standpoints and to see particular issues from those positions. As difficult as this may seem, it should also enlarge our horizon for understanding the meaning and significance of this period of transition. This is precisely the experience of those who participated in the second New Ecumenical Research Association (New ERA) Conference on "God: The Contemporary Discussion," at which these papers were initially presented in a section that dealt with religion and society.

As scholars rooted in Buddhist, Christian, Hindu, and Jewish traditions and working out of social scientific, historical, philosophical, religious, and theological disciplines, the writers of these essays have selected their own focuses within this larger theme. The result we have before us is a number of different studies, all of which seek to illuminate particular issues, questions, or cases relevant to our time of transition. In this volume we have organized the essays around four themes that emerged from the essays themselves: religion and modernity: the social dimensions of religious traditions; religion and society; issues and cases; and religion and society: some future directions. Let us now briefly review the essays in each section, so the reader may have an initial orientation to what lies ahead.

In Part I, "Religion and Modernity," we have included the essays by Richard Rubenstein, a Jewish theologian and cultural analyst from the United States; Rita H. Mataragnon, a social psychologist from the Philippines; and Padmasiri de Silva, a Buddhist philosopher from Sri Lanka. These essays deal with distinct but interrelated aspects of the theme of religion and modernity. Professor Rubenstein offers a striking analysis of the impact of modernization on Western civilization and calls for the resacralization of the political order. Rubenstein thus dissents from secularization theorists in pointing to the necessity for societies, even modern and technological societies, to ground themselves in the sacred dimensions of life. Professor Mataragnon asks whether religion and modernization must move in opposite directions as some social scientists claim. She then examines the social scientific literature on this question to see if it has uncovered any significant correlations. Contrary to widespread belief that there is an obvious and significant correlation, she finds that the issue is still unresolved, that no significant correlations have been established. Professor de Silva examines Freudian psychotherapy—often a modern substitute for classic religious care of the soul—from a Buddhist perspective. Although he respects the contributions of Freud, de Silva raises crucial questions about the adequacy of the Freudian tradition to address the profound spiritual dimensions of the self's quest for enlightenment that are often latent in psychological disorders. De Silva suggests that this modern therapy might profit from an encounter with Buddhist analyses of the self.

In Part II, "Social Dimensions of Religious Traditions," we have included four essays that deal with three different religious traditions: Judaism, Buddhism, and Eastern Orthodox Christianity. Professor Manfred Vogel, a Jewish historian of religions, offers a phenomenological explication of the social dimension of faith in Judaism. His perhaps surprising conclusion is that a sovereign national state is necessary to the full realization of Judaism in its classic form. Only in this way, Vogel argues, can the horizontal or social dimensions of Judaism be realized. This view in Judaism stands in marked contrast with Gesche Tsepal's presentation of the meaning of liberation in Buddhism. A Tibetan Buddhist, Tsepal argues that in a Buddhist perspective suffering and social malaise are only overcome through an inward, spiritual liberation. Suffering arises not because of structural features of society, but because of an inward disorder that is overcome through religious discipline. Another angle of vision on Buddhism is provided in the essay by Professor Siddhi Butr-Indr. A philosopher and head of the Department of Human Relations at Chiang Mai in Thailand, Butr-Indr presents the humanitarian virtues of Buddhism that could, in his view, support universal brotherhood. And finally, in this section we have an essay by Dr. Constantine Tsirpanlis, a Greek Orthodox historian and theologian, which offers an exposition of the social and political dimensions of Orthodoxy. This strand of Christianity, argues Tsirpanlis, did not develop in a way that leads to the separation of church and state as a desirable goal. Instead, the thrust in Orthodoxy has been to attempt to suffuse the social and political orders with the power of transcendent love. Each of these essays, then, attempts to present the social dimension of a particular religious faith.

In Part III, "Religion and Society: Issues and Cases," the focus shifts to four studies that examine particular issues or cases that cast light on the relationship of religion and society in different cultural contexts. Professor Olusola Olukunle, a Nigerian professor of religious studies, examines the social uses and abuses of religion in developing, especially African, societies. The result is a sharp critique of the way in which religion has often served colonial and imperial interests rather than its own proper purposes. A parallel theme is explored in the essay by John St. John, but here in relation to English Christianity and society. Mr. St. John reviews the history of the relationship of faith to social issues in the English context and then calls for a new synthesis of political and religious consciousness to address the current social crisis. Dr. Gustavo Benavides, a Latin American student of religion who teaches in the United States, offers an important critical analysis of Latin American liberation theology. He views liberation theology as an attempt to deal with emerging sociopolitical realities in Latin American societies, but raises important questions about the adequacy of such responses. And in the final essay in this section, Professor Ninian Smart, a Scottish historian of religions who divides his time between the University of Lancaster and the University of California at Santa Barbara, examines the notion of liberation within Eastern and Western traditions. Professor Smart finds in these types of religious liberation an implicit critique of modern politics, which would have us believe that the whole of human destiny is linked to the life of modern national states. The religious types of liberation see the issue in broader terms. In these essays, then, we glimpse something of the complexity and variety that confronts us when we examine the relationships between religion and society.

In Part IV, "Religion and Society: Some Future Directions," we have included the essays by Helmut Fritzsche, a Lutheran theologian from East Germany; T. K. Oommen, a social scientist from Jawaharlal Nehru University in New Dehli; and M. Darrol Bryant, a Christian theologian teaching in Canada. Each of these essays proposes some new directions either for relating to developments within contemporary society (Fritzsche) or for understanding the relationships of religion to society (Oommen and Bryant). Professor Fritzsche argues that the modern focus on freedom as central to the social project has roots within the Judeo-Christian tradition. Nonetheless, modern societies turn in an increasingly secular direction. Christians, Fritzsche argues, should respect this turn even though they have a more complex notion of freedom than that current in secular societies. Speaking then from the context of a socialist society, he argues that Christian freedom embodies itself in *service* as the form freedom takes in our time. Another direction is proposed by T. K. Oommen, who calls for a new understanding of the divine, the human, and nature, in their mutual relationships. This, he argues, is necessary if we are to move beyond the antagonisms that too often characterize our present situation. For Oommen, the traditions of Hinduism offer important correctives to the overly dualistic tendencies of Western religions in relation to their social context. And finally, M. Darrol Bryant, a student of religion and culture, explores the thought of the little-known Christian social thinker Eugen Rosenstock-Huessy. Bryant finds that in Rosenstock-Huessy we have the beginnings of a fresh approach to discerning the life of the spirit in society. These more exploratory essays conclude the volume.

In these fourteen essays, then, many different aspects of the relationship between religion and society are explored. Using the insights of their particular disciplines and traditions, and acknowledging their distinctive commitments, each of the authors addresses the common issue of the place and role of religion in social life. Yet the content of each study is diverse since all writers deal with religions or societies they know best. Given all of these divergences, it is significant that a careful reading of this collection also reveals some point of convergence. All of the writers, with one exception, are agreed in their rejection of reductionism in their approaches to the study of religion and society. Religion, whatever its form, cannot be reduced to a function of some other sphere of culture. Reductionism has been a constant temptation in studies of the relationships between religion and society, but that temptation is resisted in these essays. In the most characteristic forms of reductionism, religion has been reduced to mere ideology or to a superstructure of underlying economic processes. But the writers, with one exception, though they come from differing religious traditions and disciplines, respect the integrity of religion as such. Religion is therefore regarded as having an integrity of its own whether that religion be Buddhism, Christianity, Hinduism, or Judaism. This respect for the integrity of religion is apparent even though most of the authors are sensitive to the impact of the social context on religious beliefs, practices, and institutions.

A second point of convergence shared by most of the writers in this volume is that religion will continue to play a vital role in the social life of humankind. This point too is often missing in contemporary literature, despite the abundant evidence provided by history and the sociology of religion for the continuing, albeit changing, role of religion in age after age. Although several of the writers call for new syntheses in religion, or for new directions, or for recoveries, they nonetheless acknowledge the crucial role that religion plays in social life. Thus, even though the fortunes of a particular religion in a particular place may wane, such fluctuations should not blind us to the spiritual and social vitality that is present within the religious traditions when we consider the matter from a global point of view. In saying this we are not affirming that every outburst of spiritual vitality and renewal is necessarily desirable, but simply that when we judge the state of religion it is best to consider the matter from a global perspective.

But when we explore the relationships of religion and society in a global perspective, we are not, as these essays make clear, in a territory that allows for easy generalizations. Instead, we find ourselves participating in the beginnings of a global conversation that requires us to acknowledge the partiality of our own views and the different assumptions and vantage points that others bring to the conversation. The differences between religions are real and have impressed themselves on the societies in which they have been significant; likewise, the differences between societies are significant and have made their impact upon the religions of the world. This multiform relationship between religion and society must, then, be respected if we are to deepen our understanding of the realities of our global situation. These essays will serve to instruct us in some of the currents and countercurrents that shape the impact that religious beliefs and practices have made—and continue to make— upon the world. They should also serve to instruct us in the requisite humility and sensitivity to multiformity that will be increasingly required of us all as we search for ways of living together on our common planet.

Part One
RELIGION AND MODERNITY

1

Civic Altruism and the Resacralization of the Political Order

RICHARD L. RUBENSTEIN

One of the most fundamental and intellectually fruitful distinctions made by Hegel in his political philosophy is that of state and society. Although Hegel's frequently misunderstood and misinterpreted doctrine of the state is exceedingly complex, for our purposes it is sufficient to note that his model for the state was the ancient polis. Hegel was under no illusion that the polis could be reconstituted in modern times, but there are certain characteristics of a state that are perennially indispensable to the maintenance of a genuine community, one of the most important being civic altruism. It was Hegel's opinion that, like the ancient polis, the ethical basis of a true state is solidarity rather than the quest for individual self-aggrandizement. Without the willingness of citizens to risk and sometimes give their lives for the security of the community, perhaps the most imporant act of civic altruism, no state could long endure. Hegel thus rejected the bourgeois conception of the state as the institution whose purpose is to render secure its citizens' pursuit of their individual self-interest. If any modern political institution can truly be regarded as a state as understood by Hegel, it would be characterized by universal altruism.[1]

According to Hegel, with the advent of the modern period, the public sphere began to differentiate itself into a class concerned with the management of public affairs and a class concerned "exclusively with their own affairs."[2] This class was the bourgeoisie, and it constituted the social basis of civil society, whose operative values Hegel saw as in profound tension with those of the state. Hegel acknowledged the extraordinary achievements and power of bourgeois society: "Civil society is the tremendous power which draws men into itself and claims from them that they work for it, owe everything to it, and do everything by its means."[3] Nevertheless, Hegel was under no illusions concerning the destructive egoism and individualism upon which civil society was ultimately based. As citizens of the state, men relate to each other altruistically. As members of civil society, their relationships are, according to Hegel, motivated by universal egoism. Members of civil society have little choice but to treat their peers as a means to their own personal self-aggrandizement: ". . . individuals in their capacity as burghers in this state are private persons whose end is their own interest."[4] Put differently, in bourgeois civil society the private interests of the individual (or individual corporation) take precedence over the well-being of the commonwealth. Community threatens to explode as society comes to consist of a congery of self-regarding atoms whose interest in others is purely instrumental. There is absolutely nothing like the Confucian conception of the union of ethics and politics in bourgeois individualism.

Nevertheless, in spite of the tension between state and society, it was Hegel's conviction that the individualism of bourgeois society could be reconciled with the altruism of the political order, that the rights of man could be reconciled with the duties of the citizen. Unfortunately, at least in the West this conviction does not seem to have been validated by experience. To this day, the contradictory claims of state and society continue to beset modern men and women. Insofar as private individuals accord primacy to maximizing their personal interests, there appears to be little room for altruistic concern or involvement in the well-being of others, especially where large resources are at risk. On the contrary, socially irresponsible business behavior such as the following appears to be characteristic: dumping poisonous wastes as cheaply as possible with no concern for the health of the adjacent population; shutting down large-scale manufacturing operations, even when they are profitable, because they fail to yield a rate of return on investment deemed satisfactory;[5] and the manufacture of automobiles with fuel tanks known to be unsafe and possibly lethal because the estimated cost of legal judgments holding the company responsible for loss of life is calculated to be less than the cost of changing the fuel tank design.[6] These examples are meant to be illustrative rather than inclusive. Unfortunately, in the domain of business and commerce, cost-effectiveness rather than concern for the well-being of the community is normally the overriding imperative.

Because economic egoism in both its individual and corporate manifestations seems to be ultimately destructive of genuine community, one would imagine that it would be rejected by society out of hand. This was certainly the case before the beginning of the modern period. In our times. however, such individualism has, more often than not, been interpreted by social theorists as in the long-range public interest. Sometimes the legitimation of individualism has been combined with faith in the benevolent effects of the self-regulating market economy, as in the thought of Adam Smith. In other legitimations civilization has been regarded as an evolutionary development whose viability depends on the ability of strong and gifted individuals to meet the test of survival in a mercilessly competitive struggle. I refer, of course, to Social Darwinism with its doctrine that survival of the fittest is nature's means of furthering the evolution of the species both within society and in the larger biological context.[7] Social Darwinism rejects altruism and elevates egoism to the status of a biological and social imperative. Given the perspective of Social Darwinism, those who fall by the wayside deserve their fate because they have failed nature's test. Social Darwinism naturalizes human society and uses the animal kingdom as the interpretative model for understanding human economic and social relationships, a view rejected by classic political theorists. Put differently, legitimation of self-aggrandizing individualism has been made possible by the naturalization and the radical desacralization of political values and institutions.

In no nation of the Western world has the elite of the business community consistently maintained a more important position in the leadership of public affairs than in the United States. This is undoubtedly partly due to the fact that even in the colonial period American civilization was fundamentally postfeudal. By the time of the founding of the Massachusetts Bay Colony, England was well on its way to becoming a predominantly bourgeois-capitalist society. Moreover, even in the seventeenth century, the ability to emigrate normally presupposed a degree of mobility available only to those who were emancipated from feudal obligations. Thus, the earliest emigrants to English North America were predominantly men and women whose livelihoods were dependent upon a market economy rather than the old subsistence economy of agrarian feudalism. This arrangement was obviously conducive to business leadership of the larger community.

Another factor making for the predominance of business leadership in America was the country's distinctive religious inheritance. Although the United States has been overwhelmingly Protestant since its inception, there was from the outset a profound difference between Protestantism in Europe and in the United States. In

Europe most people were members of the established church. In America the vast majority were dissenters, in spite of the establishment of the Anglican church in Virginia and the Congregational church in New England. The Congregational church was a dissenting church, as were the Presbyterians, Baptists, and Quakers. These four were the dominant American religious groups until the Revolutionary War.

In Europe it was generally assumed that every member of the community was automatically a member of the established church. In rural England, the parish was responsible for the rendering of assistance in times of distress. Those who were not members of the established church had no right to turn to the parish for sustenance when other means failed. In America the parish system did not last. Only Virginia and New England had it to begin with. What sociologists call "church-type religion" was not the predominant way religion was to develop in English-speaking North America. The early Puritan settlers regarded the church as the covenanted community of the select and the elect. The church in North America was inherently a church of outsiders who stood apart from the established church, and hence to a large extent from the established political order as well, except in New England.

As historian Oscar Handlin has observed, the dissenter had to rationalize his separateness.[8] In general he did this by emphasizing the elect character of his group and the decisive role it was destined to play in God's plan for the salvation of mankind. In addition to the element of dissent and the conviction of election, the hazardous ocean journey could be interpreted as a kind of baptismal experience in which the old European man was reborn as the new American Adam in the virginal and paradisiacal wilderness.

The dissenters' social location also tended to differ from that of the majority of their original compatriots. The emigrants tended to be townspeople, burghers, rather than peasants.[9] They were therefore predisposed to a certain element of rationality and system in the conduct of their affairs. As masterless men, they could not rely on a human external authority to impose order on their lives. Order was either self-imposed or disorder would rule, with predictable economic and social consequences.[10] The tendency toward rationality was also fostered by the fact that the townspeople were dependent upon a money economy long before the peasantry. Not surprisingly, the dissenters tended to value literacy far more than did the churches of the peasants and feudal lords.

Among the important consequences of the predominance of dissent in America was the fact that the laity achieved an importance in religious affairs in the New World that it did not have in the old. Convinced of their election, the dissenters stood in awe of no man-made office, whether it was that of the altar or the throne. God's elect were humanity's true aristocrats.

In the New World, the experience of election gave the businessman a sense of authority and dignity he had possessed in few other societies. In cultures as widely separated as ancient Greece, medieval Europe, and premodern Japan, there was a profound distrust of those engaged in commerce. Unlike the warrior, who was prepared to risk his life for the sake of his community, the merchant was distrusted because of his seemingly asocial pursuit of gain. The modern elevation of the businessman to primacy of status constitutes an extraordinary transvaluation of values. Nevertheless, it could not have occurred until the businessman's sense of his own status was radically transformed. No one is accorded high dignity who does not first perceive himself as worthy.

The Calvinist belief that prosperity in the pursuit of one's calling constituted a credible certification of election contributed decisively to the unprecedented sense of authority and dignity of the successful businessman. It must be remembered that before the bourgeois-capitalist era mere possession of wealth was normally insufficient to confer a sense of preeminent dignity and status on an individual. Since the dignity of other status groups, such as the clergy and nobility, had been religiously legitimated in premodern Europe, an effective claim to high status on the part of the commercial class had to be religiously legitimated as well. This was accomplished by the Calvinist doctrine of vocation and the experience of election. As Max Weber has pointed out, the Calvinist doctrine of double predestination left the individual bereft of a mediating institution capable of offering him credible assurance of election and salvation.[11] Because of the intolerable existential uncertainty this situation engendered, believers came to look for hints of election in the way an all-powerful, supramundane deity had guided them in the pursuit of their calling. Vocational success came to be the most credible sign that one had been elected to salvation. Within Calvinism the successful businessman came to enjoy a sense of divinely ordained status that gave him an authority and dignity in his own eyes the commercial classes had never before known. At the same time, the doctrine of double predestination carried with it a baleful evaluation

7

of those who failed to prosper. Lack of prosperity was as credible a sign of eternal rejection by God as prosperity pointed to election. The successful businessman was assured of the primacy of his status and the dignity of his vocation; he was further assured that the indigent had been accounted worthless by the just and all-powerful deity. The new ethic was thus accompanied by a new harshness in the way the poor were regarded, a phenomenon amply documented by other scholars.[12]

A far-reaching consequence of the rise of lay authority within the church was the unprecedented elevation of the authority of a class that had never before enjoyed a comparable dignity. As the political order was desacralized and the connection between religion and public life severed, the bonds of community between persons tended to weaken. As religion became privatized, those who were convinced that they alone were elect citizens of the heavenly commonwealth, the only true commonwealth, saw little reason to create a genuinely altruistic commonwealth in the here and now. In the United States, the attenuation of communal bonds was aggravated by a lack of ethnic homogeneity in the general population.

As noted, a particularly striking example of the destruction of the bonds of community can be seen in the tendency of American-controlled multinational corporations to transfer operations to countries in which labor and other costs are significantly lower than in the United States with no concern for the unemployment such transfers cause at home. Until recently, corporations transferred manufacturing operations but left their office staffs intact. Currently, satellite technology makes it possible to transfer data- and word-processing operations from American urban centers, where office labor is relatively expensive, to the island nations of the Caribbean, where English-speaking office workers command far lower wages. The examples could continue, but the point is obvious. There are business enterprises prepared to accept the destruction of the economic base of whole communities in their native land if their operations can be rendered more profitable by moving elsewhere. This phenomenon has been worsened by the consolidation of large-scale enterprise. Corporate decisions concerning the closing or relocation of plants are made in distant offices by executives with no involvement in the life of the affected communities.[13]

The ascription of primacy to economic values is dangerous to a community in any age. In the age of the microprocessor revolution, it could prove to be an unprecedented disaster. According to a recent in-depth study in *Business Week* magazine, within the next two decades approximately 45 percent of all jobs in the United States, approximately forty-five million in number, will be displaced because of computerized automation.[14] A very significant number of those rendered workless in the current recession will never return to the jobs they lost. When one considers the worldwide implications of the microprocessor revolution; the demographic and social problems confronting the rapidly increasing populations of the developing nations; the rise of the nations of East Asia as successful industrial, technological, and economic competitors of the West, it becomes apparent that the unemployment crisis besetting the United States and other industrial nations is not merely a consequence of the current business downturn and will not be resolved by what will be characterized as an "economic recovery." On the contrary, each "recovery" since the 1960s has left the United States with a new definition of what constitutes an acceptable level of "normal unemployment."[15] Moreover, as "normal unemployment" continues to rise in the United States, millions of desperate Hispanics seek to enter the American labor market because of the even worse conditions facing them at home.

We could elaborate further on the nature of the economic and social problems confronting the United States and the Western world, but such elaboration is not necessary for our purposes. If this analysis has merit, it would appear that Hegel's distinction between the state and civil society as the respective domains of universal altruism and universal egoism has special relevance for our time, in spite of Hegel's misplaced optimism concerning the degree to which the realms could be reconciled. Unfortunately, if the realms cannot be reconciled, sooner or later we shall be confronted with large-scale social catastrophe. There are, for example, basically only two ways of solving the problem of unemployment: a jobs program in which the federal government becomes the guarantor of full employment, employing all whom private industry is unable to employ; and elimination of the unemployed by radical means. Indeed, one wonders whether there is any connection between the fact that unemployment has risen to its highest levels since the Great Depression and that responsible government officials are for the first time stating that the United States must be prepared to win a "protracted" nuclear war in which twenty million deaths would be considered a sustainable casualty rate.

Assuredly, there must be a better way to solve the growing

problem of unemployment than getting rid of the unemployed. We must, however, recognize how difficult it will be to implement any other solution. A government sponsored jobs program would have a profound effect on society. In all likelihood it would involve redistribution of the total national workload and possibly re-distribution of resources as well. Such redistributive efforts have never been welcomed before and it is not likely that they will find easy acceptance even if the unemployment crisis becomes far worse than it is today.

Insofar as the United States retains a predominant bourgeois ideology, which accords primacy to economic over political values, redistribution will be resisted. As we have seen, the primacy of economic values has been religiously legitimated within American culture. Those who, at any level, regard their prosperity as certify-ing divine election are not likely to consent to share part of what they have for the poor, whom they believe God has in any event rejected.

The viability of a program involving redistribution is further weakened by the fact that most Americans do not see the political order as an end in itself, as did Aristotle, but as a means to private felicity. Most Americans would agree with John Locke: "The great and chief end of men uniting into commonwealths and putting themselves under government is the preservation of their prop-erty."[16] Locke's instrumental view of government accords with the Judeo-Christian view that the political order is justified only if it serves an end beyond itself. Although we cannot go into detail, there would appear to be a significant connection between the subordination of the political order to a divine plan in biblical religion and its subordination to the economic order in Locke and in bourgeois ideology. By contrast, the instrumental view of the polit-ical order does not accord with Aristotle's view: ". . . as all associa-tions aim at some good, that one which is supreme will aim at the supreme good. That is the association which we call the Polis, and that type of association we call political."[17] Unlike Locke and Hobbes, Aristotle did not see the political order as an instrument of a higher good. It aims at the supreme good. Similarly, Hegel saw the state in noninstrumental terms. One of his most controversial statements held: "It is the way of God in the world, that there should be [literally, is] a state."[19] Although Hegel's statement has been taken as a glorification of state power, in reality Hegel was really interested in reminding us that it is the existence of a viable political order that makes both civilization and freedom possible. Hegel identified the state as "freedom universal and objective."[20] In civil society, self-realization implies lack of concern for the fate of one's peers, save as they serve one's interests. In a genuine political order, self-realization is mutual. It should, of course, be remembered that Hegel was fully cognizant of the shortcomings of actuality.

If Aristotle and Hegel are correct that the state aims at the highest good, there may be a limit to the degree to which the political order can be secularized, a limit we are rapidly approaching as the unemployment crisis worsens. In a purely secular order, there is simply no credible rationale for civic altruism. We are left with the economic egoism of civil society and universal mistrust and fear. Neither the purchase of handguns nor anticrime programs will halt the trend toward social atomization. In reality, there is no humane alternative to the rediscovery of civic altruism. Without it we are likely to be confronted with ever greater civic disorder punctuated by war and mass violence whose latent purpose can only be to eliminate physically those who have already been eliminated economically.

It is my conviction that some credible form of resacralization of the political order is indispensable. Given America's religious pluralism and the claims of so many of its denominations to possess exclusive religious truth, there is little likelihood that resacralization will be based upon unanimity of religious opinion. However, one of the most important lessons the civilizations of the Orient have to teach us may be that genuine coexistence of different religious traditions within a common community is altogether possible. Perhaps an even more important lesson is that the sacred need not necessarily be theistic in the way Western monotheistic exclusivism has been. In the West the dichotomy of sacred and secular has meant that without theism all relationships and obligations have been secularized. Having secularized our politics, the major political alternatives envisaged by Western intellectuals have been some form of free-enterprise capitalism, with its tendency toward economic egoism and social atomization, on the one hand, and some version of bureaucratically administered collectivism on the other. Regrettably, both secular alternatives can engender disastrous social consequences. We have noted some of the negative effects of economic egoism. Yet, as undesirable as the phenomenon may be, it still permits a measure of personal freedom that has wholly disappeared

11

from secular, bureaucratically administered collectivism. Moreover, the horrors of Stalinism may not be accidental but intrinsic features of such collectivism. Where the only rationale for state behavior is the mythical future well-being of the group as a whole, there is, as we have learned, nothing to stop those in power from the most murderous demographic violence in the name of that ever-receding felicity. If technology produces the kind of social crisis we have outlined above, only a resacralization of human relations could offer a hopeful alternative to free-enterprise capitalism or bureaucratized collectivism.

It is ironic that at a time when so much attention is being paid by managers of American business enterprises to Japanese managerial methods, very little of the discussion has focused on Japanese religious and ethical teaching, although it is obvious that Japanese management techniques cannot be divorced from the fundamental ethos of Japanese society. There has been one significant exception, the publication of a mass market paperback edition of *A Book of Five Rings* by Miyamoto Musashi (1584–1645), a leading samurai of the Tokugawa period.[21] In his book Musashi notes the difference between the various Ways ("Michi" or "Do", or in Chinese "Tao"). According to Musashi, there is the Way of Confucius governing the Way of learning, the Way of salvation by the law of the Buddha, and the doctor's Way of healing. There is also Musashi's Way, the Way of the warrior, which he informs us is "the resolute acceptance of death."[22]

It would, however, be a mistake to see the Way of the warrior as one of either excessive morbidity or gratuitous longing for death. On the contrary, the real meaning of the Way of the warrior is the utterly selfless acceptance of the path of service in the performance of one's duty. The editor of *A Book of Five Rings* quotes Yamamoto Tsunenori, another seventeenth-century samurai, to clarify what Musashi meant by "resolute acceptance of death": "If you keep your spirit correct from morning to night, accustomed to the idea of death and resolved on death, and consider yourself a dead body, thus becoming one with the Way of the warrior, you can pass through life with no possibility of failure and perform your office properly."[23] Clearly, the Way of the warrior precludes egoistic self-preoccupation and concern for anything whatsoever but the dis-charge of one's duty. Paradoxically, the warrior who is resolute in his acceptance of death is far more likely to survive a continual round of life-and-death struggles than the self-preoccupied warrior.

Musashi knew whereof he wrote. By the age of thirty, he had killed over sixty opponents in duels. Yet, he was no brute. He had a profound feeling for art and poetry and was deeply religious. He understood his Way to be supremely honorable in his society and was utterly faithful to it. Put differently, for Musashi his Way was holy even unto death. He wrote *A Book of Five Rings* while living in a cave a few weeks before his death. We might note that for Musashi there is a Way for every meaningful human role.

It is not our purpose to enter into the complicated question of the extent to which the religious traditions of the Orient influenced Musashi, although it is clear that Confucian, Taoist, and Buddhist elements are present. We need only note that for Musashi the Way of the warrior was sacred without being theistic. This is apparent in the last book of *A Book of Five Rings*: "The Book of the Void." It is brief and deserves to be quoted extensively:

The Ni To Ichi Way of Strategy is recorded in this Book of the Void.

What is called the spirit of the void is where there is nothing. It is not included in man's knowledge. Of course the void is nothingness. By knowing that things exist, you can know that which does not exist. That is the void.

People in this world look at things mistakenly, and think that what they do not understand must be the void. This is not the true void. It is bewilderment.. . . .

. . . To attain the Way of strategy as a warrior you must study fully other martial arts and not deviate even a little from the Way of the warrior. With your spirit settled, accumulate practice day by day, and hour by hour. Polish the twofold spirit heart and mind, and sharpen the twofold gaze perception and sight. When your spirit is not the least clouded, when the clouds of bewilderment clear away, there is the true void. . . .

In the void is virtue, and no evil. Wisdom has existence, principle has existence, spirit is nothingness.[24]

It is interesting to note that Musashi wrote his meditation on the void within weeks of his death, an indication of the fundamental seriousness with which he wrote. There is irony in the way Musashi's work reached the American mass market. In their quest to understand Japan's managerial success, well-informed American corporate managers have discovered that *A Book of Five Rings* serves as a guide for contemporary Japanese business executives. The Way of the samurai has become the Way of the business executive. Having attempted to uncover the secret of Japanese managerial technique to enhance their own economic self-interest, American executives have come upon a guide that is thoroughly imbued with the spirit of nontheistic, mystical selflessness. If the American executives who read this book attempt to emulate their successful Japanese counterparts, they will be compelled to change more than their managerial techniques; they will have no choice but to change themselves and their fundamental values. There is no place for egoistic self-enhancement in Musashi's Way.

The intention of the American businessmen who have turned to works on Japan has been to find a technique with which to meet Japanese competition. Ironically, there is no technique to master. Like Musashi, they will have to learn to find and be faithful to their Way and they will have to learn, as did Musashi, that "in the void there is virtue and no evil." This will require a conversion, not from Christianity to Buddhism, Confucianism, or Taoism, but within themselves and their culture as Christians, for they can no more start wholly anew than can other civilized men. They must build on who they are and what they have been. For the first time, they have come into contact and competition with the East in a way in which everything is at risk. Of necessity, they will be changed by that contact.

Although I can offer no blueprint for the form the resacralization of politics could take in the West, it is possible to give expression to what resacralization could mean: put simply, to sacralize an institution or a domain of activity is to accord ultimacy to it. This was clearly understood by Musashi, who accorded ultimacy to the Way of the samurai. As he makes unmistakably clear, even life itself must be subordinated to the Way. One may object and say that to accord ultimacy to the political order is a form of idolatry. This certainly has been the perennial conviction of the Western religious tradition, a conviction that contributed greatly to the long-range secularization of Western politics. It can, however, be argued that the political order deserves ultimacy because it is that which makes possible the distinctively human form of existence as distinguished from that of animal existence. That is why the ruler and the warrior have historically been accorded greater respect than the merchant. It is the political order that enables men to create a physical and cultural space in which they can protect themselves from the ravages of both physical nature and the worst aspects of human nature, thereby forming the basis of civilization. We know what happens to men and women when the political order breaks down or becomes impotent.

Since the political order alone makes civilization possible, it alone must be regarded as self-validating and self-legitimating. That is why the institution of divine kingship so long commanded the loyalties of men in widely scattered cultures. This is also why Aristotle saw the polis as aiming at the highest good and why Hegel claimed, "It is the way of God in the world that there should be a state." Even the hermit who utterly flees the society of men is in his use of knowledge, his prayers, his memories, and his meditations the child of the political order. To resacralize the political order is merely to come to understand the true nature of the political order and to abandon the Way of the bourgeois for that of the citizen. Of special importance is the fact that if membership in the political order were regarded as the highest good, no citizen would be regarded as superfluous because he or she had been rendered vocationally redundant by technology. The first concern of the community would be to abort the drift toward wasted lives on the part of those whose jobs had, through no fault of their own, disappeared.

Briefly stated, the resacralization of politics would mean the end of economic egoism and the restoration of shared obligation within the community. Compare the samurai's selfless commitment to his Way with the concept given expression by Adam Smith—and currently enjoying renewed respectability—of why men perform their tasks: "It is not from the benevolence of the butcher, the brewer, or the baker that we expect our dinner, but from their regard to their own interest. We address ourselves, not to their humanity but to their self-love, and never talk to them of our necessities but of their advantages."[25] There is an optimistic component in Smith's thinking that his successors did not share. Implicit in his thinking was the view that the sum total of private selfishness could somehow yield the common good. Ironically, if American executives continue to act out of egoistic self-love, they will lose that which they prize most, their ability to win the contest of life in their chosen field of endeavor. They will be no match for those who are selflessly committed to their Way not out of self-interest but because of the ultimacy of that obligation. The resacralization of politics means at the very least a selfless commitment to the common good, an end to the privatism, self-indulgence, and self-preoccupation that so destructively besets contemporary society.

Conclusion

It is easier to discern the need for resacralization than to predict with confidence when and how it will come about. That is not my purpose in writing. I can do no more than analyze the increasingly problematic character of secularization and to point to what must eventually follow. America remains both a young and a rapidly changing country. Sooner or later the sacred will find its place in American life. When it does, it is my conviction that we will understand it as the same ultimate reality as the holy nothingness of the Western mystics, the *en sof* of the kabbalists, and Miyamoto Musashi's void.

NOTES

1. Shlomo Avineri, *Hegel's Theory of the Modern State* (Cambridge: Cambridge University Press, 1972), 134–35.

2. Georg W. F. Hegel, *Political Writings,* trans. T. M. Knox (New York: Garland Publishing, 1984), 202.

3. Georg W. F. Hegel, *Philosophy of Right,* trans. T. M. Knox (Oxford: Clarendon, 1942), addition to par. 238.

4. Hegel, *Philosophy of Right,* par. 187.

5. Carol Teich Adams, "The Flight of Jobs and Capital: Prospects for Grassroots Action," *Community and Capital in Conflict: Plant Closings and Job Loss,* ed. John C. Raines, Lenora E. Berson, and David McL. Gracie (Philadelphia: Temple University Press, 1982), 12–13; see also Barry Bluestone, "Deindustrialization and the Abandonment of Community," *Community and Capital in Conflict,* 38–61.

6. The company in question is the Ford Motor Company. The car with the defective gas tank was the Pinto. See "Ford Study: Death, Injury Cheaper than Fixing Cars," *Tallahassee Democrat,* October 14, 1979. This was a *Chicago Tribune* wire service dispatch.

7. Richard L. Rubenstein, *The Age of Triage: Fear and Hope in An Overcrowded World* (Boston: Beacon Press, 1983), 217–23.

8. Oscar Handlin, *The Uprooted,* 2d ed. (Boston: Little, Brown, 1973).

9. Richard H. Tawney, *Religion and the Rise of Capitalism* (London: J. Murray, 1926), 197ff.

10. Christopher Hill, *The World Turned Upside Down: Radical Ideas During the English Revolution* (London: Temple Smith, 1972), 39–56.

Civic Altruism

11. Max Weber, *The Protestant Ethic and the Spirit of Capitalism,* trans. Talcott Parsons (New York: Scribner, 1958), 110 ff.

12. Rubenstein, *The Age of Triage,* 56–103.

13. Adams, "The Flight of Jobs and Capital."

14. "The Speedup in Automation," *Business Week,* August 3, 1981.

15. For a visual representation of this phenomenon see the charts on "The State of the Economy," *New York Times,* October 29, 1982, p. 11. The charts on unemployment use data supplied by the Bureau of Labor Statistics.

16. John Locke, *Two Treatises of Government,* book 2, chap. 9, 124.

17. Aristotle, *The Politics,* book 1, chap. 1.

18. Hegel, *Philosophy of Right,* addition to par. 258.

19. Walter Kaufman, ed., *Hegel's Political Philosophy* (New York: Atherton Press, 1970), 279.

20. Hegel, *Philosophy of Right,* par. 33.

21. Miyamoto Musashi, *A Book of Five Rings,* trans. Victor Harris (Woodstock, N.Y.: Overlook Press, 1974).

22. Musashi, 38.

23. Yamamoto Tsunenori, *Hidden Leaves* (Ha Gakure) cited in the notes to Musashi, *A Book of Five Rings,* 39.

24. Musashi, 95.

25. Adam Smith, *The Wealth of Nations* (Harmondsworth, Middlesex: Penguin, 1974), 119.

2

Modernization and Religion: Must They Move in Different Directions?

RITA H. MATARAGNON

The term *modernization* has been popularly used in the study of social change despite its lack of a consensual definition, conceptual clarity, and precision. The appeal of the term apparently lies in its capacity to evoke generalized, universalistic images of an evolutionary process moving from one set of attributes called traditional to another set of attributes called modern.

Although a distinction is properly made between modernization (a process or the product of a process) and modernity or modernism (a set of attributes), it is clear that the study of modernization would ultimately have to rely on the variable of modernity or modernism, which is the more tractable and measurable variable. "Changes in the proportion of people holding modern values, or changes in the extent to which individuals have gone modern constitute modernization."[1]

Indeed, one of the undisputed assumptions in modernization theory and research is that there are certain characteristics and behaviors that can be identified for the modern man, i.e., a class of attributes called modernity or modernism. The question is: does this class of attributes include a decreased interest in, or even disavowal of, religion? Do individuals in a modernizing society become less religious? Does modernization necessarily move in a direction away from religion?

Modernization and Religion: Ambiguity of Relationship

An investigator interested in establishing the relationship between modernization and religion soon discovers, to his surprise, a virtual absence of empirical evidence that directly relates modernization to religion or vice versa. Furthermore, an examination of the tangential contexts in which religion is mentioned in modernization studies suggests a serious ambiguity in the relationship between modernization and religion. It appears that the problem is not just a matter of the magnitude of relationship, but the nature of the relationship.

In several studies in which the components comprising a measure of modernity are listed, religion or religiosity is cited as one component. Typically, a measure of modernity is developed through item analysis: to identify salient characteristics, items that comprise the different components are initially scored in what is *felt* to be the modern direction and correlations are then computed between each item and the total score to determine which ones are more highly related to an overall measure of modernization.[2] Although in some cases respondents are employed to judge which response constitutes the modern direction of each item, the fact remains that subjective judgment is used to determine that religious behavior is more unmodern. Since the measurement of modernity becomes its operational definition, if the items on religion are significantly correlated with the total score and the items are adopted, an inverse relation between modernity and religion becomes automatic. The original basis, however, was intuitive.

To give a flavor of religious components in the modernity or modernism scale, the following are offered as examples. Kahl posited fourteen dimensions in which attitudes may change with modernization.[3] One of them was "low religiosity." Inkeles started with thirty-three themes, which included, "religious causality" and "religious-secular orientation." Although these themes did not comprise the final salient characteristics, several of the final chosen themes could be tangentially related to religiosity—faith in science and medicine rather than fatalism, subjective efficacy, or belief in man's control over the environment. Inkeles's final shortened scale of ten items included this one characteristic of the modern man: he is willing to acknowledge that a man can be good without being religious.[4] Schnaiberg included among his Modernism Items a short religiosity index in which items concerned type of marriage, frequency of prayer, and length of fasting.[5] Finally, Stephenson's culturally derived Modernism-Traditionism Scale included religion as one of the seven value areas. It must be noted that although the judgments about the direction of modernism for each item were derived from indigenous judges, the seven "value areas" were determined as bases for classification prior to judging. Using a Guttman scale, Stephenson also showed that among the seven value areas religion is the next-to-the-last area to be changed, i.e., it is not so vulnerable as opinions about innovation and education.[6]

It can be readily seen that scholars and laymen alike often intuitively see an inverse relationship between modernization and religion, or modernity and religiosity. This is especially evident in the tendency of many, though not all, investigators to include at least initially a component of religion or religiosity among the areas of attitudinal and value changes expected to be affected by modernization processes. It is also reflected on the part of scholars in their choice of the unreligious attitude or behavior as "the more modern one." Although in some careful studies the religiosity component does not come out as a critical factor, still the fact that certain areas are chosen and not others reveals underlying assumptions and value judgments about the end-state of modernization.

Although one does not get much insight from correlating modernity and religiosity if the latter were a subsumed component and therefore part of the definition of the former, this state of affairs, if uniform, would at least leave no doubt about the nature of the relationship between modernization and religion. However, the relationship is apparently more elusive than that. First, the studies that initially included religion as a component have yielded equivocal outcomes in their eventual enumeration of critical or salient components. In some, religion has weak, marginal significance, whereas in others it provides no contribution whatsoever to overall modernity.

Second, there is no explicit agreement that religion or religiosity is under the rubric of modernization or modernity rather than an external variable that affects or is affected by modernization. A number of studies have used religion, or changes in religious values, as an intervening variable to explain or interpret the effects of modernizing structures on behavioral changes. For instance, Coombs and Freedman concluded that changes in familial and religious values mediate between urbanization and family life.[7] As Fawcett has pointed out, prominent among the themes that relate modernization processes to fertility change are the effects of changes in cultural and religious values.[8]

The shifting back and forth of religion as a subsumed variable under modernity or as an external variable to be correlated with modernity partly reflects the theoretical imprecision of the modernization concept, something for which it has often been criticized. It is perhaps worth noting, though, that religion, whether subsumed under the modernity rubric or treated as an externally correlated variable, does not seem to have the same strength, consistency, and centrality other components of modernity show, such as openness to change and subjective efficacy. In fact, the latter two are never treated as external variables but always make up part of the definition.

Thus, the supposed inverse relation of religion to modernization can be said to be more intuitive than empirical. There is little direct evidence and little serious attention to a formal relationship between modernization and religion. References to a "relationship" are frequently assumed or inferred from other variables that are tangential to religion, such as fatalism, time orientation, and subjective efficacy.

Measurement Problems

Where religion/religiosity has been included as a component or external intervening variable, operational definitions and measurements of this variable have been wildly discrepant. The following are examples in Goldberg's study. Turkish women were asked, "How often do you pray? Do you fast during Ramadan?" The same questions were asked of the women about their husbands, along with "How often does he go to the mosque?" Mexican women were asked about themselves and their husbands: "How often do you (or does he) go to mass?" "How often do you take communion?" "How often do you pray outside of church?" "What type of religious instruction have you had?" "Have you ever gone to a religious school?"[9]

Consider the religiosity index of Schnaiberg, also used in a study of Turkish women, which had the following items: (1) Couple has had a civil marriage only; (2) Wife prays less than five times a day; (3) Wife does not fast for the entire period of Ramadan.[10] Another study by Bose, this time on Indian peasants, establishes a negative relationship between religious inclination and adoption of innovation just on the basis of one item about religion: "After death the soul is not destroyed but passes on to the next world."[11] Another single item for a whole component of religion, found in Stephenson's Modernism-Traditionism Scale, was: "The old Bible (the King James Version) is the only true word of God."[12] Still another study by Coombs and Freedman on Taiwanese women defined a religiosity index in terms of observance of ceremonies for ancestors.[13]

Although many investigators do not publish their questionnaires, the ones that have been published suggest an explanation for the status of the religion/religiosity variable in modernization research. Commonly the most traditional belief or the most conventional ritual is represented. The very broad and rich concept of religion, with its endless variations of personal beliefs and forms of observation and participation, is tragically oversimplified. Not only are there not enough items exploring cognitive ideas and overt behaviors, there are virtually no items on affect or feelings about the supernatural and on one's relationship with the supernatural. In general, there is a significant lack of content validity in the measure of religion/religiosity as a variable in modernization research. Notwithstanding, data based on one or two statements are often used in asserting relationships between religiosity and modernity.

Is religion merely the observance of religious ceremonies? Is it merely the subscription to the King James Bible as the Word of God? Is it having a religious wedding ceremony? These are traditional expressions of religiosity and are likely to be present in individuals who came from traditional families that expect them to toe the line with regard to basic practices. Religiosity measured in this simplistic manner is frequently correlated with familism. Furthermore, since the type of religiosity tapped involves the observance of highly traditional practices, it does not allow a fair test of personal religiosity, which could take more serious forms such as "spirituality," "faith," "strength of belief," "significance of God in one's life."

In this connection, it is important to point out the distinction between tradition and traditionalism. Religion is often associated with tradition. People talk of religion and tradition together, or in some cases even of religious traditions. But religion need not be traditional in its expression. "Tradition refers to the beliefs and practices handed down from the past; as we reinterpret our past, our traditions change. In contrast, traditionalism glorifies past beliefs and practices as immutable. Traditionalists see tradition as static; they urge that men do things only as they have been done before. Traditionalism, by virtue of its hostility to innovation, is clearly antithetical to the development of modernization; traditions, which are constantly subject to reinterpretation and modification, constitute no such barrier."[14]

Misplaced Polarities

In an oft-cited article, Gusfield raises the point that tradition and modernity are misplaced polarities in the study of social change.[15] The same thing could be said about religion and modernity. Gusfield presented seven fallacies in the assumption of the tradition-modernity polarity. These fallacies can be examined in the context of the religious tradition. Although several of these fallacies overlap with each other, (notably fallacies four, five, six, and seven), they will be presented one by one, as they were in Gusfield's analysis.

Fallacy one is that developing societies have been static societies. Religion, as it is present in any culture, has not always existed in its present form. Conquests of foreign powers and the growth of social and cultural movements have deeply influenced religious beliefs. In the same way it can be expected that modernizing influences will continue to influence religion but not destroy it.

Fallacy two is that traditional culture is a consistent body of norms and values. The distinction between popular or folk religion and the religion of the literate elite have coexisted in many cultures, making it difficult to characterize "the religion" in a given society. Individuals who subscribe to the same religion in one culture may show wide variation with regard to their specific religious beliefs and practices. There is room for both the traditional and the modern.

Fallacy three is that traditional society is a homogeneous social structure. Although Weber referred to "the Protestant ethic," the specific sects that carried the ethic were by no means typical of all Protestant groups. The Jews in Europe, the Muslims in West Africa, the Chinese in Southeast Asia, the Indians in East Africa—all are examples of groups whose marginality has spurred them toward entrepreneurial achievement. In India, the Parsees and Jains have been potent carriers of economic innovation and the development of large-scale industrial production. Asian religions, viewed by many Westerners as an obstacle to modernization, have in many cases proven to be capable of positive adaptation to social change.[16] What is characteristic of all these communities, according to McClelland, "is an intense religiously based feeling that they are superior to other people around them and that in one sense or another they hold the key to salvation."[17]

Fallacy four is that old traditions are replaced by new changes. "The acceptance of a new product, a new religion, a new mode of decision-making does not necessarily lead to the disappearance of the older form."[18] Paganism and Catholicism have often been accommodated together in a new form of ritualism. Many modern schools teach science and religion side by side. Interaction results in fusion and mutual penetration. Far from being replaced, religion has been the guardian of culture and civilization across the centuries. It has built schools, hospitals, and community centers. It continues to be a repository of all that is best and enduring in a culture, a reflection of its *zeitgeist* and stage of development.

Fallacy five is that traditional and modern forms are always in conflict. The picture of a conflicted society undergoing development or of a tormented individual choosing between traditional and modern options does not seem to hold. The "traditional" society often contains sufficient diversity of content to allow it to accept some and refuse other components of modernization. Japan is unlike the West in the ways in which feudalism and industrialization have been fused to promote growth. A collectivist orientation and commitment to emperor and family also allowed it to reject the individualism of the West. In individuals, fusion as well as compartmentalization allow a sane adjustment to modernization. Modern forms of communication and transportation allow him better access to religious activities. Role inconsistencies are tolerated by compartmentalization. In the words of the famous informant who told the British anthropologist, "When I put on my shirt and go to the factory I put off my caste."[19] Inkeles and Smith's study on personal adjustment of urban and rural dwellers in each instance compares favorably on psychosomatic symptoms with control samples of the rural population. The notion of psychic stress in urban life is probably due not so much to an incorrect view of city life as to a mistaken image of relative security and emotional support in traditional village life.[20]

Fallacy six is that tradition and modernity are mutually exclusive systems. Religion ranks with the extended family as the institution most often identified as both an obstacle to economic development and a victim of the same. As has been pointed out under *Measurement Problems,* this is because religion has always been operationally defined as the traditional expression of religion. "Systematic evidence for this proposition is, however, much less ample than one might imagine."[21] The caste system in Indian life has been exaggerated as an impediment to economic growth through failure

24

to consider its role in the division of labor and in caste mobility as an impetus to growth.

Fallacy seven is that modernizing processes weaken traditions. Modernized structures, especially mass media, allow the rapid dissemination and reinforcement of whatever are the predominant values of the society. People are discriminating about what is meaningful to them and what impinges on important aspects of their lives. Mass media can broadcast propaganda incessantly, but if friends and relatives preach different values, the mass media are not likely to win. "The persistence of belief in God in countries where atheist propaganda has gone on for decades is a case in point."[22]

The trickle effect of ideas from the accepted indigenous elite to the masses increases rapidly with modernization. Thus, Srinivas contends that, whereas higher social levels appear to be "Westernizing" their life-styles, lower and middle levels seek mobility by becoming more devotedly Hinduistic, following more Brahminical styles, and otherwise Sanskritizing their behavior: ". . . tradition may be changed, stretched, and modified, but a unified and nationalized society makes great use of the traditional in its search for a consensual base to political authority and economic development."[23]

Portes has in fact theorized that modernity, presumably because it leads to Western attitudes, can interfere with mass mobilization.[24] On the other hand, traditional structures can do the job better. Indirect support comes from a panel regression study, which concludes that indigenous modernizing institutions such as school or education registers a more substantial contribution to economic development, whereas exposure to exogenous modernizing institutions such as imported cinema actually hinders economic development. The authors argued that "the cinema impedes economic growth by transmitting and promoting Western values incompatible with the social ethos that must accompany programs of national economic development."[25] This is still more evidence that indigenous religion and modernization need not be polarized, but that one can in fact be the impetus for the other.

Symbols and Myths amid Changing Times

Modernization is a concept that evolved in the social sciences to depict a phenomenon of the twentieth century. Compared to religion, modernization is a relative new-comer; yet, at best, it allegedly threatens to undermine religion; at worst, to send it on the way of the brontosaurus. Equivocal empirical evidence so far does not warrant such apprehension. At this point, some perspective is needed.

People have always sought, and will always seek, meaning in their lives. This impulse is in recognition of man's mortality and the need to transcend it. Each age and culture provides its own symbols and myths, which form a structure of meaning from which people generate values by which to live. Myths here do not refer at all to falsehoods, but to lasting truths shared by a people.[26]

Whether modernization will solve more ills than those it unleashes is for future history to decide. In the meantime, however, it has to be reconciled to some of the symbols and myths that have for years provided a comfortable structure of meaning for individuals in a culture. Breakdown in cherished symbols and myths leave a people bereft of guideposts for coping and rules for living. Experimentation in different life-styles and the flourishing of new psychotherapies may be viewed as modern attempts to discover personal meaning. Modern interpretations and expressions of religion, modern forms of religion, and even modern religions also come to the rescue.

The challenge is to discover new forms of cultural symbols and myths. The rebirth of symbols and myths is creative, dynamic, and unending.

Generations have trod, have trod, have trod;
And all is seared with trade; bleared, smeared with toil;
And wears man's smudge and share man's smell: the soil
Is bare now, nor can foot feel, being shod.
And for all this, nature is never spent;
There lives the dearest freshness deep down things; . . . [27]

Such is the inexhaustible essence of religion and of things spiritual that defies the imperative of human societal transition.

NOTES

1. John B. Stephenson, "Is Everyone Going Modern? A Critique and a Sug-

gestion for Measuring Modernism," *American Journal of Sociology* 74 (1968): 265–75.

2. David H. Smith and Alex Inkeles, "The OM Scale: A Comparative and Socio-Psychological Measure of Individual Modernity," *Sociometry* 21 (1966): 353–77.

3. J. A. Kahl, *The Measurement of Modernism: A Study of Values in Brazil and Mexico* (Texas: University of Texas Press, 1968).

4. Alex Inkeles, "Making Men Modern: On the Causes and Consequences of Individual Change in Six Developing Countries," *American Journal of Sociology* 75 (1969): 208–25.

5. Allan Schnaiberg, "Measuring Modernism: Theoretical and Empirical Explorations," *American Journal of Sociology* 76 (1970): 399–425.

6. Stephenson, 265.

7. Lolagene C. Coombs and Ronald Freedman, "Some Roots of Preference: Roles, Activities and Familial Values," *Demography* 16 (1979): 359–76.

8. James T. Fawcett and Marc H. Bornstein, "Modernization, Individual Modernity, and Fertility," in *Psychological Perspectives on Population,* ed. James T. Fawcett (New York: Basic Books, 1973), 111.

9. David Goldberg, *Modernism* (The Netherlands: International Statistical Institute, 1974).

10. Allan Schnaiberg, 399–425.

11. Santi Priya Bose, "Peasant Values and Innovation in India," *American Journal of Sociology* 67 (1962): 522–60.

12. Stephenson.

13. Coombs and Freedman.

14. Myron Weiner, ed., *Modernization: The Dynamics of Growth* (New York: Basic Books, 1966).

15. Joseph R. Gusfield, "Tradition and Modernity: Misplaced Polarities in the Study of Social Change," *American Journal of Sociology* 72 (1967): 351–62.

16. Milton Singer, "The Modernization of Religious Beliefs," in Weiner, *Modernization,* 59–70.

17. David C. McClelland, "The Impulse to Modernization," in Weiner, *Modernization,* 29–42.

18. Gusfield, 354.

19. Singer, 68.

20. Alex Inkeles, and David H. Smith, "Personal Adjustment and Modernization," George De Vos, ed., *Responses to Change: Society, Culture and Personality* (New York: D. Van Nostrand Company, 1976), 214–33.

21. Alex Inkeles, "A Model of the Modern Man: Theoretical and Methodological Issues," Cyril E. Black, ed., *Comparative Modernization,* 320–48.

22. Ithiel de Sola Pool, "Communications and Development," Weiner, *Modernization,* 105–18.

23. Singer, 63.

24. A. Portes, "The Factorial Structure of Modernity: Empirical Replications and a Critique," *American Journal of Sociology* 79 (1973): 14–44.

25. Jacques Delacroix and Charles Rogin, "Modernizing Institutions, Mobilization and Third World Development: A Cross-National Study," *American Journal of Sociology* 84 (1978): 123–52.

26. Rollo May, "Psychology Today/The State of the Science," *Psychology Today* 16 (May 1982): 56–58.

27. Gerard Manley Hopkins, "God's Grandeur," *Poems of Gerard Manley Hopkins* (New York: Oxford University Press, 1970).

3

Mental Health and the Dilemmas of Freudian Psychotherapy: An Eastern Perspective
PADMASIRI DE SILVA

Sigmund Freud wrote a stimulating paper toward the latter part of his life entitled "Analysis Terminable and Interminable."[1] Apart from raising some significant queries regarding the question "Is there such a thing as a natural end to an analysis?" it also contains some significant conflicts and tensions regarding the main concerns of this essay: the "normal" and the "abnormal," and "sickness" and "health." I wish to refer to the issues of normal/abnormal and sickness/health as tensions rather than clear dualities, tensions that emerged due to Freud's ceaseless exploration of the human predicament on the one hand, and the cautious voice of science, which made him disclaim any moralistic purpose in his writings, on the other. There were also other types of conflicts. There was a technical demand on the termination of analysis: if continuous analysis is a time-consuming business, how do we accelerate the slow progress of analysis? Can we set a fixed time limit? Freud, however, expressed a willingness to spend a number of years with one patient; even the well-being of one human being, he felt, is a matter of "ultimate concern."[2] When the work "Analysis Terminable and Interminable" is placed against the wider background of Freud's other writings, it may be said that in Freud we see a kind of oscillation between a limited ideal of therapy and a more ambitious one, as well as optimistic and pessimistic conceptions of cure and therapeutic transformation.

Already in Freud's "Studies in Hysteria," we find the celebrated passage: "No doubt fate would it easier than I do to relieve you of your illness. But you will be able to convince yourself that much will be gained if we succeed in transforming your hysterical misery into common unhappiness."[3] On similar lines, in the work, "Analysis Terminable and Interminable," Freud comments: "Our aim will not be to rub off every peculiarity of human character for the sake of a schematic 'normality', nor yet to demand that the person who

29

has been 'thoroughly analysed' shall feel no passions and develop no internal conflicts. The business of analysis is to secure the best possible psychological conditions for the functions of the ego; with that it has discharged its task."[4]

From a very specific eastern perspective, I found another contrasting vision of the goals of therapy mentioned in "Analysis Terminable and Interminable" more interesting:

". . . but we reckon on the stimuli that he has received in his own analysis not ceasing when it ends and on the processes of remodelling the ego continuing spontaneously in the analysed subject and making use of all subsequent experiences in this newly acquired sense. This does in fact happen, and in so far as it happens it makes the analysed subject qualified to be an analyst himself."[5]

The path of continuous self-exploration that is mentioned here has attracted some contemporary writers, such as Anthony Storr, on the concept of "cure." He says quite clearly that psychoanalysis certainly offers something more than mere relief from symptoms, and as the patients often lose interest in the symptoms for which they wanted to be treated, they seek the process of analysis as an end in itself. Storr says that in this manner analysis is sought not so much as treatment but more as a way of life.[6] This is the sort of dimension in which analysis as both therapeutic transformation and growth of self-knowledge offers a point of convergence for an Eastern, and more particularly, a Buddhist perspective.

A possible objection to my approach is that Freud grappled with the neurotic and the abnormal and that we have no right to use these insights to understand the normal mind, and, even more, to bring them into the Buddhist context. Though Freud was primarily interested in the mentally sick, his psychology had a broad basis. In fact, Philip Rief, who deals at great length with the therapeutic dimensions of Freudian psychology, claims that both Freud's dictum that "we are all somewhat hysterical" and his claim that the difference between so-called normality and neurosis is only a matter of degree comprise a central Freudian position rather than a peripheral one. In fact, we also know that Freud dealt at a very deep and intensive level with what may be called the "pathology of normalcy," as found in his *Psychopathology of Every Day Life*.[7] Freud certainly went beyond the narrow confines of a therapy for mentally sick patients. As MacIntyre points out, "The scope in principle of Freudian explanation is all human behaviour: had it been less than this Freud would have been unable to draw the famous comparison between the effect of his own work and that of Copernicus."[8] Here again, "Analysis Terminable and Interminable" confirms this standpoint: "Every normal person, in fact, is only normal on the average. His ego approximates to that of the psychotic in some part or other and to a greater or lesser extent; and the degree of its remoteness from one end of the series and of its proximity to the other will furnish us with a provisional measure of what we have so indefinitely termed an 'alteration of the ego.'"[9]

After this brief glimpse into our special interest in Freud's study of the termination of analysis, in the rest of this essay, I will divide my discussion into three phases: first, I will present a summary of "Analysis Terminable and Interminable," then briefly discuss some parallels to and differences from the Buddhist concern with sickness and health, and next examine some of the Freudian dilemmas that stand in the way of a terminable analysis. I will try to make you understand this tangle from a Buddhist position. I will conclude with a few remarks that will relate this essay more closely to our theme of religion and society.

Before I conclude this introductory discussion, I should mention two special reasons for selecting this particular essay by Freud for detailed analysis. First, in spite of the conflicting strands of thought regarding the ideal of mental health, it is possible to agree with James Strachey that in this work the skeptical, pessimistic outlook dominates. This is especially so compared with the more optimistic outlook in works such as the *New Introductory Lectures,* which preceded it, and the *Outline of Psychoanalysis,* which followed it. But in a rather paradoxical manner, such pessimism seems to increase our interest in schemes of therapy that go beyond the accepted patterns of scientific psychology. Perhaps, as Charles Rycroft says, "psychoanalysis could be regarded as a semantic bridge between science and biology on the one hand and religion and humanities on the other."[10] The dilemmas of Freud call for a widening of the frame that we can use to plot the perennial conflicts inherent in the human situation.

The second reason, which I consider quite significant, is the insight that is available from Freud's own dilemmas regarding the crucial role of the ego in this interminable analysis. At this point, I wish to open up a line of inquiry from a Buddhist perspective and place it before you as an exercise in exploration. Apart from the complexities of psychoanalytic writings on the subject, there appears to exist a semantic thicket that has to be cleared. It is to the credit rather than discredit of Freud that he stumbled on this during the latter stages of his research and left it to future workers (including his daughter Anna Freud) to find an answer.

Analysis Terminable and Interminable: A Summary

Psychoanalytic therapy, which is designed to free people from neurotic symptoms, inhibitions, and abnormalities of character, is a time-consuming business. Attempts have been made to shorten the duration of analysis. Apart from the technical problem of how to accelerate the slow process of change, there is the "more deeply interesting question": is there such a thing as a natural end to analysis?

From a practical point of view, it is easy to answer the question: "An analysis is ended when the analyst and the patient cease to meet each other for the analytic session." Normally, such an end is reached when the patient is free from the symptoms he had and has overcome his anxieties, and the analyst feels that a certain amount of repressed material has been made conscious and intelligible and internal resistance has been conquered. At this point, "there is no need to fear a repetition of the pathological process concerned." The other meaning of the "end" of analysis is a kind of absolute normality, where all the patient's repressions have been resolved and gaps in the memory filled. Freud was not only skeptical about the more ambitious ideal of psychic normality, but he came across three factors that interfered with the decisive termination of analysis.

In the early days, Freud dealt with a large number of patients who wanted to be dealt with as quickly as possible. He later dealt with a smaller number of severe cases, where the therapeutic aim was no longer the same: "There was no question of shortening the treatment; the purpose was radically to exhaust all the possibilities of illness and to bring about a deep-going alteration of their personality."[11] Now, there were three factors that interfered with the decisive termination of an analysis: the influence of traumatic events, the constitutional strength of instincts, and the "alterations of the ego." As the attempt to deal with the traumatic factor had good results, the traumatic factor (as compared with the constitutional factor) was not a major obstacle. Thus here we are mainly concerned with the two other factors: the strength of instincts and the alterations of the ego.

The key question for Freud here is: "Is it possible by means of analytic therapy to dispose of a conflict between the instinct and the ego, or of a pathogenic instinctual demand upon the ego, permanently and definitively?"[12] The terms *permanently* and *definitively* do not mean that they cause the demand to disappear, but rather that there is a kind of "taming of the ego," where the instincts are brought into complete harmony with the ego.

Though the aim of analysis is thus to replace repressions that are insecure with reliable ego-syntonic control, this is not always achieved. In the defensive struggle, the ego gets dislocated and restricted. This unfavorable situation stands in the way of a permanent cure. The "constitutional strength of instincts" adds to the difficulties. Though attempts were made to maintain the autonomy of the ego in harmony with the demands of the instincts, Freud discovered that the ego is developed from the id, and at some point the topographical distinction between the ego and the id collapses. There are other obstructions to a permanent cure, such as the "adhesiveness of the libido" and the conflict between eros and destructiveness. These dilemmas, especially those springing from the ambiguous role of the ego in therapy, are of special interest for an Eastern perspective on the question and will be discussed in the subsequent sections.

At this point, it is necessary to appreciate that, following the logic of his own system, Freud honestly encountered these difficulties and stated them. It appears that the development of what may be called "ego psychology" has not done very much to ease the situation. It is possible that ego psychology is merely moving in a vicious circle. These are built-in difficulties in the Freudian ego concept, and unless the question is approached from a different angle, as for instance from an angle found in the Buddhist tradition, we may well come up against a wall and a conceptual thicket. Take the overburdened ego of the Freudian system: it is a part of consciousness and control, perception and motility; it is a drive (the self-preservation drive); it is a reservoir of libido; it is the cause of repression; it conforms to reality (identical to the reality principle); it is a reaction to the drive and it constitutes the basis of character; it carries out reality testing.[13] In the final analysis, Freud discovered that the ego is developed from the id. The poor ego is at the same time, "a precipitate of object losses" and the seat of sanity, order, and reason. It is not only that in a semantic sense it is an overworked concept, but that the inherent psychological ambiguities drive Freud into the real difficulties honestly voiced in "Analysis Terminable and Interminable." The inherent ambiguities in the "self and world" relation, "self and other" relation, as well as the self attempting to relate to itself are meticulously worked out in the Buddhist sutras.[14]

Analysis Terminable and Interminable: A Buddhist Perspective

There have been three attempts to view Freudian psychotherapy from a Buddhist perspective that are relevant for this discussion: Erich Fromm's *Zen Buddhism and Psychoanalysis,* from a neo-Freudian standpoint; David Levin's "Approaches to Psychotherapy," where a critique of Freud is presented from the standpoint of Tibetan Buddhism, with basic sympathies for a Jungian position; and my own *Buddhist and Freudian Psychology.*[15]

I have found Fromm's definition of well-being very much in line with the early Buddhist position: "Well-being is possible only to the degree to which one has overcome one's narcissism."[16] Fromm says that "well-being means, finally, to drop one's Ego, to give up greed, to cease chasing after the preservation and the aggrandizement of the Ego, to be and to experience one's self in the act of being, not having, preserving, coveting, using."[17] If the Buddhist is asked to recommend a general working norm of health and sanity, at least to be approximated in varying degrees, overcoming narcissism is one I prefer and find conducive in light of the Buddhist tradition. It may even be a point of convergence for a general religious perspective on therapy, and not merely for an Eastern position. In spite of the dilemmas of ego psychology, it is also a concept that makes sense to a Freudian, especially in the light of Freud's paper on narcissism. Fromm has not merely revitalized the Freudian concept of narcissism, but he takes it beyond this and brings it close to the doctrine of the Buddha. Fromm comments: "The awakened person of whom the Buddhist teaching speaks is the person who has overcome his narcissism, and who is therefore capable of being fully awake."[18]

Fromm says that, quite contrary to popular assumptions, Freud's system transcends the traditional Western concepts of "illness" and "cure." According to Fromm, Freud's system is concerned with the "salvation" of man rather than a mere therapy for the mentally sick:

Psychoanalysis is a characteristic expression of Western man's spiritual crisis, and an attempt to find a solution. This is explicitly so in the more recent developments of psychoanalysis, in "humanist" or "existentialist" analysis. But before I discuss my own humanist concept, I want to show that quite contrary to a widely held assumption, Freud's own system transcended the concept of "illness" and "cure" and was concerned with the "salvation" of man, rather than only with a therapy for mentally sick patients.[19]

For Fromm the liberation of the individual from neurotic symptoms is a task with a quasi-religious mission.

Some of these converging lines between psychotherapy and Buddhism have become relevant to the post-Freudian world, and more so in the world in which we live today. The patients who came to Freud in the early stages of his career were those who suffered from certain symptoms, such as a paralyzed arm or an obsessional symptom or a washing compulsion. The difference between these patients and those who went to the regular physician for treatment was that the cause of their symptoms was not organic but mental. But there was a common pattern of cure: once the symptom was removed, the patient was cured. The new kind of patient who came for treatment was not sick in the traditional sense and had no overt symptoms. These patients were not insane or considered sick by their relatives. Yet they complained about being depressed, not enjoying their work, and so forth. Though these people thought they suffered from certain symptoms, their apparent symptoms were perhaps socially recognized ways of grappling with their inner deadness and lack of vitality. Fromm describes the situation well: "The common suffering is the alienation from oneself, from one's fellow men, and from nature; the awareness that life runs out of one's hand like sand, and that one will die without having lived; that one lives in the midst of plenty and is yet joyless."[20]

In spite of these converging lines between Buddhist therapy and Fromm's "humanistic psychoanalysis," the Freudian system as such was subject to tensions between descriptive clinical diagnosis and the norms of therapeutic recommendation. The medically oriented psychologist talks in terms of "psychological maturity" and "ego strength," whereas in nonmedical contexts one speaks of the authenticity of moral concern and personal integrity. These dual worlds seem to separate in Freud's work due to a scientist's respect for the recognized idiom and the proper semantics of communication, but these worlds run into each other. As Freud said, "The aim of psychoanalysis is not to tell the person what is good or bad, or right or wrong in a specific context, but to 'give the patient's ego freedom to decide one way or another.' . . . The medical aim is thus in substance a spiritual aim. It is to help the individual become an agent and cease being a patient, it is to liberate not to indoctrinate."[21]

The Dilemmas of Ego Psychology and the Buddhist Theory of Motivation

According to the psychology of early Buddhism, the mind can be considered a dynamic continuum that extends over a number of births. As such, it is composed of a conscious as well as an unconscious mind in which is contained the residue of emotionally charged memories, going back not merely to childhood but to past lives. The mind is viewed in this way as a continuum subjected to the pressure of the threefold desires of sense gratification, egoistic pursuits, and self-annihilation, which have some strange affinities to the Freudian concepts of the libido, the ego instinct, and the death instinct. The drive for selfish pursuits, which is fed by the illusion of an indestructible ego, is the most relevant concept for the present study. The Buddha considers the ego the seat of anxiety and the attachment to a false sense of the ego nourished by unconscious proclivities as a base for the generation of tension and unrest. Although the ego-anxiety linkage offers an interesting point of intersection for Freudian and Buddhist therapies, the Freudian system is darkened by the ambiguities inherent in the ego concept as used by Freud.

I wish to make three specific points in the light of the Buddhist theory of motivation, very briefly outlined here: First, there are two significant uses of the term *ego* that have to be clearly distinguished. Sometimes it is used to describe an aspect of the personality that coordinates mental functions. It is also used in a completely different sense to convey a strong self-interest. Thus, in the latter sense, the word *egotistical* is used to refer to people with a "strong ego" in a negative sense. When Freud finds that the ego is rooted in the id and yet it has to control it, and that the ego derives it strength from the id, he creates a veritable tangle. As Freud remarks:

When we speak of an "archaic heritage" we are usually thinking only of the id, and we seem to assume that at the beginning of the individual's life no ego is as yet in existence. But we shall not overlook the fact that id and ego are originally one; nor does it imply any mystical overvaluation of heredity if we think it credible that, even before the ego has come into existence, the lines of development, trends and reactions which it will later exhibit are already laid down for it."[22]

It is because of this impasse that we in the East, when we speak of personality growth, do not speak of strengthening, adding or accumulating. Rather our root metaphor is "let go" and "give up." These metaphors are now gaining entry into the humanistic psychotherapies.

This is the reason those like David Levin feel that, compared with the Buddhist approach of the analyst, the Freudian approach is coercive. What is necessary is an open, nondirective approach: "Freudian analysis is indeed reflective. But its way of reflecting is very different from the Buddhist's. The latter is like a clean mirror, or like the calm surface of a mountain lake; the former is more like an Expressionist portrait painted to reveal the sitter's true self."[23]

The dynamic psychology of Buddhism also provides a scheme of evaluating motives that are nonegotistical, nonaggressive, springing from detachment, compassion, knowledge, etc. The basic springs of human motivation are analyzed into three unwholesome roots—greed, hatred, and ignorance—and three wholesome roots—nongreed, nonhatred, and wisdom. There is no ambiguous ego structure or a flow of energy running both ways; the ways of parting for healthy and unhealthy actions are clearly laid down, and the tricks played by the ego concept, whether they be "conceptual" and semantic or experiential, are cautiously handled. They are not merely handled at an intellectual level, but also at the deeper levels of a "meditative" therapy, of tranquility meditation and insight meditation.

The second point that makes the termination of a successful analysis difficult according to Freud is the duality between Eros and destructiveness that generates conflicts. The Buddha's analysis sheds a great amount of light on the Freudian position—the inherent conflict between the two instincts. The drive for self-preservation and that for self-destruction, paradoxically, emerge from the same root of an ego illusion; they are like the two sides of the same coin. Buddha's psychological insight lay in pointing out that such apparently contradictory attitudes as narcissistic self-love and self-hatred or ambivalent attitudes such as the desire to live and to die stem from the same root. Suicide for example is paradoxically a strong form of self-love.

The enigmatic puzzle for Freud was "how can one who is infected with such an amount of self-love consent to his own destruction?" Freud came within the very doors of an interesting solution to unravel this puzzle, when he saw a link between "wounded narcissism" (injured self-love) and the state of depression described in "Mourning and Melancholia," but this was never integrated into his complete system as it could have been done.[24] In the Buddhist context, self-destruction would be "reactive" rather than "appetitive." But all the same, the two forms of craving, the craving for self-preservation or egoistic pursuits and the craving for self-annihilation are not "opposites"; they are merely the contrasting attitudes of a man who is subject to the illusion of a separate and indestructible ego.

The Buddha describes the vagaries of ego attachment with a graphic image: "just like a dog, brethren, tied up by a leash to a strong stake or pillar—if he goes, he goes up to that stake or pillar; if he stands, he stands close to that pillar or stake; if he lies down he lies close to that . . ." The pillar represents the "ego" (fivefold grasping group). Thus, if we take the "body" (which is one of the five grasping groups) as an example, whether we adorn the body, or like Narcissus fall in love with the reflection of one's own body in the pond, or we inflict torture on the body, we are like the dog tied to the pillar going round the same illusory pillar—the ego.

It is unfortunate that the first expounder of the concept of narcissism in psychoanalytic theory, Sigmund Freud, could not completely get out of the spell of the strong sexual overtones of his writings. It remained a mission for Erich Fromm to revitalize the Freudian notion of narcissism: "Narcissism is a passion the intensity of which in many individuals can only be compared with sexual desire and the desire to stay alive. In fact, many times it proves to be stronger than either. Even in the average individual in whom it does not reach such intensity, there remains a narcissistic core which appears almost indestructible."[25] It is true that the Buddhist doctrine of egolessness offers a clue to the besetting dilemmas of the narcissistic man, but Fromm feels that it is a dimension that fits in with all the great religions of the world, East or West.

Third, the constitutional strength of instincts and the "adhesiveness of the libido" are all accepted in the Buddhist concept in its recognition of the deep-rooted nature of craving. The Buddha does not exaggerate the role of sexuality as Freud does nor consider the duality between the life-and-death instinct as leading to a kind of interminable analysis. While accepting the strength of instincts, they can be tamed, redirected to sublimated goals, or even completely mastered. Although the ideal of harmonious living is sought by the householder, the recluse who has renounced the world seeks a path for the "elimination of all conflicts."

When Freud said that he was merely translating "hysterical misery into common unhappiness," he was underrating the potential of his own system. "Analysis Terminable and Interminable," though it is colored by a heavy tinge of pessimism, paradoxically contains within itself a deeper search for the roots of human happiness. I shall conclude this analysis with the observations of Robert H. Thouless, who wrote when searching for a wider mission for psychoanalysis:

One can speculate on the possibility of a future development of the therapy based on psycho-analysis to do more than this, to produce a radical mental reorientation that led to the complete disappearance of internal sources of unhappiness. If such a development of psychotherapy did take place, one can predict that it is likely to demand more time and energy than those of the few hours per week taken up by psycho-analysis. It is more likely to be a lifelong activity as is that of those striving for the final achievement of the Buddhist saint.[26]

Instincts, Society, and Civilization: Summing Up

It is known that people have limited problems of adjustment, specific symptoms that disappear due to the impact of analysis, weakness of memory, oddities, compulsions, and so forth. Some of these and more of a similar type can certainly be handled within the limited goals of psychotherapy. But types of patients and patterns of sickness have changed; the nature, effectiveness, stature, and status of modern analytical therapy is being reexamined; new cross-cutting pathways across psychoanalysis and other disciplines have emerged. In this context, a second glance at "Analysis Terminable and Interminable" can be a rewarding venture. The work also provides a good meeting ground for therapeutic orientations and metaphors of "health" and "sickness" found in the East and the West, as well as for exploring well-being within society.

Freud had conflicting notions regarding the relationship between instincts and society. He very clearly believed that society was so constituted that men were subject to emotional disturbances. Culture and civilization led to the repression of instincts. Freud also saw a strong element of aggression integrated into the development of the superego, the voice of morality and religion. If society is so constituted that it aggravates man's anxieties, why not change society? Though he seems to have favored revolutionary changes he did not turn to such a task. He also has a limited vision of the more positive and creative role that social interaction could play in the development of love and understanding. As Reuben Fine has pointed out, Freud became curiously hesitant at this point and seems to even accept the idea that it is not society that is at fault but the instincts themselves.[27] Freud also saw a kind of ambivalence and circular dialectic built into the notion of instincts such that attempts to control or tame them appeared to be difficult. In the clinical context he advocates rational and conscious encounter as the panacea for these ills, but works such as *Civilization and its Discontents*[28] provide a more perennial note of discordance and for this reason makes the case for the close understanding of "Analysis Terminable and Interminable" even more important.

NOTES

1. Sigmund Freud, "Analysis Terminable and Interminable," *The Standard Edition of the Complete Psychological Works of Sigmund Freud,* ed. James Strachey (London: Hogarth Press, 1966), 23: 216–53.

2. See Erich Fromm, in *Zen Buddhism and Psychoanalysis,* ed. Erich Fromm and D. T. Suzuki (New York: Harper, 1960), "Zen Buddhism and Psychoanalysis," 77–142.

3. Sigmund Freud, "Studies in Hysteria," *The Standard Edition,* vol. 2: 305.

4. Freud, "Analysis Terminable and Interminable," 250.

5. Ibid., 249.

6. See Anthony Storr, "The Concept of Cure," *Psychoanalysis Observed,* ed. C. Rycroft (London: Constable, 1966), 53.

7. Freud, "The Psychopathology of Everyday Life," *The Standard Edition,* vol. 6: 278.

8. Alasdair C. MacIntyre, *The Unconscious: A Conceptual Study* (London: Routledge & Kegan Paul, 1958), 25.

9. Freud, "Analysis Terminable and Interminable," 235.

10. Charles Rycroft, "Causes and Meaning," *Psychoanalysis Observed,* ed. C. Rycroft (London: Constable, 1966), 21.

11. Freud, "Analysis Terminable and Interminable," 224.

12. Ibid., 224.

13. See Dieter Wyss, *Depth Psychology: A Critical History,* trans. Gerald Onn (London: George Allen & Unwin, 1966), 121.

14. A more fruitful connection between Buddhism and Freudian analysis might begin with Freud's paper, "On Narcissism: An Introduction," *The Standard Edition,* 14:73–102, which is a great contribution. See my discussion of the Freudian notion of "narcissism" in the light of the ego concept in early Buddhism, in Padmasiri de Silva, *Buddhist and Freudian Psychology* (Colombo, Sri Lanka: Lake House Investments, 1978), 127–32.

15. See Fromm's "Zen Buddhism and Psychoanalysis"; David Levin's "Approaches to Psychotherapy: Freud, Jung and Tibetan Buddhism," in *The Metaphors of Consciousness,* ed. R. S. Valle and R. Von Eckartsberg (New York: Plenum Press, 1981), 243–74.

16. Fromm, "Zen Buddhism and Psychoanalysis," 91.

17. Ibid., 92.

18. Erich Fromm, *The Heart of Man* (New York: Harper & Row, 1964), 88.

19. Fromm, "Zen Buddhism and Psychoanalysis," 80–81.

20. Ibid., 86.

21. Herbert Fingarette, *Self-Deception* (London: Routledge and Kegan Paul, 1969), 142.

22. Freud, "Analysis Terminable and Interminable," 240.

23. Levin, "Approaches to Psychotherapy," 255.

24. Sigmund Freud, "Mourning and Melancholia," *The Standard Edition,* 14: 243–58.

25. Fromm, *The Heart of Man,* 72.

26. Robert H. Thouless, "Foreward," *Buddhist and Freudian Psychology,* viii–ix.

27. Reuben Fine, *The Development of Freud's Thought: From the Beginning* (New York: J. Aronson, 1962), 74.

28. Sigmund Freud, "Civilization and its Discontents," *The Standard Edition,* vol. 22: 143.

Part Two
SOCIAL DIMENSIONS OF RELIGIOUS TRADITIONS

The Social Dimension of the Faith of Judaism: Phenomenological and Historical Aspects
MANFRED H. VOGEL

The purpose of this essay is to examine the stance that Judaism takes with respect to the political dimension in life. We should note, therefore, at the very start that we are concerned here with the stance that Judaism takes rather than with the stance that Jews may or may not take toward the political dimension. It is important to note this, as it is by no means the case that the stance that Jews take is always and necessarily the same as the stance that Judaism dictates. The needs and requirements of the former are by no means always and necessarily identical with those of the latter. Indeed, the whole history of Judaism and of the Jewish people (and it is rather a long history) bears witness to the continuous tension between the two. What Jews as human beings wish and require is not necessarily what Judaism wishes and requires for them. Conversely, therefore, it also follows that what is good for the Jews is not necessarily good for Judaism, and vice versa, what is good for Judaism is not necessarily good for the Jews. This ironic discrepancy characterizes the situation throughout Jewish history, but it certainly comes to the fore and is most pronounced in the modern era in the context of the emancipation. There can be no denying that in this context the interests and needs of the emancipated Jew often collide head-on with the interests and needs of Judaism. Thus, what we may claim on behalf of Judaism may not at all be what the emancipated Jew would want to claim as his or her position. But be this as it may, our concern is with the position of Judaism and not with the position of Jewry, specifically, emancipated Jewry. We are not concerned with the historical, sociological, or psychological analysis of the attitude taken by a certain collectivty of people, but rather with the philosophical analysis of a certain *weltanschauung,* that is, a certain view of the world and man's place and vocation in it, that we call Judaism; or rather, as we would be inclined to say, we are concerned with a philosophical analysis of the structure of faith that constitutes Judaism.

We must realize, however, that Judaism in its historical manifestation, as, indeed, all other historical religions, encompasses a number of structures of faith. It is not monolithic; rather, it is a mixture of different structures of faith held together by shared symbols, rituals, and institutions. Thus, we should specify that our intention is to deal exclusively with the structures of faith that can be encountered in the prophetic strand of the Bible and in the nonmystical halackic strand of rabbinic Judaism and that we do not propose to deal here with those structures of faith that may manifest themselves, for example, in the priestly strand or the wisdom strand of the Bible or in the mystical or hasidic strand of rabbinic Judaism. Had we dealt with these latter strands the picture that would have emerged regarding our topic would have been quite different. Our choice to deal with the former strands, that is, the prophetic and nonmystical halackic strands, is not, however, completely arbitrary. For we would want to argue that these strands represent the mainstream expression in the historical manifestation of Judaism and, what is even more significant, they represent the *distinctive* expression of Judaism. (Indeed, no less significantly, though on a different level, a case can be made that it is by virtue of the structures of faith encountered in these strands that Judaism could survive through millennia of years of diaspora existence.) But whether or not one accepts the validity of these justifications, it is important for us to be clear about the parameters of our investigation, namely that when we refer to Judaism in this essay we have in mind the prophetic and nonmystical halachic strands of Judaism.

Lastly, as clarification, we should specify that the notion of "political dimension" involved in our discussion here is used in its broadest sense, namely, as the dimension that encompasses not only the political (now, in the narrower sense) relations, but also the social and economic relations; in short, the notion is used here to signify what we may call the "horizontal dimension" of life in its totality.

Thus, the task before us in this essay is to examine in what way (and if at all) the structure of faith of Judaism (specifically, of the prophetic and halachic strands) implicates involvement in the horizontal dimension of life. Is involvement in the horizontal dimension of life a necessary, essential, and inextricable aspect of the religious life or is it of no real consequence? And if the former, in what sense does it constitute the religious vocation for Judaism?

The Social Dimension of the Faith of Judaism

We can answer this central question in a very straightforward and unqualified way: our thesis is that the structure of faith of Judaism necessarily implicates, as an essential and inextricable act, its involvement within the horizontal dimension of life in all its aspects, i.e., social, economic, and political. Take away the possibility of involvement in the horizontal dimension of life, and the very structure of faith of Judaism (i.e., of prophetic and nonmystical halachic Judaism) disintegrates. The task before us now, of course, is to justify and explain this claim.

To justify this claim should not, in our judgment, be too difficult. For it can hardly be denied that biblical prophecy by its very essence is deeply involved in the horizontal dimension of life. Take away the critique of social injustice, of economic oppression, the involvement in international politics, and what is left of biblical prophecy? And isn't the distinctive and imposing feature of the halacha the fact that it encompasses a comprehensive civil, political, and criminal law in addition to the ritual law, thus encompassing the totality of the horizontal dimension of life? The point, I think, needs no further elaboration. Indeed, biblical and rabbinic scholarship has almost universally recognized and acknowledged this point. To quote at random only a few sources: "the justice of the prophets is social justice. They demand not only a pure heart but also just institutions. They are concerned for the improvement of society even more than for the welfare of the individual";[1] "the Hebrews were the first who rebelled against the injustice of the world . . . Israel demanded social justice";[2] "our social legislation is derived from the spirit of the prophets. Also in the future will the spirit of Israel remain the instigator and awakener of social reforms";[3] "the basis of Judaism is ethics";[4] "the idea of the inseparateness between religion and ethical life arose for the first time in Judaism . . . this idea of the unit of ethics and religion passes through the whole Bible . . . and this applies equally to rabbinic literature";[5] "in any reading of Judaism the ethical dimension is of supreme importance. Judaism has always taught that God wishes man to pursue justice . . . to make his contribution towards the emergence of a better social order. This is a constant theme in the Bible and in the Rabbinic literature."[6] Any further buttressing of this assertion is not really called for; what is called for, however, is an attempt to explicate why and how this is so. This is the intriguing and challenging task and we will try to accomplish it in the remainder of this essay.

We would submit that the key to the understanding of why the structure of faith in these strands of Judaism necessarily and essentially implicates the involvement within the horizontal dimension of life lies in the fact that the very structure of faith here formulates itself from the ethical perspective rather than from the ontological perspective. What do we mean by this? We mean that the fundamental predicament of man is not perceived here to lie in the "way man is constituted" but rather in the way in which he expresses and realizes himself within the possibilities and limitations of his given ontological constitution. The fact that man is constituted, to use Buberian terms, as an It-Thou being, as body and soul, as material and spiritual, as divine and earthly—as the bearer of the divine image and a being of nature, a member of the animal kingdom—is not perceived to constitute the fundamental predicament. There is nothing wrong with the way man was created; by and large, there is no pessimism or desperation about this—the judgment about creation is positive, that it was good. Rather, where the fundamental predicament, the problematic, is perceived to lie is in the balance that man, all too often, strikes between these two dimensions in the way he expresses and realizes himself. The problematic lies in the fact that man all too often realizes and expresses himself as a beast—albeit a sophisticated beast but therefore also, all too often, as a very mischievous beast—rather than as the bearer of the divine image. To use Buberian terms again, the predicament lies in the fact that man, all too often, acts and relates to others in the I-It rather than in the I-Thou context. Therefore, the salvation that is envisioned and yearned for does not involve the ontological transformation of man, the new creation of man as a "new being," but rather the steadfastness of man in striking and maintaining the proper balance between the two dimensions constituting his being—indeed it is a redemption rather than a salvation that is envisaged.

It should be clear that as such the perceived predicament and the envisaged redemption are centered here not on the way man is constituted, on his ontological makeup, but on his actions, on his relations with others. Consequently, the perspective involved here, that is, the perspective in terms of which the structure of faith formulates itself, is evidently an ethical perspective. For the evaluation of actions and relations, specifically of *man's* actions and relations, is precisely what constitutes the business of ethics.

But a structure of faith that formulates itself from the ethical perspective would necessarily implicate involvement in the horizontal dimension of life. For in being concerned with the proper balancing between the It and the Thou dimension in man's expression and realization of himself in his actions and relations, it must of necessity encompass the action and relations of man with respect to the world, specifically, to the human world, that is, to the human horizontal dimension of life. The horizontal dimension of life cannot be left out of the picture as inconsequential precisely because the perceived predicament and thus the envisioned redemption necessarily involve here (at least in part) man's actions and relations that impinge upon the horizontal dimension of life. Thus, man's actions and relations with respect to the horizontal dimension of life become an inextricable part in the forumulation of the two basic categories of the structure of faith, that is, of the category of the fundamental predicament and that of redemption.

But even more to the point (and this, indeed, is the very crux of the matter), the very actions and relations of man with respect to God and, conversely, God's actions and relations with respect to man must be "refracted," mediated, through the horizontal dimension of life. For we must not overlook or forget that the It dimension in man is not to be extirpated, which is tantamount to saying that man is to remain a this-worldly being.[7] But this, in turn, means that all actions involving man, thus including the actions and relations that express the Thou dimension, must inevitably be "refracted" through the It dimension. Thus, even man's action and relation with respect to God, which in terms of God being a pure Thou being (the eternal Thou) are to belong exclusively to the pure Thou dimension, must be "refracted" here through the It dimension, that is, through the horizontal dimension, because of the inextricable presence of the It dimension in the constitution of man. This, of course, means that the most fundamental and central aspect of the religious life, namely, the relation between man and the divine, must be mediated through the horizontal dimension. Indeed, in the prophetic and nonmystical halachic strands of Judaism the burden of the expression of the relationship of man to God, namely, the burden of the expression of faith and of worship, is not expressed in direct vertical relationships, but rather in indirect relationships, that is, in relationships that go through the horizontal dimensions, specifically, the human horizontal dimension (seeing that man is the only being in nature endowed with the Thou dimension).[8] Or to make the same point, but this time not with respect to the divine, it is indeed the case that in the structure of faith of the prophetic and nonmystical halachic strands of Judaism's God, who is constituted as a pure Thou and as transcending the world, is nonetheless represented as deeply and essentially involved in the relations of man to the world, again, specifically the social world of man. God, the pure Thou, the transcending God, is affected in the most real and profound sense by what man does or does not do with respect to the world, especially with respect to his fellow man.[9] Thus, in the prophetic and in the nonmystical halachic strands of Judaism, man can fully witness to God, in the last analysis, only through the world—he can fully establish his relationship to God only through the world, he can work for redemption and redemption that can be realized only through and in the world. Take away man's involvement in the horizontal dimension of life, and the whole structure of faith collapses. Thus, in the strands of Judaism represented here one cannot separate the vertical from the horizontal, the sacred from the profane, relegating the religious concern, that is, faith, exclusively to the former. The religious concern, that is, faith, which of course must ultimately come to rest in the vertical, is nonetheless inextricably intertwined within the horizontal.

But let us be clear about the precise meaning of the relationship that exists between faith and the horizontal dimension of life. Clearly, it is diametrically opposed to the model whereby faith, taken as the direct vertical relating of man to the divine, is completely (one is tempted to say hermetically) separated from the horizontal dimension (a model that may be found, for example, in some formulations of German Lutheranism). But let us note what may not at first sight appear so clear—that it also differs from the model whereby faith, still constituted as the direct vertical relating of man to the divine, is now connected with the horizontal dimension; where faith is brought to bear upon the horizontal dimension, for example, by molding and guiding it or by manifesting its fruit within it (a model that may be encountered, perhaps, in Calvinism or in Catholicism). For in Judaism the very constitution of faith is effected through the horizontal dimension. It is not that faith is constituted here independently as a direct vertical mode of relating, which is then brought into relation with the horizontal dimension of life; rather, faith is constituted here as an indirect mode of relating, which is refracted through the horizontal dimension of life. Without relating through the horizontal dimension of life there can be no faith. Perhaps we can put the matter thus: the relation of faith to the horizontal dimension of life is not established in the context of sanctification; it is established in the very context of justification.

But to return to our main line of argument, there is an all-important aspect that the formulation of the structure of faith from the ethical perspective further implicates for the prophetic and nonmystical halachic strands of Judaism. In implicating the involvement of religion in the horizontal dimension, it also implicates an inextricable bond between religion and the category of the ethnic-national entity. This is to say, it establishes religion as being primarily not the affair of the individual but rather the affair of the collectivity, specifically, of the ethnic-national entity. (It is not surprising, therefore, that the human pole in the divine-human relation, both when it is the active agent and when it is the receiving object in the relation, is represented primarily by the ethnic-national collectivity and not by the individual.)

The claim that religion must implicate the collectivity rather than the individual as the primary context of its expression can be seen in the consideration that, inasmuch as religion formulates itself from the ethical perspective, it impinges not on questions concerning the being of man, but rather on questions concerning the actions and relations of man. As such, it cannot impinge exclusively on the individual person, but must impinge on man and the object of his actions or on man and his partner in relation. Because of a number of considerations that cannot be elaborated on here, this partner, this "other" must be a fellow man. (Suffice it to say that inasmuch as the ethical perspective involved here represents an ethics that is grounded in accountability and responsibility, it must impinge on actions and relations that arise exclusively between man and his fellow man and not upon actions and relations that may arise between man and the inanimate objects of nature.) Thus, religion cannot impinge upon man in his monadic individuality; it must impinge upon both man and his fellow man. But a twosome, that is man and his fellow man, already constitute a collectivity, a human community.

The claim that the collectivity implicated here cannot be just any collectivity but must be specifically the ethnic-national collectivity can be seen from the consideration that only the ethnic-national collectivity can encompass the full gamut of relations constituting the horizontal dimension of life on which a religion formulating itself from the ethical perspective would optimally have to impinge.

All other subnational or extranational collectivities (as, for example, the family, the clan, or any of the social, cultural, professional, ideological, or political associations) can present only some of these relations, but never all of them. Thus, if the horizontal dimension of life is to be made available to religion in all its relations—the social, economic, and political—the collectivity that is to be implicated must be specifically the ethnic-national collectivity.

It must be clear, however, that the ethnic-national entity cannot really fulfill its function optimally with respect to religion, that is, it cannot make fully available to religion the horizontal dimension of life, unless it has sovereignty. The ethnic-national entity must have the power to shape, regulate, and determine the relations constituting the horizontal dimension of life. It must have the power to impose its wishes and judgments with respect to these relations. In other words, it must possess a horizontal dimension—a horizontal dimension must rightfully belong to it. It must be at its disposal freely to determine its destiny.

We have thus far argued, therefore, that the prophetic and non-mystical halachic strands for Judaism in formulating themselves from the ethical perspective implicate an indirect relating to the divine, a relating that is "refracted" through the horizontal dimension of life, thus involving Judaism in a very fundamental and essential way in the matrix of the horizontal dimension of life in all its aspects bar none. We have further argued that this implicates an inextricable bond between Judaism and an ethnic-national entity. And last, we have argued that for Judaism to optimally express and realize itself, the ethnic-national entity that is inextricably bound to it must possess sovereignty.

Indeed, in light of these considerations one can come to understand and evaluate the major transformations in Jewish history not only from the vantage point of the fortunes or suffering of Jewry, but from the vantage point of the needs and requirements of the structure of faith of Judaism. We can gain different insights into the strengths and weaknesses that will be judged now not from the vantage point of how they impinged on the well-being of Jewry, but rather from the vantage point of how they impinged on the viability of the structure of faith of Judaism.

Thus, from this vantage point, the essential strength and advantage of the biblical period lies in the fact that it provided sovereignty and consequently that it could place the horizontal dimension in all its relations at the disposal of Judaism. In such a context Judaism could express itself fully and in this sense it was indeed the fulfillment of the promise. Indeed, the tradition knew this for its continuous yearning for restoration signified for it not only the liberation from the physical sufferings of exile, but the renewal of the opportunity for Judaism to express itself *fully* (in its language: the renewal of the opportunity to observe *all of God's* commandments). It is not a coincidence that the tradition links its messianic hope to the restoration, making the former contingent upon the latter.

On the other hand, the essential predicament and problematic that diaspora existence presents must be seen to lie principally in the fact that diaspora existence signifies the abrogation of sovereignty. But more specifically, the problematic of the abrogation of sovereignty must be seen here to lie not so much in the scattering of the Jews or in their dependence for their very physical survival on the good graces of others, but in the fact that the abrogation of sovereignty threatened the availability to Judasim of the horizontal dimension of life. For without a horizontal dimension at its disposal Judaism could not survive.[10] Indeed, Judaism managed to survive in diaspora existence only because it succeeded, partly due to fortuitous circumstances, to establish what has been called "a state within a state," namely, only because it succeeded to create in diaspora, and thus without sovereignty, a portable horizontal dimension that was at its disposal. True, this horizontal dimension provided by "ghettoized" existence was limited and consequently the expression of the structure of faith of Judaism in these circumstances could only be a truncated expression. Still, it evidently was sufficient to allow for the survival of Judaism.

By this very same logic, however, when things are to be viewed from the vantage point of the interests and requirements of the structure of faith of Judaism, the crisis that the emancipation precipitates in modern Jewish life must be seen now to lie essentially in the fact that the thrust of the emancipation is to abrogate this limited horizontal dimension that Judaism managed to establish for itself in the context of diaspora existence. For what the emancipation really signifies is the exit of Jewry from its ghettoized existence and its entry into the life stream of the host nation, and the real crisis that this represents when viewed from the vantage point of the structure of faith of Judaism, is the loss of the horizontal dimension to Judaism. For the horizontal dimension, albeit the limited, truncated horizontal dimension, that Judaism managed to constitute for itself in the context of ghettoized existence could not be transferred into the life stream of the host nation. This meant that to the extent Judaism did manage to accompany emancipated Jewry, albeit in a restricted and mitigated way, into the life stream of the host nation, it was nonetheless, in terms of its own structure, made impotent in the process. Thus, from the vantage point of the structure of faith of Judaism the real crisis that the emancipation precipitates for Judaism must be seen to lie in the fact that the emancipation abrogates the horizontal dimension that was at the disposal of Judaism and that consequently it necessarily emasculates Judaism and renders it impotent.[11]

Finally, the real significance of the reestablishment of the state of Israel (again, when viewed from the vantage point of the structure of faith of Judaism) must be seen to lie in the fact that it rescues for Judaism the horizontal dimension in terms of emancipated Jewry—and indeed it rescues the horizontal dimension no longer in a truncated form but in its full extention. For only in the context of the reestablished state of Israel can Jewry reenter the life stream of history, can Jewry be emancipated from its ghettoized existence, in a way that allows Judaism to accompany it fully and in a viable manner. If Judaism is to survive in the context of the emancipation, therefore, the reestablishment of the state of Israel becomes a condition sine qua non. For only in the context of the reestablished state can the horizontal dimension in terms of emancipated Jewry be placed at the disposal of Judaism. And indeed, because the horizontal dimension is provided here with sovereignty, it not only allows Judaism to survive, namely, to hold the fort and mark time (as the horizontal dimension in the context of ghettoized existence did), but it should allow Judaism once more to pursue its vocation in full force.

Thus, we have tried to argue that by its very structure of faith, seeing that it formulates itself from the ethical perspective, Judaism must express itself in the horizontal dimension. It must impinge upon the horizontal dimension in all its aspects. The availability, therefore, of the horizontal dimension is essential to Judaism. Without a horizontal dimension at its disposal, Judaism would disintegrate. *In no other religion* is this requirement—to be involved in the horizontal dimension, to impinge upon it in all its aspects—more central or essential than it is in Judaism. But we've also tried to argue that Judaism can impinge upon the horizontal dimension only if the horizontal dimension rightfully belongs to it, only if it possesses sovereignty over it. It can impinge upon the horizontal dimension only in its own "backyard," in its own "home." But this means that the most that Judaism can do in the context of diaspora existence is to constitute, if allowed, a limited horizontal dimension, as an enclave separated and isolated from the life stream of the host nation, upon which it can impinge. Evidently, it cannot impinge upon the horizontal dimension of the host nation. No host would allow it and rightly so.

But one may contend that although this argument may be valid with respect to host nations that are homogeneous, it would have to be greatly mitigated if the host nations had pluralistic societies. For shouldn't Judaism in these circumstances have a partial rightful claim on the horizontal dimension of life and shouldn't it therefore be allowed to impinge, at least in part, upon it? Thus, if the emancipation is to take place in the context of a pluralistic society, shouldn't the problematic that it precipitates for Judaism be greatly mitigated? There is no question that at first sight the pluralistic alternative appears very attractive. But after a closer look, we would submit, its attractiveness is greatly diminished. First, there are any number of very difficult practical problems that a pluralistic situation presents. How, for example, would such an arrangement work when there are several religions claiming the right to impinge upon the horizontal dimension? Would it work by finding the least offensive common denominator of these religions and allow only the common denominator to impinge upon the horizontal dimension; or would the horizontal dimension be partitioned among the various religions, allowing each to impinge on only part of it? Clearly, neither of these alternatives would be satisfactory to Judaism nor, I dare say, to any other religion. But as far as Judaism is concerned, there is even a more serious problem, not of mere practicality but of substance. To see this we must ask, what kind of pluralism are we talking about? Are we talking of a pluralism that is merely religious or are we talking of a pluralism that is actually ethnic? If it is the former, then Judaism, unlike other religions, may well be unable to avail itself of its opportunities. For, as we have seen above, Judaism is inextricably bound to a specific ethnic-national entity and it would perforce be excluded by virtue of this ethnic bond. Thus, for pluralism to present meaningful possibilities to Judaism in diaspora existence, one must envision a pluralism that is specifically ethnic. But given the way the world is, I'm not at all sure that such an ethnic pluralism is feasible. I certainly do not know of any instance of authentic pluralism that is stable and viable and that appears to be a permanent state of affairs (let alone any instance that would also incorporate Judaism as a full-fledged ethnic partner).[12]

Thus, we must conclude that as far as diaspora existence is concerned, Judaism, in the context of the emancipation, is not really in a position to impinge upon the horizontal dimension of life. (What *emancipated Jewry* does is, of course, quite a different story.) This is somewhat ironic because Judaism, perhaps more than any other religion, is a religion that by its very essence requires that it impinge upon the horizontal dimension of life. But then, this is part of the price that diaspora existence exacts.

NOTES

1. Julius Wellhausen, *Israelistische und Juedische Geschichte* (Berlin: Vereingung Wissenschafllicher Verloger, Walter de Gruyter Co., 1921), 114.

2. Ernest Renan, *Histoire du Peuple d'Israel,* 3 (Paris: Calmann-Lévy, 1889), vi–vii.

3. Herman Gunkel, *Deutsche Rundschau,* 2 (Berlin: Verlag von Gerbrüder Baetel, 1875), 231.

4. K. Kohler, *The Ethical Basis of Judaism,* (New York: The Young Men's Hebrew Association, 1887), 143.

5. Isidore Epstein, *Emunat Ha-Yahadut* (Jerusalem: Mossad Harave Kook, 1964), 18–19.

6. Louis Jacobs, *A Wish Theology* (New York: Behrman, 1973), 231.

7. See, for example, Martin Buber, *I and Thou* (Edinburgh: T. & T. Clark, 1958), vol. 11, 34.

8. See my essay, "The Distinctive Expression of the Category of Worship in Judaism," in *Bijdrachen,* 43, no. 1 (December 1982): 350–81.

9. For a striking description of this aspct of the divine in prophetic literature see Abraham J. Heschel, *The Prophets,* (New York: Harper & Row, 1969), vol. 2, chaps. 1, 3, 4.

10. Max Wiener, *Judische Religion in Zeitalter der Emanzipation* (Berlin: Philo Verlag, 1933).

11. For a fuller analysis of the problematic that the Emanicipation precipitates for

Judaism see my essay, "The Dilemma of Identity for the Emancipated Jew," reprinted in *New Theology*, no. 4, ed. Martin E. Marty and Dean G. Peerman.

12. For a further critique of the notion of pluralism as it impinges on the state of Judaism and Jewry in diaspora see my review article, "The Impact of the Emancipation on Continuity and Change in Judaism," in the *Journal of Religion*, 59, no. 4 (October 1979).

5

Liberation in Social Life: A Buddhist View

GESHE LOBSANG TSEPAL AND ACHARYA KARMA MONLAM

Namoguru Manjugoshaya (Homage to Manjugosha)

In this essay, I would like to throw some light on the possibility of liberation in social life based on the teachings of Buddha. Rationality will be the means through which this topic will be discussed. This seems appropriate since in this atomic age, science based on logical reasoning dominates all social activities. Here, seemingly, only logical reasoning has a part to play.

In our view, where the three baskets of the teachings of Buddha prevail, together with a noncontradictory understanding and practice of the three Disciplines, there abides the teachings (shasna) of Buddha, the Enlightened One. Where the sublime remedy (upaya) is accompanied by compassion, there is said to prevail the teachings of Mahayana. Moreover, there is provision within Mahayana to practice equally investigative and fixed meditations and for the practice of Sutra and Tantra in combination. Therefore the questions are: What is to be practiced? How is it to be practiced? And what can we achieve as result of such practice? It is also important to understand these practices in the right context.

Whoever desires to be happy by intellectual means has to search for the remedies that can liberate us from the sufferings of cyclic existence (samsara). Moreover, such a person must learn what the appropriate things are that can be observed for attaining liberation. The intellectual way of investigation must be based on the four Relying-on's. First, we must not rely on the person but on the dharma, the words or teachings. Second, we should not rely on the words alone but on their meanings. But in respect to the meanings of words, we must—and this is the third—rely on their *definitive* meaning rather than on their *interpretative* meaning. And fourthly, in the investigation of meaning we must not rely upon the mind, but on wisdom. In this context, to rely on or not to rely on means to confide in, to believe as true.

The first two ways—relying on dharma and meaning—are to be accepted while we acquire knowledge. That is, one should be fully concerned with the subject (even if it turns out that it does not show the correct way of liberation or is not helpful) and not about the person who is talking or teaching the subject at hand. One may be of any social status or have any type of personality. Likewise, when regarding the subject at hand, one should investigate and examine thoroughly the *meaning* of that subject, but not its expression. Then, when meditating or during the analysis of meanings, one should rely on and strive for the definitive meaning of the subject, that is, the correct understanding of that meaning. Interpretive meanings should only be regarded as complementary for understanding the definitive meaning.

While practicing for the accomplishment of liberation, one should not be satisfied with the knowledge of learning alone. Rather one should be seeking the deeper knowledge of actual experience through meditation. Thus one must rely on the fourth element: wisdom. (The necessity of relying wholly on wisdom is thoroughly explained by Acharya Asanga.)

The practice of the four Relying-on's enables a person to create a deep respect for the profound dharma, to practice the profound knowledge, to avoid misunderstanding the meanings of prophecy, and to obtain the wisdom-without-passion. As it is said in the *Sutra-Alangkara* by Arya Maitrinath: "One likes and practices, hears correctly from others and by inexpressible wisdom, one will not be betrayed."

In regard to Buddhism one who accepts the Triple Gem (Trirattana) as the ultimate refuge is said to be Buddhist. The way of accepting the Triple Gem is explained by Bodhipadhpradipam as arising from (1) understanding the virtuous qualities of the Triple Gem, (2) understanding their characteristics, and (3) by not accepting through the four means. The view that *going for refuge* is the watermark for differentiating a Buddhist from non-Buddhist is unanimously accepted by Acharya Shantideva, Atisha, and rJe Tsongkhapa. And it is a very important point.

Establishment of the Correct View

Here it seems important to briefly review some other views, that of nihilism, for instance. Nihilists assert in their philosophy: "Pleasure should be sought till death. After death there is nothing to enjoy as the body is turned into ashes and there is no question of rebirth. Therefore, there is neither life nor future incarnations." They assert that there is no previous birth because purush (soul) originates from the body, and the body itself is composed of the great elements. Thus there is no previous life. They also deny future rebirth on the grounds that at the time of death the body disappears into the four great elements and the soul likewise disappears. The analogies often cited are alcohol and its power of intoxication, the lamp and its light, and a wall and its paintings.

To refute such views, many logical, rational discussions have been furnished by Acharya Chandrakirti and also by Acharya Bhavaveveka in *Tarkajaval*. Here we will not go into detail on their arguments in order to save space and time. But nonetheless, the question arises: How can we prove the existence of previous lives and future births? What is the cause of the first moment of the mind of a new born common person? Its cause is a former mind. There is also the case with the present mind. Likewise, the last moment of the mind of a common man at the time of death causes the mind to continue and make chain connections for the future births because it is a mind with continuity of attachments. Thus the mind continues and causes reincarnation or the next life.

In this way, then, we can prove former and future life. We can also prove that one can gain enlightenment. Compassion and wisdom, which are the inevitable means of Buddhahood, can be practiced for many lifetimes, and such practices can develop to infinity. Moreover, such qualities of mind are steadfast and once gained remain. In each successive life, then, they come automatically without repeated effort. This creates a steadfastness in the mind. It is a quality in the nature of the mind that will not require repeated effort because, once created, compassion will remain on the mental continuum and no additional effort is needed to create it again.

To those who are of the view that there cannot be an enlightened person purified of all sins, we ask the following questions: (1) Do they believe so because they believe faults such as passions are permanent?; (2) Do they believe that if these faults are impermanent there is no remedy to overcome them?; (3) Do they believe that even if there is a remedy there is no one who understands it?; (4) Do they believe that there is no one who puts forth the effort to know it?; (5) Do they believe that though there might be someone who seeks to know it, there can't be anyone to teach that remedy?

Now let us repudiate these views one by one. First, passions cannot be permanent because they have causes behind them, that is, they can be destroyed by the removal or negation of their causes. Second, we are not without a remedy to remove these passions. Rather, as we focus our practice on the origin or cause of these faults, they will be completely uprooted. Third, the remedy can be understood because when the nature of the cause is known its overcoming can be understood. And fourth, it is also not the case that there is no one who would try to know the remedy. Rather, as a person arrives at the conclusion that he himself is suffering worldly sorrows and pains, he understands that it is the causes that make him suffer. And, by understanding the causes of suffering, we turn to annihilate that suffering by bringing the causes to an end. Finally, the assertion that there is no one to teach the remedy is also invalid, because when a person gains enlightenment, then he will show the way or method through his own experience to overcome suffering. This would be done without any selfish motive, but because of his compassion for suffering beings.

Such reasoning is in accordance with the logic of the teaching of Chandrakirtri. As he said, "As there is cause, it can be annihilated by practicing the antagonism of it." This means that by putting an end to causes, things such as suffering can be eliminated forever. Thus, we can deduce that the mind by its own nature is pure, clear, and faultless; but it is obscured by temporary clouds of faults.

Four Noble Truths

The essence of the path to be practiced for liberation consists of the sixteen features of the Four Noble Truths. Consequently, we would like to briefly introduce these elements. Since each of the Four Noble Truths has four features, there are sixteen elements in all.

(1) The four features of "True Suffering" are based on misunderstandings of being clean, happy, permanent and on the existence of an I or atman. (a) We are void of anything clean for there is no I or atman which is different from the suffering body itself. (b) This physical body, which is the real samsara, is not happiness because it is completely under the control of action (karma) and afflictions (klesha). (c) This body cannot be permanent because it is undergoing change at every single moment. (d) The causal body is without an I or atman, as there does not exist such an I or atman.

(2) The four features of "True Case" are: the cause, the all-

growing, the effectively encouraging growth, and the agent. (a) These are the roots of all sufferings, karma, and cyclic existence with passion, the true cause. (b) Likewise, karma and cyclic existence with passion is all-growing, because all kinds of pains and sorrows are caused by them over and over again. (c) Karma and cyclic existence effectively encourage the growth of suffering for they create very strong sufferings. (d) They are also the agents since the passion for cyclic existence is the spontaneous agent of sufferings.

(3) The four features of "True Cessation" are: cessation, calmness, complete satisfaction, and sure liberation (definite deliverance). These are the remedies of the four misunderstandings regarding cessation, namely, believing in the nonexistence of liberation, mistaking some passioned aspect for liberation, looking for liberation above the end of suffering, and believing that there cannot be definite deliverance. (a) The elimination of suffering forever through antagonistic methods is cessation. Here one is free of sufferings. (b) As it is devoid of all afflictions, it is calmness. (c) It is completely satisfying because it is the supreme stage of bliss and liberation. (d) Once this liberation is achieved there is no losing it, thus it is definite deliverance.

(4) The four features of "True Path" are: suitability, accomplishment, path, and definitely giving forth (definite emergence). (a) Wisdom, actually knowing the nonexistence of I or atman is the path because it leads to liberation. (b) This wisdom is suitable for it is the direct antidote of afflictions. (c) It is also accomplishment as it correctly knows the real state of mind. (d) It has the aspect of definitely giving forth because it brings forth the esteemed object.

Logic of Establishing the Nonexistence of I or Atman

The logic for establishing the nonexistence of I through understanding the main causes binding us to worldly existence is discussed in the Madhyamika Shastras, the texts of the central philosophy of Buddhism. This logic can be categorized into two groups, based on the person and phenomena. These two—the person and phenomena—are the main causes of cyclic existence (samsara). Thus, they should be the main subject of discussion when establishing the nonexistence of the two selves. It is said in *Dan-nge-nam-jed:* "attachment to the person, regarding which one thinks it is Me, the I and the phenomena on its continuum are the main binders, thus they are also the main subject of belief in the existence of Self. Therefore, the logics are also condensed for the repudiation of these two Selves."

The main logic for establishing the nonexistence of the phenomenal self is the logic of not originating through the four ends. Acharya Nagarjuna, while commenting on the theory of entering the sixth Bhumi (stage) by ten equal aspects, observed that the "equal aspect of nonoriginating is the most important." Thus, it is mentioned at the very beginning of the *Mula Madhyamikakarika:* "Neither from self nor from others . . . ."

Likewise, Acharya Chandrakirti discussed nonorigination through the four ends in the *Madhyamika-avatāara.* Thus the main logical reason for establishing the nonexistence of the phenomenal self is reached by discussing nonorigination through four ends. This does not mean that there is self-origination. Now, let us discuss the logical reasons for establishing the nonorigination through four ends in their own perspectives. They are: (1) originating from self, (2) originating from other than self, (3) originating from both, and (4) originating without cause.

For example, a grown sprout need not grow again because it is already grown. A thing which has obtained its identity does not need to grow again. Otherwise, there is no end to growth and a grown thing would be required to grow again. It is also said in *Buddhapalita,* "Things do not grow or originate from themselves because there is no purpose and moreover, there will never be completion of growth, which is absolutely irrational." Something that has obtained itself need not grow again as there is no purpose for such growth. If a thing originates from such causes having self-definition then it must grow from everything, as everything has the same aspect of being other. Thus it is said in the twentieth chapter of the *Mula-Madhyamika-karika:* "If a different fruit grows from a different cause then there is no question of one and not the other being the cause of a thing. So, from the above two reasons it is clear that there can't be origination from both. Nothing occurs without any cause, otherwise, everything must grow from everything in all times".

The nonexistence of the self or person (purush-atman) can be established by examining the seven aspects of the example of a cart. A cart is composed of several elements and parts, which together are called a cart and serve the purpose of a cart. But each component part is not the cart. By assembling all the parts together into their right places, a cart comes into existence. It is the same case with the self or person. Thus it is said in the *Madhyamika-avatāara* when discussing this example: "A cart can neither exist apart from its component parts, nor be the same as its parts, . . . nor is it only the composition, nor the shape so formed." This means that a cart does not exist in these seven aspects, but by depending on the parts we can be sure that there is a cart which can actually be used for certain purposes. It is the same with the self.

Furthermore, it would be a mistake to identify the self or person with the physical body. First, such an identification would be meaningless because the physical body is caused by causes. Second, such a self would be as many as there are parts of the physical body. Thirdly, if the physical body is the self then the self must be born and must also die together with the physical body. Here a question can arise: what is wrong in accepting the self as being born and dying? If it is just an etymological fact, there is nothing wrong with this view. But when birth or death of self means "independent by one's own self," it is mistaken in three ways. If the originating and ceasing of the self is independent and by its own self then (1) there can't be anyone who remembers his or her previous birth or life, (2) such efforts or collection of deeds (karma) would be of no importance, and (3) one can suffer or enjoy the fruit of a thing with which one has no relation whatsoever.

But we can't hold that the self is completely separate from the body. Otherwise, we can't accept the originating, ceasing, and lasting of the self as we know it. So, in the *Madhyamika-karika* it is said "If the self is completely separate from the physical composition, then there can't be the existent nature of the self."

Just as the composition of the aggregate can't be accepted as the self, neither can we assume that the shape of the aggregate is without any form. By this analysis, the self cannot be regarded as having an independent nature. Thus the self does not exist by itself. There is no self as such except in an etymological sense.

Various aspects of the nonexistence of the self are taught by the Enlightened One. These teachings are designed to suit intellectual powers of different individuals. They include the views of a permanent single, independent I, an independent, substantial self, the absolute that is void of subject and perception. All such phenomena exist in an etymological but not in an absolute sense. These matters are crucial to the principle of cause and effect as well as the overcoming of worldly bondage and the attainment of liberation. The former views are the steps of understanding the later ones and there is no contradiction in gradual practice.

We have thus briefly discussed how our basic bondage to cyclic existence can be recognized in order to be able to practice the methods of liberation. So, in short, those having ability should practice in accordance with the five texts by Arya Maitrinath, the six texts on central philosophy by Acharya Nagarjuna, and the graded course to enlightenment by Acharya Tsongkhapa.

Therefore, we have to practice wholeheartedly while we are in contact with such precious guidance for liberation in order to make this human life meaningful for oneself and others. By doing so we can lead a happy and benevolent social life and guide fellow beings toward a better future and ultimately gain liberation from all worldly chains. It is not necessary or essential to remain solitary or torture oneself to such extremes in the name of such practice for liberation.

As man is a social animal, he should seek happiness and liberation while being in society by conquering his own mind and eliminating all negative views and thoughts. Thus there is the possibility of liberation in social life.

MAY ALL SENTIENT BEINGS GAIN THE WISDOM OF PERFECTION.

6

The Social Philosophy of Dhammology
SIDDHI BUTR-INDR

A Thai Preface

According to the "domino theory," a country such as Thailand was internally vulnerable and would tend to fall in whatever direction her neighboring countries of Indochina moved. This view contains an assumption that can be shown to entail a logical fallacy: *ignoratio elenchi*. Moreover, this view failed to recognize the possibilities inherent in Thai culture itself. In this essay, I want to show a way that overcomes the domino theory. My essay is extracted and revised from a larger work in progress entitled "The Social Philosophy of Humanism." There I philosophically explore, after an introductory chapter, the topics of man and man, man and nature, man and culture, and the future of humanity. My purpose there, as here, is to develop a social philosophy from an Eastern, Buddhist perspective. It is formulated within the intellectual culture of Buddhist humanism. But I also seek to engage some Western views. Its final aim is to initiate or propose some form of a dialectical principle that, however limited, might contribute to the creation of new patterns of philosophizing that can serve the *social unification of man*.

My research method is to adapt the Four Noble Truths of the Buddhist tradition to a more contemporary style and situation. This is what must be done since, to my knowledge, the Four Noble Truths are well known and familiar to Eastern peoples, especially to those raised in Buddhist civilizations. My approach, then, proceeds step by step along this path. First, I point out the real, effective phenomena in human society today, the things we are actually experiencing. It is the experience of a world full of difficulties and suffering. Next, I try to explain what the root causes of this situation in the world are and why they remain. In this context, I show that the root cause of this misery can be traced to man's intellectual and spiritual illusions, especially to his dogmatic clinging to philosophical particularity.

Then, I argue that by human striving and endeavor there can be a positive cessation of the root causes that underlie social crises and suffering. The pragmatic truth of the human potential for well-being and human welfare sustains and supports the logical principles proposed. Thus the social philosophy outlined here is neither a dream in the air, nor a fallacious speculation, but a real existence. And in the last section of this essay, I suggest the means and ways that will lead to the extinction of social evils (the negative) and to the establishment of an ideal world (the positive). Central here is the universal cultivation and development of social conscience.

For about three decades now, we in Thailand have been subject to undue stress and strain caused, in part, by the imported philosophical systems of Western culture. These philosophical systems have manifested themselves in socioeconomic and political ideologies and movements. They show, in essence, two historically contradictory elements: dogmatic capitalism and dogmatic communism. Both stand for extremes. But in the Thai perspective these are relative or conditional goods. Democracy based on liberalism is conditionally good and socialism is also, to a degree, agreeable. Yet these elements can be dialectically analyzed and synthesized into "one" through their critical unification in terms of "the Middle Way of Life." This would free us from the extremist cultures these social philosophies—democracy and socialism—have given rise to in the West. This unified social philosophy would be "the social philosophy of humanism," whose essence is embedded in dhamma. If it were to be introduced in the Thai way of life it would surely overcome the domino theory and lead us toward a more promising future.

General Statement

The present age signifies an age of humanism in need.[1] Philosophical interest has shifted from the older interpretations of God, matter, and science to man. Man is a dhamma being. With the dhamma he goes beyond and lives free from the illusive bondage of categorical ideologies and particular systems: religious, philosophical, social, political, and economic. Universal brotherhood based on truth, righteousness, goodness, and peacefulness underlies the social philosophy of dhammology. The social philosophy of dhammology is blooming above the fashions of so-called capitalism, socialism, and even democratic socialism. Without the application of the dhamma to our situation it is impossible to achieve unification in human society.

Human life and society are essentially corporate. Any solution of present-day problems, which are complex in their components and vast in their scope and manifestations, must be a cooperative enterprise. This enterprise may be everlasting so long as humanity continues to inhabit the world.

The world, which has become ecumenically one, longs to be consciously one. No nation, however great, can now live in isolation. It cannot survive by seeking to have a life of its own. It needs to share what others are and have. The brotherhood of nations is important and necessary. It is important no matter how men in any particular society, or in any particular language—political, economic, or philosophical—come to express this idea. Developed countries are as much concerned about the brotherhood of nations as are the developing countries.

In the world today, we have pledged ourselves to international cooperation and to efforts to establish the peace. There is no isolation anymore, even though there remains a great deal of geographical, social, cultural, political, and religious differentiation. The humanist philosophy, with its spirit of cooperation, must be carried beyond the nation to the ecumenical community of mankind. We must employ a democratic way to reinforce such a spirit.

Everyplace is thus called to democracy. It is a social system and method by which we attempt to raise the living standard of people and to give opportunities to every man to develop and fulfill his personality. Democracy becomes a common denominator of social philosophy today. It is crucial in all of our dealings for the welfare and well-being of mankind. It is what is required for the utilization of the principles of wisdom, cooperation, harmony, and mutual respect, based on humanitarianism.[2]

All leaders of democratic societies admit that we should give all members of society the opportunity for a full and fruitful life.[3] This way of life requires us to move toward peaceful coexistence and cooperative living. It asks and urges us to strive patiently and persistently for mutual understanding and to explore every avenue to reach synthetic agreement through the principle of reciprocity.

Living reciprocally, we must have faith in the spirit of man—the spirit capable of suffering and compassion, of endurance and sacrifice, the spirit that has inspired human progress and prosperity. At the same time, we should admit the fallibility of man as a constant factor in human affairs. Yet we do not ask for submission, which is the product of despair, or appeasement, which is the result of demoralization.

We are well advised not to be governed by fixed ideas or ideologies. The basic issue is no longer the victory of this or that nation, of this or that group, of this or that social ideology. What is at issue is the survival or suicide of man. Ours is a time for decision, not despair. The choice is either extinction or human brotherhood. It cannot be left to the vagaries of chance. The test of a nation's right to survive today is measured not by the size of its armaments, but by the extent of its concern for humanity as a whole.

Man is a social and ethical being, with sentiments and emotions developed in the direction of other men. Human personality develops and takes shape in a social environment. The ethical situation leads not only to an intensification of his own inwardness, but also to a recognition of the same inwardness in others. Man is a religious being, craving and searching for cosmic and divine support for his life and activity, and desiring communion with the truth.

Man is a rational being, questioning himself, evaluating his thinking, verbalizing, acting, wondering if he is mistaking fancies for truths or truth for falsity, right for wrong and good for evil. He is a complex creature, leading an inward and outward life and craving stable support both ways. And above all, man is a dhamma being, always striving for the ecumenicalization of the truth, the right, and the good.

Man now wishes to come to face his fellow man more closely, to understand and appreciate him intimately, and to avoid conflicts that involve the entire planet. There is a growing realization in such a risky situation that we have only two alternatives before us: a recognition of the brotherhood of man or the annihilation of man. This necessity to understand and recognize each other—each other's point of view, each other's culture, values, religion, and philosophy—paves the way to establishing what we wish to call "unification in human society," according to the social philosophy of dhammology.

Dhamma and Social Unification

I agree with Professor Northrop when he writes that ours is a paradoxical world.[4] The achievements that are its glory threaten to

69

destroy it. The nations with the highest standard of living, the greatest capacity to take care of their people economically, the broadest education, the highest grade of democratic culture, and the most enlightened enterprise in religious mission exhibit the least capacity to avoid mutual violence and destruction in war of various forms. It would seem that the more civilized we claim to become, the more incapable of maintaining civilization we are.

Probably a better answer to clarify the above situation would suggest that we lack and need the practice of dhamma. One of the main purposes of this thesis is to seek and make available to each culture the values of the others in their common essence, so that each can develop by incorporating all that is valuable in the rest. And the value of any culture can be appreciated only with reference to the value of human brotherhood.

According to the social principle of dhamma, man is the same everywhere and can assimilate the values of every culture and benefit from them. The welfare of humanity based on the conscience of brotherhood, which leads to a fuller and deeper life for man on earth, is much more important and urgent than the spread, by competition and contest, of one's own religion or philosophy for the defeat of all others.

Although we have old rivalries and conflicts of ideas, these must become synthetic moments of the advancing force of the dhamma ethos by which people of different cultures are united and bound into one march of humanity. On this faith depends the hope of the future of mankind. All leaders of humanity—the Buddha, Jesus, Muhammad, and others—realize, I believe, this ecumenical principle of oneness and sameness in humanity. Otherwise, it is nonsensical and useless for UNO and UNESCO to attempt to make available the values of all cultures to each other and to utilize these values.

The principle of dhamma and the social unification of mankind are very intimately related.[5] The possibility of the latter is based in the application of the former. The principle of dhamma formulates the middle way philosophy for mankind. It encourages and establishes unity, harmony, sameness, oneness, brotherhood, and peace in the human community, which becomes finally only one community.

According to the principle of dhamma, the delusion of and attachment to the mistaken conceptual principles of categories, species, accidents, and particularities lead people to become intoxicated by the differentiation of ideologies and systems: philosophical, religious, social, economic, political, etc. The truth is that the more we think and speak of different philosophies, religions, and social ideologies, the more splitmindedness will arise. Thus it is important to understand that all differences are only on the surface of the mind. If we have an enlightened understanding, then we will realize the essence of the truth, we will recognize the fallacies in these differentiations. Then terms such as *ultimate reality, God,* the *Buddha,* the *kingdom of God, nibbana, capitalism, socialism*—call them what you will—will appear as the same in their essence. And that essence is dhamma.

But, as we know, an ordinary man is under the impression that there are many different religions and philosophies and that they are all different to the extent of being hostile and opposed. Thus he considers Buddhism, Christianity, Islam, and so on as incompatible and even bitter enemies. Precisely because of views like this, there exist different religions and philosophies hostilely opposed to one another. If, however, a person has penetrated into the fundamental nature, essence, and purpose (dhamma) of religions and philosophies, he will regard them all as essentially similar. Therefore, the truth, the right, and the good (dhamma) constitute the heart of all religions and philosophies, even though their interpretations and expressions are different and diverse.

But particular religions, philosophies, and social systems are not essentially different. The label "Buddhist social philosophy," for instance, is attached only after the fact. This is also the case with other systems of social philosophy. All leaders of humanity are seeking to teach the truth, the right, and the good—the dhamma. Although we call ourselves Buddhists or Christians or Muslims, we have not yet attained the truth (dhamma) of Buddhism or Christianity or Islam. At this stage, we are simply aware of the shell, the outer covering, which makes us think our religion or philosophy is different from this or that other religion or philosophy. And we are probably inclined to look down upon other religions or philosophies, while praising and supporting our own. We tend to think of ourselves as a separate or superior group: outsiders are not part of our fellowship. They are wrong; only we are right. Such judgments show our ignorance and foolishness.

People who quarrel, who interfere with others, who violate others, or who lose patience with others lose their humanity. They are not really human beings due to the lack of certain qualities of loving-kindness and the like and are depraved. Thus, people who think and claim that other religions and philosophies are different from, inferior to, and incompatible with their own—attitudes that cause hostility, persecution, violence, and mutual destruction—are the most stupid and ignorant of people.

When religions and philosophies are regarded as in opposition and conflict with one another in their beliefs and practice the result is that people become enemies. Everyone concerned thinks: "We are right; they are wrong." This leads to quarreling, fighting, and destruction. Such people only display their foolish egoism. What they are quarreling about is only the outer, conventional form of things. This is due to their ignorance of the inner essence of dhamma. When people of dhammic intelligence and humanitarianism get together over essential matters concerning religions and philosophies, they recognize that they are all the same.

Though outwardly religions and philosophies seem to be contradictory, the person of dhamma knows that the inner spirit and purpose is the same in all cases. The inner essence is similar no matter how different the external forms. Consider the analogy of water: the essential nature of water, in Asia, America, or outer space, is always the same no matter how filthy it appears on the outside. The water is not dirty. It is the other elements and conditions mixed in with the water that are dirty. The essential nature of water is composed of two parts hydrogen and one part oxygen; this is the same everywhere.

Whenever there exists a quarrel, conflict, or violence, whether it is among the rich, the poor, capitalists, socialists, theists, or atheists, it may be likened to people drinking polluted water. In this case the pollutants are prideful bias and egoistic self-centeredness, and just as impure water must be distilled before it is consumed, so we must be purified by means of enculturation of the fourfold dhamma. This will give rise to the purified social consciences to be discussed below.

The problems that arise in a social group have their origin in the desire to satisfy selfish feelings that lead to mutual conflicts and break down human solidarity and unity. When we analyze closely the clashes between nations or between opposing blocs, we discover that there, too, both sides are slaves to their feelings of selfish interest. A war is not fought simply because of adherence to a doctrine or an ideal or anything of the sort. In point of fact, the motivation is the satisfaction of the feelings of craving, lust, hatred, fear, and so on. Each side sees itself making all sorts of gains, scooping up benefits for itself. Such a doctrine is just camouflage or, at best, a purely secondary motive. The most deep-seated cause of all strife is really subservience to feeling. To understand feeling is, then, to know an important root cause responsible for our falling slaves to mental defilements, to evil, to mutual violence, and to the suffering experienced by all humanity.

When dhamma is realized and reached, however, we will reach the central heart of all religious, philosophical, and social truths and come to recognize that Western, Eastern, American, Thai, Chinese, Muslim, capitalist, communist, and so on are all of one and the same humanity. We will finally come to enjoy the union of universal fraternity, which will lead to the complete cessation of suffering.

Development of Social Conscience

Social life is a matter of interorigination, interdependence, and interexistence. That implies a continual process of living according to the principle of what I call "reciprocal altruism."[6] This points further to the more deeply ethical-spiritual interpretation of human brotherhood that any conception of genuine social unity implies and requires certain virtues that produce social consciences culminating in "like-mindedness or one-heartedness" in the people and a certain recognition that their good (and interest) is a common one. It is on this philosophy that the social ideal of fraternity can be built up and worked out.

Men live together and are bound to each other, not by mere instincts and impulses, but by the rational application of certain moral and spiritual values. These values are enculturated, ultimately speaking, by a conscience that may be called "the human conscience of social bond." Accordingly, to establish, maintain, develop and strengthen the social bond and to live together happily and peacefully, people must be advised to cultivate a sense of "fraternity,"[7] to practice the virtues of loving-kindness, compassion, sympathetic joy, and impartiality toward each other and to learn to develop the idea of identity with all others. For, as one's own self is everywhere most dear to oneself, so it is with others; therefore, one who loves oneself should not inflict evil upon others.[8]

Loving-kindness (metta). The virtue of loving-kindness is one of the factors most beneficial both to spiritual development and to the development of a sound pacific relationship in society. With this virtue, people should neither allow their minds to become per-

73

verted with enmity nor utter any evil speech. The thought of loving-kindness should free us from hatred and harmfulness. We should show kindness and love toward persons. By starting with one person we should extend this virtue until it suffuses the whole world with the heart of loving-kindness. Loving-kindness would thus become far-reaching, widespread, immeasurable, without enmity and malevolence.[9] "As low-down theives might carve limb from limb with a double-handled saw, yet even then whoever sets his mind at enmity," said the Buddha, "he, for this reason, is not a doer of my teaching."[10]

A man of loving-kindness wishes others to be happy. That is clearly to his own advantage, since, at least, it makes them so much more pleasant to live with. Thus, it is by cultivating within oneself interest in the welfare and well-being of others and feeling their happiness as one's own that we realize loving-kindness. "Just as I want happiness and fear suffering and just as I want to live and not to die, so also others do. . . ." Loving-kindness will encourage one to be able to regard one's enemy without resentment but with the same friendliness as one regards one's own admired, dearly beloved companions.

One should extend loving-kindness toward all living beings equally without making any difference between oneself and others, or between one's own beloved, favorite, pleasant, and agreeable people and those who are neutral to oneself, and even one's enemy. We should always be thinking: "May all living beings be without enmity, without ill will, untroubled; may they keep the self well . . . may they all be safe with the disappearance of all fear and calamities; may they be satisfied with physical pleasure and may their hearts rejoice with all mental bliss."[11]

To remove the evil habit of anger or hatred and to replace it with the virtue of tolerance or patience, one develops the social conscience of loving kindness. One should not allow one's own thought of enmity and ill will to grow against others, even though they might do something wrong to oneself. On the contrary, one should keep one's mind in balance, think of the virtues possessed by others, and forgive faults done to oneself. The exercise of loving-kindness leads, finally, to the path of nonviolence (ahimsa). Ahimsa consists in delighting in the happiness of others, doing no harm to anyone, and cultivating sentiments of loving-kindness. One is meek and kind, compassionate and merciful, benevolent and useful to all living beings, laying aside all sorts of weapons. "Among human beings all should learn to be of one mind with nonviolence," said the Buddha. "They should not violate, destroy, and quarrel with one another as beasts always do."[12]

Compassion (karuna). The virtue of compassion characterizes the social conscience that expresses itself in a sense of participation with others in their time of troubles and difficulties, making one's head tremble and quiver at the sight and thought of suffering experienced by others. Compassion even arouses the desire to take upon oneself these things, to put an end to them and to strive to do something, to help and release others from them.

When a compassionate person sees or hears or even thinks of others who live in troubled circumstances, his heart becomes overwhelmed with compassion. The virtue of compassion has for its characteristic the activity of removing from other people those bad conditions of life that cause trouble; it has for its essence the inability to neglect others' sufferings; it has for its function the establishment of selflessness, and for its basis the sight of helplessness of others in such bad conditions. In a word, a compassionate person is unhappy at seeing others in trouble, he feels himself in solidarity with them and furthermore attempts to make them happy. He counts the harm and other bad conditions of others as his own. In this way he identifies himself with others who are in pain, depression, frustration, misery, calamity, lamentation, horror, and so on. Therefore, the social emotion of compassion signifies the virtue that is cultivated with a view, on the one hand, to uproot the ill will to harm others and decrease the evil habit of selfishness and, on the other hand, doing good to them, to make people sensitive to the troubles and difficulties of others to such an extent that they do not wish to increase them further, but to decrease and remove them.

In order to cultivate and develop the virtue of compassion one goes through a process similar to that of loving-kindness. Those toward whom compassion is to be expressed are those who are in trouble and difficulty. Those toward whom one feels compassion one strives to help and make free as much as possible from such situations. Psychologically speaking, compassion is closely allied to cruelty and the two may be easily mistaken for one another. They are the opposite sides of the same medal. Both the compassionate and the cruel are sensitive to the troubles and difficulties experienced by others and keen in observing them. But the sharp difference is that the former experience pain, while the latter derive pleasure from what they see, hear, or even recollect. That is, the compassionate person shares his heart and emotion with those who are in suffering; the cruel one keeps them away and even tries to make them suffer more.

Sympathetic Joy (mudita). The virtue that makes one glad and joyful when seeing or hearing of or even recollecting the success and happiness of others is called "mudita."[13] It has for its characteristic the state of (mutual) rejoicing, for its essence the absence of envying, for its function the suppression of disgust, and for its basis the cheerful acknowledgment of good fortune and prosperity achieved by others. From the above description we see that the virtue of sympathetic joy requires a deliberate effort to identify oneself with those who live successfully and happily and that it enables a person to feel a genuine joy at the happiness of others as much as at his own. It also enables one to share with others their joy of possession, their material or spiritual success, their promotions to positions of civil or national or other importance, or their receipt of titles and glories. It counteracts conceits of all kinds. Its growth and development checks craving's grip in the heart of man. A person, particularly one who is under the influence of jealousy, is advised to cultivate this social emotion of sympathetic joy. He should arouse within himself thoughts that foster this emotion and cultivate the habit of sincerely congratulating those who are released from troubles and difficulties and attain the fulfillment of their wishes. He should rejoice with them in their welfare, prosperity, and well-being. On seeing or hearing or even remembering others to be happy, cheerful, or joyous, the man of sympathetic joy thinks within himself: "Verily, how good, how excellent it is that this fellow lives happily." He treats all people, and even all living beings, with wholehearted gladness in the same manner as he does himself and his own beloved person. And, moreover, he prays that their good fortune, prosperity, and well-being may last long.

The virtue of sympathetic joy helps a man to learn how to appreciate, with a sincere heart, the prosperous conditions of others, to be heartily pleasant in his dealings with them, and to share their happiness even by making it resound in his own heart. It also furthers the sense of altruism and subdues the latent feelings of grudge or ill will against people in superior positions. By virtue of his ability to identify himself with others, the sympathetic man always welcomes with joy the happiness of his fellow man and never welcomes their miseries, and gets rid of what we might call mental isolation caused by selfishness. In the depth of their hearts, some people harbor a definite aversion to dwelling on the happiness of others, since egoism and jealousy are a strong and deep-seated, though rarely admitted, counterforce in their minds. All the time, we find men jealously comparing their lot with that of others and begrudging others their good fortune. Therefore, to remove this evil attitude and habit, the cultivation of the social spirit of sympathetic joy is introduced.

Impartiality (upekkha). This principle, in its literal sense, implies the virtue enabling one to keep one's own mind in a balanced state.[14] The virtue of impartiality (or even-mindedness) has the characteristic of evolving the mode of being balanced as regards beings; its essence is seeing the equality of beings; its manifestation is the suppression of aversion and bias. Turning to the kammic point of view relating to the practice of impartiality, we find that it implies the arousing of an equal attitude toward all living beings and makes one see them as equals in as far as there is a possibility, according to the law of kamma, for all of them to act and react freely and live in accordance with their own actions. In this respect, the virtue of impartiality points to two considerations. First, one is advised to realize that all beings are equal in all their aspects and conditions: as "beings," all are essentially the same under natural law. And second, one should consider the effect that the actions of beings have on themselves, the reason they act as they act and endure what they endure. Thus one realizes that one's action determines one's own fate and destiny, that whatever befalls one has been brought upon by oneself, and that only oneself can alter one's own fate and destiny. Consideration of the workings of this law of action leads us to understand that whatever is, is so because it must be, that everyone must manage one's own affairs, and that everyone must discharge one's own duties. In regard to the mode of mutual conduct in society, the modern discussion also uses the term "upekkha" to explain the virtue of impartiality in the sense of just, fair, or righteous treatment. In this regard, it is closely related to its other above-mentioned aspects and to the first three virtues already discussed.[15] Thus a person of impartial spirit does act differently toward those who are beloved, pleasant, or favorite and those who are otherwise, but he behaves toward others in accordance with the principle of dhamma. In his dealings with others he avoids the four ways of unfair treatment, based on either favoritism or personal preference, hatred, illusion, and fear.[16].

Given its deeper, spiritual implication, the virtue of upekkha relates to the principle of nonattachment (anupadana)—the thought of "I-ness" and of "mine-ness." The purpose of this is to teach us that acting in a nonegoistic way helps us to destroy impurities. Such a viewpoint results from not having an ego, not being attached to "myself," not conceiving relationships to anything in terms of "I" and "my," which exist only on a conventional level but not at the dhammic level of nonattachment.

With the presupposition of "I" and "my," people are driven to conflict, quarrels, violence, destruction, war, and away from achievement of world peace. Many people, moreover, have restless or agitated minds filled with the dark clouds of egoistic delusion. Consequently, they are wary, gloomy, and insecure. Eventually, they may suffer severe depression and nervous breakdown. Disorders of the mind, diseases of insecurity, anxiety, and neurosis result from clutching at and clinging to such things as fame and money, to being caught up in such matters as profit and loss, happiness and unhappiness, ease and disease, praise and blame. In such a situation, people are advised to practice the social virtue of nonattachment, which underlies the principle of impartiality. They should practice this virtue always thinking: "Do work of all kinds with a mind that is void, and then to the voidness give all of the fruits."[17]

NOTES

1. There are several forms of humanism: the naturalistic, the evolutionary and pragmatic, the communistic, the scientific, the theological, and the atheistic. For more details, see Siddhi Butr-Indr, *The Philosophy of Humanism* (Chiang Mai: Faculty of Humanities, Chiang Mai University, 1980), chap. 1.

2. For a more detailed explanation, see Siddhi Butr-Indr, *The Philosophy of Humanism,* 274–85.

3. For a more detailed explanation, see Siddhi Butr-Indr, *An Introduction to Sociopolitical Philosophy* (Bangkok: Phrae Pitya Publishing House, 1979), 211–19.

4. See Filmer S. Northrop, *The Meeting of East and West* (New York: Macmillan, 1946), 1.

5. In the original Pali language, the term *dhamma* (*dharma* in Sanskrit) is used to refer to all the intricate and involved things that make up what we call nature. In the main, according to Buddhadasa's interpretation, dhamma embraces nature itself, the law of nature, man's duty to act in accordance with the law of nature, and finally the benefits to be derived from acting in accordance with

the laws of nature. See *Buddha Toward the Truth,* ed. Donald K. Swearer (Philadelphia: Westminster, 1979), 60.

6. For more details, see Siddhi Butr-Indr, *The Social Philosophy of Buddhism* (Bangkok: Mohomakuta Rajvidayalaya Press, 1973), 130–34.

7. Ibid., 183 ff.

8. Ibid., 246, 256.

9. For more details, see ibid., 129 ff.

10. Ibid., 166 f.

11. Ibid., 244, 245, 342 ff.

12. Ibid., 211.

13. Ibid., 268.

14. Ibid., 246.

15. Ibid., 246. As a matter of fact, the climax of the first three virtues—of metta, karuna, and mudita—suggests that one should identify oneself with others. In this respect, one learns to treats oneself as righteous and is not given to the habit of partial, unjust treatment toward others.

16. Ibid., 1ff.; see also note 31, above.

17. Buddhadasa, 95. For further material, see T. W. Rhys Davids, ed., *Digha Nikaya,* 3 vols. (London: PTS, 1949); V. Fausboll, ed., *The Jataka,* 6 vols. (London: PTS, 1962); M. Leon Feer, ed., *Samyutta Nikaya,* 5 vols. (London: PTS, 1960); H. Oldenberg, ed., *Vinaya Pitaka,* 5 vols. (London: PTS, 1964); V. Trenckner and R. Chalmers, eds., *Majjhima Nikaya,* 5 vols. (London: PTS, 1960); and H. C. Warren, ed., *Visuddhimagga* (Cambridge: Harvard University Press, 1950).

REFERENCES

Butr-Indr, Siddhi. *The Social Philosophy of Buddhism.* Bangkok: Mahamakuta Rajvidayalaya Press, 1973.

———. *An Introduction to Socio-political Philosophy.* Bangkok: Phrae Pitya Publishing House, 1979.

———. *The Philosophy of Humanism.* Chiang Mai: Faculty of Humanities, Chiang Mai University, 1980.

Davids, T. W. Rhys, ed. *Digha Nikaya.* 3 vols. London: PTS, 1949, 1960.

Fausboll, V., ed. *The Jataka.* 6 vols. London: PTS, 1962.

Feer, M. Leon, ed. *Samyutta Nikaya.* 5 vols. London: PTS, 1960.

Northrop, F. S. C., *The Meeting of East and West*. New York: Macmillan, 1946.

Oldenberg, H., ed. *Vinaya Pitaka*. 5 vols. London: PTS, 1964.

Swearer, Donald K., ed. *Toward the Truth*. Philadelphia: Westminster, 1974.

Trenckner, V. and Chalmers, R., eds. *Majjhima Nikaya*. 5 vols. London: PTS, 1960.

Warren, H. C., ed. *Visuddhimagga*. Cambridge: Harvard University Press, 1950.

7

Social and Political Dimensions of Eastern Orthodoxy
CONSTANTINE N. TSIRPANLIS

What is the Orthodox understanding of the terms *politics* and *society?* The word *politics* in the Eastern Orthodox experience means not only the "art of governing a city or polis" (the *politiké techne* of Aristotle), but also the art (*politiké areté*) of developing right personal, social, and existential relations based on the Trinitarian interpersonal life and relations. Thus, politics is not just a useful compromise in social life, but a problem of truth, a problem that determines the meaning of human life and existence, the spiritual and cultural goals that transform time and matter and make perfect man's humanity as God's creation.

Accordingly, the Orthodox do not divide this world into "two kingdoms" or "two cities," in the fashion of Saint Augustine, since this world is also God's creation and as such cannot be separated into sacred and profane. This truth does not, however, ignore the fact that this ontological unity of God's creation was broken with man's fall, with his alienation and separation from his creator. Hence, restoration of personal and cosmic unity, harmony and peace, constitutes the main objective of a genuinely humanitarian political system. The antidote to the political pessimism of Augustine and Tertullian was of course Eusebius's theocratic "harmony" of the two authorities, divine and human, church and state. Thanks to a political system that stresses organic unity comparable to that of the soul and the body, and the close cooperation but not identity between church and state, with common spiritual values and goals, the famous Byzantine Empire prospered and survived for more than a thousand years, a unique event in world history. Certainly, the Byzantine pattern of church-state relations cannot be applied to our contemporary political systems in all aspects. However, our politicians and church leaders must be willing to learn important lessons from Byzantine political philosophy and church history.

The Orthodox church, considering herself witness of God's kingdom and of a continuous spiritual event of God's incarnation,[1] a continuous catharsis of man throughout the centuries, rather than a legalistic or hierocratic institution, does not exclude from her loving care sinful kings and politicians, heretics and criminals. She does not have enemies as human persons. Her only enemy is sin per se, not human beings. Eastern Orthodox humanism is rooted in and based on the truth of the human person as a God-centered social and loving being, contrary to Western humanism, which is anthropocentric or self-centered, and as such doomed to despair.

The Orthodox church as the "assembly of sinners" (the expression of Saint Ephrem of Syria) and as eucharistic *koinonia* (Christ's society and communion of love) views herself as a community of love, of "saints" who strive to restore themselves from the temptations of fallen nature—narcissism and self-love—within the world, but not according to the world's standards. Nevertheless, the entire world in the eyes and experience of Eastern Orthodoxy is sacrament. The term *sacrament* is not a didactic reduction of the Word, a *verbum visible,* as Augustine put it. The Greek word *mystery,* used by Eastern Christians for the Eucharist, has two connotations: being initiated into the heavenly choir surrounding the presence of God, and an act of love between God and his universe through the mediation of man in Christ. The two are linked. Initiation implies participation, and true participation is love, a mutual *perichoresis* in which God and the universe embrace and penetrate each other. In a sense, this is why marriage is a sacrament or mystery: not because through it grace is given, but because the marriage relationship at its best is the reflection and sacrament of this mutual self-giving, this mutual embracing and interpenetration of God and the universe of love.

This union with God and with each other in Christ is also the true meaning of the Eucharist. This eucharistic union, in which we are one with the whole creation in our responsive self-offering to God, is the mystery that fulfills human existence. And this mysterious reality is depicted in our initial offering (of bread and wine) in the Eucharist, an offering not merely of two things, but also of our whole world, our whole life in all its dimensions.

In the first chapters of Genesis, we find a clear statement of this sacramental character of the world. God made the world and then man; and he gave the world to man to *eat* and *drink.* The world was God's gift to us, existing not for its own sake, but in order to be transformed, to become life, and so to be offered back as man's gift to God. Hence, in our relation to nature we have to walk the precarious path and live in the difficult rhythm between *mystery* and *mastery*. It is not technology and theology or science and theology that need to be reconciled. It is, rather, these two attitudes—mastery of nature and mystery of worship—which have to be held in balance. Our mastery of the universe is like the mastery of our bodies; it is not that we may have it for our own use, but that we may give nature, as our extended body, into the hands of the loving God in the great mystery of the eucharistic self-offering. This is the mystery of the cross. Christ gave himself, with humanity and nature, to God in self-denying love, and thereby saved humanity and nature. It is in that eternal act of sacrifice and love that we too are called to participate. Technology is a way of humanizing the world of matter in time-space, and thereby of extending the human body to envelop the whole universe. But that humanizing and extension, if it is to be salvific, must find its proper culmination in man's offering of himself and the universe to God in love. A secular technology of mastery of nature for oneself is the "original" sin of refusing our mediatory position between God and the universe, dethroning God, and claiming mastery for the sake of indulging our own cupidity, avarice, and greed.

The Roman Catholics as well as the Orthodox are criticized by the Protestants for laying too much stress on the priest's difference from ordinary men, on the supernatural character of his function. This criticism has much truth in it. But as an Orthodox theologian of Russian descent puts it:

In such matters, we should perhaps understand the "supernatural" as being the natural in an extraordinary degree. Man was created as a priest: the world was created as the matter of a sacrament. But sin came, breaking this unity; this was no mere issue of broken rules alone, but rather the loss of a vision, the abandonment of a sacrament. Fallen man saw the world as one thing, secular and profane, and religion as something entirely separate, private, remote and "spiritual." The sacramental sense of the world was lost. Man forgot the priesthood which was the purpose of meaning of his life. He came to see himself as a dying organism in a cold, alien universe.[2]

Christ as the new Adam, the perfect man, restored that priesthood, the simple original act that man failed to perform, and with it matter and nature were restored in its original unity with humanity.

This point is stressed in the prayers and experience of the eucharistic liturgy and it is declared by Saint Paul in Romans 8. God includes the whole universe in his creation as well as in redemption in Christ. This does not remove all distinctions between humanity and the rest of creation. Humanity has a special vocation as the priest of creation, as the mediator through whom God manifests himself to creation and redeems it. But this does not make humanity totally discontinuous with creation, since a priest has to be an integral part of the people he represents. Christ has become part of creation, and in his created body he lifted up the creation to God; humankind must participate in this eternal priesthood of Christ. This participation becomes possible in the liturgy, which is not only a message of Christ's incarnation, death, and resurrection, but is especially a taste of God's kingdom, a participation in his glorified body and blood through the real presence of the Holy Spirit, a living reality that belongs both to history and to eschatology. For Orthodox Christians, liturgy does not simply mean a specific cultic act, but a definite life-style (the work of people), which, while certainly rooted and focused in the eucharistic liturgy, *also embraces the whole life of the person*. For the Orthodox faithful, liturgy in this sense means "bringing the heavenly into the earthly, in the way that John Chrysostom suggested when he heard the singing of the heavenly choirs and the harmonies of an eternal song in the very midst of the things of time. But at the same time liturgy is the elevation of the earthly into the heavenly places, the fulfillment of every immanent creaturely *telos* (goal) and its transfiguration by grace."[3]

As a representative Greek Orthodox bishop and theologian expressively wrote:

The Liturgy is not an escape from life, but a continuous transformation of life according to the prototype Jesus Christ, through the power of the Spirit. . . . Each of the faithful is called upon to continue a personal "liturgy" on the secret altar of his own heart, to realize a living proclamation of the good news "for the whole world." Without this continuation the Liturgy remains incomplete. Since the eucharistic event we are incorporated in Him who came to serve the world and to be sacrificed for it, we have to express in concrete diakonia, in community life, our new being in Christ, the Servant of all. The sacrifice of the Eucharist must be extended in personal sacrifices for the people in need, the brothers for whom Christ died. Since the Liturgy is the participation in the great event of liberation from the demonic powers, then the continuation of Liturgy in life means a continuous liberation from the powers of the evil that are working inside us, a continual reorientation and openness to insights and efforts aimed at liberating human persons from all demonic structures of injustice, exploitation, agony, loneliness, and at creating real communion of persons in love.[4]

The Orthodox Emphasis on Eucharistic Ecclesiology

It is not accidental that in recent years Orthodox theologians have placed strong emphasis in Orthodox ecclesiology on the eucharistic understanding of the church. There are two main reasons. First, there is a strong trend today toward changing the church into a mere sociopolitical institution or into an ally of the established government. Therefore, many Orthodox theologians, laymen as well as clergymen, constantly urge the churches to persevere trustingly in their appointed role as "bond-servants to God," for only by so doing can they maintain their freedom over against ideologies and political systems, which the church cannot under any circumstances or for any considerations of expediency enter into coalition or even identify herself with, but of which she must always remain the prophetic "crisis." Second, there is the modern misunderstanding of the nature and mission of the church, which was originally understood and experienced as Christian *diakonia,* witness and promotion of God's kingdom on earth, and as a contribution to the creation of a fellowship of solidarity, in the sense of a metamorphosis of "natural" orders and the outlook of a society composed of individuals into a *koinonia* of persons. Of course, this remains a constant task of the church, but one that is supremely urgent today when modern conceptions and conditions of life are forcing appalling *paramorphoses* (deformations) on human society, *paramorphoses* that aim at obliterating the very fact that man has been created in the image of God (moral and intellectual freedom). Precisely this fact lays upon us an inescapable obligation to defend the human dignity of the person in all its aspects. Consequently, *cultura agri* (living conditions), *cultura animi* (sanctification, *theosis*), and *cultura Dei* (Eucharist, doxology) are inseparably connected. The Orthodox emphasis is placed on the individual and his spiritual powers to act in a morally right way. The state cannot be venerated or respected except as an agency representing the will and interests of the people, and hence individuals are obligated to give to society what it needs to perform its mission so that human beings can live

85

in an atmosphere that guarantees the free exercise of man's spiritual powers. The primary witness of the church as a eucharistic community living the Trinitarian life on earth is to generate and sustain the specificity and uniqueness of persons to the end that persons-in-relation do not sunder the community, nor does the community suppress or destroy the specificity and uniqueness of each member. Such a relationship of mutuality in love and freedom eliminates the need to compete with each other or to affirm oneself by suppressing the other. It excludes domination, repression, or exploitation and seeks to conserve the dignity and freedom of all persons. It also means that we must respect and foster cultural, racial, political, economic, or other group identities, making sure, however, that no group identity becomes closed or absolutized.

The Christian attitude, according to the Orthodox experience, is never that of the abstract idea of the good, is not defined through a system of impersonal relations; it is always an interiority, a conversion, a call for the love that God has for us in Jesus Christ, an obedience that renews us, so that God may reveal himself through us to our neighbor as the lover. Even Orthodox monasticism, in its genuine spirit, is a strong witness—*martyria* and *martyrion* (martyrdom)—for the kingdom of God on earth, since the kingdom has been promised to the poor.[5] Making oneself actually poor for the love of and as a sign of that kingdom, which is our *only* wealth, becomes an undisputed criterion of perfection and of evangelical authenticity. Further, this means that the church should totally identify herself with the outcasts, with those who suffer and are persecuted because of their devotion to God's justice and love. This is also the reason an effective lack of an assumed or a voluntary poverty among Christians will make them lose the consciousness of their pilgrimage on earth. The gospel will then lose its savor. This *martyria*, or witness, recalls the remark of the Epistle to Diognetos of the second century: "they spend their lives on earth, but they are citizens of heaven." And that is possibly the special gift of Orthodoxy. "Let the dead bury their dead" is spoken to the living to remind them of the resurrection of the dead and to orient history beyond its boundaries. In the words of Paul Evdokimov:

The traditional Priesthood contemplates in Christ the perfect bishop and the perfect layman and knows that in Christ there is neither Jew nor Greek, neither man nor woman, neither bishop nor layman, for each finds there his fulness and his overflow (Col. 3:9–11). The body is well organized, hierarchically without any confusion about equality. No layman exceeds a bishop, but the bishop can exceed himself in his sanctity: "we are not the masters of your faith, we are the *servants* of your joy" (the joy of final liberation). The only real power of a bishop is that he presides in love, with the gift of tenderness and of enlightened charity. His only power persuasion is martyrdom.[6]

One also notes that in Dostoyevski's eyes, the czar in his sacred vocation of noble revolutionary exceeds himself, and that Russian socialism is fulfilled in the universal church on earth.

What Sociopolitical System Does the Orthodox Church Support?

It is true that the Orthodox church as a whole has not presented the world with the sight of a limitless wealth. Orthodoxy has remained the church of the poor, of peasants, of artisans, of a large number of poor bishops and badly paid priests. However, since the church of the West has sided with the rich, the whole of Christendom has become the object of social criticism. This is a striking example of the solidarity of the Christian churches in evil as well as in good.

However, it is equally true that, first, the church must not identify herself with any of the structures of temporal existence, even if they are structures of liberation. She vigilantly maintains her freedom to enter into freely chosen relationships with any structure, in faithfulness to her own true identity. In the very interest of identification with the poor and the oppressed, she cannot as a church tie herself completely to any given structure. Second, the churches' highest priority is the renewal of their own Trinitarian–eucharistic life, in order that the church may truly fulfill her vocation as sign and sacrament of the kingdom. This means setting her own house in order, eliminating counter-Trinitarian elements in her own structures, and renewing the teaching and sacramental ministry. Third, in the very process of such renewal of her own life, she will be renewing and freeing her own members to become creative agents of transformation in society through their own God-given vocations. If members of the church, individually or as groups, felt called to engage in liberation struggles or fights against tyranny, it will be the churches' task to extend her special and discerning pastoral care to such people. The church witness is necessarily political since it is made within the city and thus disturbs some authority. An absolutely apolitical church is completely inconceivable; it necessarily is *in patria.* Did the Lord not render an eminently political judgment when he called Herod "fox"?[7] The church must always carry on the prophetic function of Christ, otherwise she ceases to be the people of God. Furthermore, social and political revolts in the history of Eastern Orthodoxy are not few, and they were supported by the church as long as they were motivated and controlled by the spirit of love of freedom, recovery of human dignity and rights, and the purpose of God's providence, which is "to *unify* by faith and spiritual charity those whom vice has sundered in various ways."[8] It should be pointed out also that the Orthodox church has consistently opposed all forms of racism. Typical of this opposition is an encyclical of the ecumenical patriarch Metrophanes III to the Orthodox Christians of Crete in 1568. At that time, Crete was still under Venetian rule. A quarrel between the Cretan Jews and Venice over the payment of certain debts provoked the Venetians to adopt anti-Semitic measures. The wave of anti-Semitism seems to have been initiated by the Latin patriarch of Venice, Laurentius Justinian. The Jews had appealed to the ecumenical patriarchate, complaining that even Orthodox Christians had taken part in hostilities toward the Jews. Whereupon the patriarch wrote that those who unjustly treat the Jews in any way are excommunicated and condemned, since injustice and defamation were wrong whoever the victim was, and no one who committed such wrong could possibly regard himself as innocent on the pretext that he had only wronged someone of another faith and not one of the faithful. For even our Lord Jesus Christ tells us in the gospel not to bully or blackmail anyone, "making no distinction and not permitting Christians to deal unjustly with people of other faiths."[9] At the very time Gobineau and Chamberlin were stirring up Europe with racist heresies, the Synod of Constantinople (1872) officially condemned contemporary racism with its nationalistic overtones (*ethnophyletismos*). This was, if not the first, certainly one of the first official pronouncements of the Christian church on this subject.

But let me go back to earlier centuries, to the Greek Fathers of the fourth and fifth centuries—Basil the Great, Gregory the Theologian, and John Chrysostom. Their message is the message of the power of their experience of God: "For the Kingdom of God does not consist in talk but in power."[10] In their experience, the Christian world becomes an actually lived social reality. The Basiliad of the great Cappadocian saint and doctor, which was the first Christian hospital for the sick, a social work of a certain breadth, is called a "new city" by Saint Gregory of Nazianzus.[11] Saint John Chrysostom considered just sharing of goods in the city of Antioch, which would abolish misery; the church sought to influence Byzantine legislation; monasteries freed all Christian slaves; judges periodically visited prisons to inspect personally the improvement of the prisoners condemned by them. The universal doctrine of the church in the East as well as in the West is that "the rich withhold the goods of the poor, even if this wealth is honestly acquired or legally inherited."[12] The church Fathers did not glorify poverty as such, nor did they condemn riches. Nor did they cherish any illusions. Saint Neilos writes, "the religious person is not the person who distributes alms to many, but one who treats no one unjustly."[13] Likewise Saint Augustine says, "you give bread to the hungry, but it would have been better that no one be hungry and that you do not give to anybody." This is not only the yeast of a social revolution, but the hope that a day will come in which the church will cease speaking of Christ, and show him forth, reveal him, become herself Christ by sharing his love for the whole of humankind.[14] Staretz Zossimus (in notes for *The Brothers Karamazov*) makes a very daring remark: "love men in their sin, love even their sins, for this is the love of God." "To love" in this case means to understand and have compassion.

NOTES

1. Cf. Gregory the Theologian, "IV Theological Oration 21," *Christology of the Later Fathers,* ed. E. R. Hardy (Philadelphia: Library of Christian Classics, Westminster Press, 1954), 193.

2. Alexander Schmemann, *Church, World, Mission* (New York: Saint Vladimir's Seminary Press, 1979), 223.

3. A. Papaderos, "Liturgical Diaconia," *An Orthodox Approach to Diaconia* (Geneva: World Council of Churches, 1980), 22.

4. A. Yannoulatos, *Martyria-Mission,* ed. I. Bria (Geneva: World Council of Churches, 1980), 66–67.

5. Luke 6:20.

6. P. Evdokimov, "Eschatological Transcendence," *Orthodoxy-Life and Freedom,* ed. A. J. Philippou (Oxford: Studion Publications, 1973), 45.

7. Luke 3:32.

8. Cf. Saint Maximus Confessor, *Capita de caritate,* English trans. with introduction by P. Sherwood (Westminster, Md.: Newman Press, 1955), vol. 4, no. 17, 194. Also see my study, "Aspects of Maximian Theology of Politics, History, and the Kingdom of God," *The Patristic and Byzantine Review,* no. 1 (1982): 1–21.

9. Luke 3:14.

10. 1 Cor. 4:20.

11. Saint Gregory of Nazianzus, "Oration" 43.63: *Nicene and Post Nicene Fathers of the Christian Church,* vol. 7, 416.

12. Saint John Chrysostom, *Patrologia Graeca* 61: 84. Cf. Homily 20 in 2 Cor.

13. Saint Neilos, *Patrologia Graeca* 79: 1249.

14. John 3: 16–17.

Part Three
RELIGION AND SOCIETY: ISSUES AND CASES

8

Social Uses and Abuses of Religion in Developing Countries

O. OLUKUNLE

Many have written on the crucial importance of religion in society, and no effort has been spared to show us that human beings are by nature religious. Writing about the Yoruba of western Nigeria, Idowu tells us that "the religion of the Yoruba permeates their lives so much that it expresses itself in multifarious ways. It forms the themes of songs, makes topics for minstrelsy, finds vehicles in myths, folktales, proverbs and sayings, and is the basis of philosophy."[1] I doubt if anyone can deny the positive use to which religion has been put and is still being put in establishing and maintaining the sanity of society. Yet few things have been subject to as much abuse as religion, which was meant to serve a salutary purpose in society. This is the point I wish to make in this short essay. My approach will be largely historical, with a few excursions into contemporary developments. I believe that we communicate with God by means of religion and try to convert others or reinforce their faith by means of religious language. Religion, then, becomes very germaine in any intelligible discussion on God. Most of the examples I use are from Africa, not only because it is the continent with the highest number of developing countries, but also because it is the terrain I know best. The fact that I am a Christian and that Christianity is virtually everywhere makes it the religion that will receive most of my attention.

For the purpose of this essay, I define *use* as proper application of something toward an end. By inference, an abuse would be an improper application of something toward a negative or even a positive end. Some things are basically good and serve a good purpose. Think, for example, of oxygen, which is absolutely necessary for the continuation of human life on this planet. On the other hand, some things are, I believe, basically evil. The example that comes readily to mind is a cancerous cell, which can only infect other cells of the body. However, some things that were initially

93

meant to serve good purposes have ended up serving negative ends too. When Alfred Nobel invented dynamite, he meant it to be used by miners to help in blasting hard rocks, thereby making the job less tiring. As we all know, it has been misapplied since then. One can see religion in the same light. It was meant to create a unique link between God and humanity and between human beings. It was to remind man of the existence of the infinite, to help in regulating the relationship between men and in promoting peace. However, religion has been used and abused to promote wars, as in the Islamic Jihad and the Christian Crusades. My point is that men can adapt good things for negative ends if they so desire. Religion is no exception.

I am not the most traveled person, but of all the countries I have visited it strikes me that religion has a greater impact on the lives of individuals in developing countries than in other countries. I will offer an explanation of this later, but let me now provide an example. In 1972, I was a graduate student in the industrial city of Birmingham in the British Midlands and I used to ride the bus past a church. When I went back to Birmingham in 1976, that church had become an electronic warehouse. I imagine that the congregation had gradually thinned out, the parish priest gave up, and the building was sold. By contrast, during this same period at least fifty new church buildings, most of them branches of established churches, were put up in Ibadan, Nigeria. Most people in developing countries take religion quite seriously. Its influence can be seen everywhere. It influenced elections in Nicaragua and it was the rallying point the Ayatollah used against the shah of Iran. (What has been done with power since the Ayatollah took control from the shah is entirely another matter.)

Although I am suspicious of definitions, since they are seldom sufficiently encompassing, I will try to indicate what I mean here by a developing country. A developing country is commonly understood as one that is economically and technologically lagging behind Europe, North America, and Eastern Europe. It is characterized as having a low per capita income. However, according to Walter Rodney, "development in human society is a many-sided process. At the level of the individual, it implies increased skill and capacity, greater freedom, creativity, self-discipline, responsibility and material well-being. Some of these are virtually moral categories and are difficult to evaluate—depending as they do on the age in which one lives, one's class of origins, and one's personal code of what is right and what is wrong."[2] The word *developing* as used by Western scholars, especially economists, refers almost entirely to that narrow issue of economic sufficiency. I take the view that human development goes beyond economic well-being. Coming from Nigeria—one of the countries classified as developing—I am suspicious of the use of this word, which is often a euphemism for underdeveloped. Both terms are used to refer to practically all the countries of Africa, Latin America, and Asia with the exception of Japan. Japan is now often considered to be one of the Western European countries, as if economic well-being obliterates geographical separation. My objection to the use of the word *developing* is twofold. First, it is a term coined and applied by the same developed countries that colonized and still inhibit the development of the so-called developing countries. Colonization, in case anyone is in doubt, had a devastating effect on the colonized. It involved years of physical and enforced rule. This was often followed, in the years after "independence," by even more fears of mental bondage. This was often a pseudoindependence since, although the colonialists officially yielded political rule, they still held the reins of economic power, using surrogates from the formerly colonized countries and multinationals from their own countries to maintain control. My second objection arises from the fact that the concept of development seems to rest unduly on technological and economic considerations. Thus, a country with sophisticated technology, high-income earnings, and a large balance of payments (never mind if most of the money comes from the developing countries) may be said to be developed. But are they developed when the resources of the developed countries East and West have enough weapons to wipe out the whole world ten times over? Civilization or development is regarded as an improvement on earlier stages, but it would appear that our present development is like terminal cancer. The world is walking on such a dangerous nuclear tightrope that we are not sure it will exist into another century. Such a disaster will not arise because God has decided to end this creation; it would, rather, be because we have become too "developed" to learn to live with others in peace. In any case, I think that a so-called developed civilization in which the family—the basic unit of the society—has all but collapsed, in which money has overtaken man, in which the spiritual has been overtaken by the material, in which lethal weapons mean power, and in which God has become a mere footnote is probably heading for destruction. Nevertheless, when I use the term *developing* I use it in the sense of its inventors so that my readers will know which part of the world I am referring to. But, at the same time, I am suggesting that our understanding of development should be expanded to include the values one embraces.

It is possible that many of my readers do not know what it means to come from a developing country. Consequently I will try to describe this situation. My intention is not to create a sense of guilt (even though the developing countries did not create the situation), but to state the way things are in the hope that things will not continue to be as polarized and as one-sided as they are in a world supposedly created by a good God.[3] Being born into almost any of the developing countries of Africa, Latin America, and Asia is an ordeal. The first challenge is to survive at all. Although there are a few exceptions, most people are born into poverty. To be born into poverty is to be born with many disadvantages conferred on you by national and international circumstances over which you have no control whatsoever. It is like going into the boxing ring with both hands tied. You will be beaten before the bout begins. Most developing countries are permanently in recession. Consequently, when the world complains of recession, one must realize that the developing countries are already in desperation.

Of course, not all the people in developing countries are poor. Indeed, the economic and political situations are such that some are so rich, they cannot see the poor. Thus, what we have is not two groups, the haves and have-nots, but two extreme groups of have-mores and have-nevers. Such is the situation in a "democrazy" as opposed to a proper democracy. There is little doubt that most of the people are poor and have little hope of getting rich. Many therefore turn to religion, often in its most aggressive mode, so as not to lose out in eternity. Religious responses in developing countries are totally different from those in Europe. A peasant cannot afford the luxury of reading the writings of Paul Tillich when he has no money to buy new hoes to till his farm. Niebuhr would be meaningful only after you and your neighbor have enough to eat and there is no suspicion that one would rob the other's poultry or goats at night. Poverty has always contributed greatly to the abuse of religion in developing countries. Most of the people who died with the Reverend Jim Jones in Guyana were poor people who found solace in a man posing as a messiah who met their daily needs. His was a religious movement gone berserk. Its Muslim equivalent—the Maitasine group in Nigeria—claimed over three thousand lives in December 1980. Poor and disinherited people do not fear death because they have nothing to lose apart from their poverty. Our discussion of the use and abuse of religion may be easier once we bear these considerations in mind.

When we speak of the *use* in this context we mean the positive ends served by religion, whereas *abuse* means the negative ends. There is sometimes an overlap, where use and abuse defy clear-cut separation.

From the coast to the hinterland in practically all developing countries, the greatest use of religion was in the spread of Western education, without which the administration of the colony could not be carried out since most of the colonialists were victims of tropical diseases. Educated local people were to man the schools, hospitals, offices, and churches of the future. Thus, religion contributed in no small measure to the initial development of the developing countries. Writing about the relevance of the Christian religious missions to education, Ayandele noted that "they adopted a two-fold attitude to the society. On the one hand they sought to effect a moral and social regeneration through their churches and schools. On the other they exerted themselves to prevent the demoralization of the society by the white man's 'fire-water' liquor."[4] There is no doubt that the use of religion to introduce formal Western education and medical facilities is a credit no one can deny.

As mentioned above, poverty is rampant in developing countries, and religion, perhaps playing the role of an opiate, as Marx noted, has helped to stabilize or tranquilize many people who otherwise may have committed suicide out of sheer despair. As long as there is hope for a better tomorrow and a secure eternity, society is bound to be relatively stable. According to O'dea, "People suffering from extreme deprivation and people suffering from anomie (some groups may be experiencing both) display a considerable responsiveness to religions which preach a message of salvation—that is, which present the world as a place of toil suffering and offer some means of deliverance from it. Christianity is a religion of this kind. It offers the believer salvation through participation in Christ's victory over evil and death."[5] Although such use must not be overstressed, neither can it be denied. The house of God is one place where no one will physically turn you back because you are poor. Religion helps to keep the family together and sustain the cherished extended family system. Since the whole family usually worships at the same shrine, church, or mosque, religion remains a useful symbol of cohesion. Finally, religion may help to keep people united in times of trouble or stress. As Susan Budd noted, "the statistics of religious attendance suggest that those whose lives are relatively uncertain, risky or uncontrollable are often more religious. The greater religiosity of women can be explained in this way."[6] This sustenance in times of stress may even be nationwide. The people of Iran were united essentially by Islam to overthrow the shah. Poland is the most recent example in which religion holds the people together. Long after martial law was imposed and trade unions and demonstrations banned, the church remains the rallying point and focus of national unity that no one can ban.

I am not a particularly religious person and so I have no business defending religion when it has been abused or misused in developing countries, but charity demands that one should add that in many cases of abuse it has been by default or accident.

An obvious instance of perhaps accidental abuse of religion in developing countries arises in almost all cases when the introduced religion, especially Christianity, came before the colonialists. Since missionaries, traders, and colonialists came from the same country, they were classed together. In fact, the missionary was seen by some as the bait the colonialists used to make the indigenous people succumb to foreign domination. This linkage was confirmed by the fact that in Nigeria the soldiers helped the missionaries if they ever got into trouble. As Ayandele put it rather succinctly, "allied with, and in many cases inseparable from the British secular arm, at least until the beginning of the twentieth century, missionary enterprise resulted politically in the suppression of Nigerian chiefs by Christian white officials."[7] The missionaries demanded and received British protection and in return turned the territory they covered over to British administration. Nigerians have not forgotten this ambidexterity on the part of the missionaries. Consequently, they began to doubt the good intentions missionaries claimed to have. To mislead people in this way in the name of religion is to abuse religion. And as Ayandele noted elsewhere, "missionary propaganda in Nigeria was not just a religious invasion. In effect it was associated with a political invasion as well. In the background was the secular arm of Britain, to be invoked when practicable."[8] It is a sad commentary on religion that it inadvertently heralded the colonialists. There is an old story that when the colonialists came, they had the Bible in their hand and told the people to close their eyes for prayers. At the end of the "prayer," the colonialists had connived with the missionaries and succeeded in taking the peoples' land in exchange for their own Bible.

Another abuse of religion arises when it is used to propagate and enforce an alien culture. Western culture has always masqueraded as superior to other cultures, and the propagators of religion were expert in this. History books are replete with examples of the arrogance of British officials and missionaries in Africa and India. Initially, they were believed because they cleverly tied their position to religion and gave their work biblical sanctity. We may consider only two examples here. Polygamy was widely practiced in Africa. In part this was because the population was mainly agricultural. It was widely held that a chief must have more than one wife since he must not eat food cooked by any woman other than his wife. He must be polygamous in case one wife took ill or died. If a man was a successful farmer, he needed a large family to help him work on his farm, especially if he could not pay for laborers and agriculture was not mechanized. Thus a man married more than one wife not to satisfy any lust, but to meet a need. In this way everything worked out well. There were no unmarried girls to constitute a potential prostitute population, there was collective discipline in the extended family and so there was hardly any delinquent youth, and it was rare to find homosexuals. In its introduction into developing countries, Christianity was used as synonymous with European culture. Nowhere does the Bible categorically condemn polygamy, but Europeans read this into their religion. As Beetham observed:

"The ruling of the first missionaries was almost universally that polygamous men should at their conversion to the Christian faith put away all but one wife; otherwise they could not receive the sacraments of baptism and holy communion. There were some who did not think it right to break the existing marriage relationships and who therefore sought to retain such a man within the fellowship of Sunday worship and Bible study, but withhold the sacraments, though doing so with a feeling that the church's practice was at odds with the spirit of the Lord."[9]

Some men, in obedience to European (not biblical) order, disbanded their harems and drove away their children. Such children grew up to become social problems and some of them who became prominent men and women never forgave their fathers and resented Christianity, which had disinherited them and displaced their mothers.

The second example has to do with dressing. For some strange reason the earliest missionaries insisted that those who received communion must attend in European dress. Some at first consented, but most resented this requirement since it was mere cultural domination.

Another instance of abuse is religious intolerance, which is rather pronounced in developing countries. Practically all the religions that one can think of advocate peace and brotherhood, but almost all of them are intolerant of other religions and therefore contradict the teachings of their founders. Intolerance takes several forms, but usually comes in the form of the abuse based on numerical superiority. Thus, in one or two states in India in which the Sikhs are in the majority, they keep harassing the Hindus and Muslims. Muslims, on the other hand, oppress the Baha'is in Iran. The Unification movement undergoes systematic and official persecution in some countries. African traditional religion went through and survived this type of persecution at the hands of Christianity and Islam; time seems to have been on its side, however, for it survived several onslaughts. Abraham remarked that "an introduced religion depends for the depth of its success on the extent to which it can overcome or accommodate elements in the society into which it is introduced."[10] By considering itself superior, Christianity definitely abused the hospitality accorded it by African traditional religion. Most Africans, for example, gladly welcomed Christianity not because they felt it was superior, but because they believed a man had a right to worship the way he chooses.

Religious abuse in developing countries may be found in hero worship, which now has very serious political repercussions. In African traditional religion some of the gods were deified ancestors who by their might and valor saved their people from destruction and suffering. Fadipe tells us that, "as an example of the culture hero subsequently raised to the dignity of an *orisa*[11] and worshipped in the community may be mentioned *Obalogun* of the *Ijesa* people who, tradition claims, saved the country from the warlike intentions of the Nupe."[12] I suspect that many leaders of developing countries, especially in Africa, sought to transfer this status to themselves. Employing the same religious pattern, they saw themselves as gods who saved their people from colonial rule and, as gods, they must be deified. Thus they sit tight in office long after their popularity has waned and postpone and rig elections for fear of losing. They thereby encourage the military to forcibly effect a change. Part of the political instability in Africa today is traceable to this self-identification of the ruler with one of the gods, which can be linked with the determination to remain in office at all cost. This is an indirect abuse of religious tradition.

Abuse of religion also comes when the moral position of religion is seriously questioned and deeds do not match words. Christianity came to Africa as a "superior" religion and with a "superior" culture and one would have thought with "superior" morality. Taylor declared that "this finished system was presented to simple peoples sanctioned by the authority and endowed with the surviving culture of the civilised world. It offered them mightier, superior and nobler knowledge, and a better ordering of life than they had known. The manner and authority of its presentation hastened its acceptance."[13] However, this "manner and authority of its presentation" did not quite fall into place with the actions of the propagators in subsequent years. Africans saw their continent arbitrarily partitioned in Berlin in 1885 as if it was a no-man's-land, they saw a nonissue begin the First World War among people who said they were civilizing others, and they were forced to fight in the Second World War, which they knew nothing about. They fought for the freedom of those who held them in bondage and did not for all that easily win their own freedom. South of the Zambezi, they listened to some missionaries use the Bible to justify the apartheid government, and they quite rightly questioned Christian morality. This, in a way, led to the foundation of the Pentecostal churches, which were protesting against a European Christianity that rallied the people but did not meet their aspirations. Beetham put it correctly when he said: "What remains crystal clear is that the Christian gospel is rejected by many Africans today because those of European race in Africa and outside, claim the name of Christ but do not do the works; their practice of racial segregation and acquiescence in unequal opportunities for the races being in fact a denial of fellowship in Christ."[14] The use of religion to rally people and unite them can also be abused to promote personal status as, in my opinion, the Ayatollah Khomeini is now doing in Iran. Certainly he cannot pretend that the war he is waging against Iraq, another Islamic nation, is for the sake of Islam. That would be a colossal contradiction.

Religion also seems to have encouraged the further stratification of an already stratified society. Instead of making people of one body, it tended to simply reinforce the stratification already in

society. Religion often fails to rise above society and quite uncon-
sciously takes on some of society's values, values that are not
necessarily positive. O'dea observed that "founded religions tend at
first to repudiate, at least implicitly, the stratification differences of
society, but that after a time they come more or less to accept these
local institutions. Important people in society consequently come to
be looked upon as important in the religious group as well."[15]
Somehow everyone would like to be thought of as important both
in the religious group and in the larger society. The result is a rat
race to get to the top by all means even if such means are neither
godly nor humane.

It was noted above that one of the salutary functions of religion in
society is the solace it gives its adherents. The optimism that makes
one look to the future and indeed to eternity with certainty is
definitely very refreshing. It deadens all rebellious desires and sustains the peace of the society. However, this may have its own
drawbacks. Carry patience too far and it becomes cowardice. Un-
fulfilled hopes in which hundreds of tomorrows fritter away and
stretch into unrealized dreams make one become a time bomb of
frustration. One more sermon of appeasement, one more word
about waiting in hope, and one more disappointment, and everything could blow up. This is why I think that when the blacks rebel
against oppression in South Africa and willingly face the gun rather
than continue to suffer, the church that has kept them waiting for so
long has no plausible answers to their questions. This is not because
the church created the problem, but because it has, until recently,
allowed itself to be used, albeit indirectly, to perpetuate injustice. As
Beetham pointedly noted:

For its members, the Church is a divinely founded fellowship within
which the Holy Spirit acts despite the human frailty of members of the
fellowship. There is for them an unknown spiritual dimension in any
equation the historian seeks to formulate. This does not exonerate us
from the attempt to assess the points of weakness and of strength of the
Church as it emerged from the colonial era; on the contrary it demands
the utmost honesty for, as the history of the Church repeatedly shows,
judgement has to begin with God's own household.[16]

To conclude, I might say that intolerance is perhaps the worst
form of abuse of religion. Ironically, intolerance is the pet child of
most of the so-called orthodox and established religions of the
world. They are often so jittery and intolerant of others that they

would do anything to maintain the status quo. They forget, however, that persecution simply helps in the spread of a new religion. Tertullian noted that "the blood of the martyrs is the seed of the church."[17] Nonetheless, intolerance is an abuse of genuine religion. There are many cases of intolerance in the world: the persecution of the Baha'is in Iran, the harassment of other Muslims by the Maitasine group in Nigeria, the Unificationists in America, and many others who labor under the intolerance that arises from the abuse of religion. Abuse in these cases arises from confusing religion with civil issues, or appending religious intolerance to issues that are not genuinely religious, or seeking to apply a religious cover to other issues so as to give them respectability and make them appear acceptable. When we consider the relationship of religion to society, we should not forget that, although religion has often contributed positively to society, there are examples of its abuse all over the world and these examples can be easily multiplied in developing countries.

NOTES

1. E. B. Idowu, *Olodumare: God in Yoruba Belief* (London: Longmans Green & Co., 1962), 5.

2. Walter Rodney, *How Europe Underdeveloped Africa* (Dar-es-Salam: Tanzania Publishing House, 1972), 9.

3. As for example in Gottfried W. Leibniz's expression of this idea in "The Best Possible World."

4. E. A. Ayandele, *The Missionary Impact on Modern Nigeria* (London: Longmans Green & Co., 1966), 284.

5. Thomas F. O'dea, *The Sociology of Religion* (Englewood Cliffs, N.J.: Prentice-Hall, 1966), 57.

6. Susan Budd, *Sociologists and Religion* (London: Collier Macmillan, 1973), 35.

7. Ibid., 5.

8. Ibid., 8.

9. T. A. Beetham, *Christianity and the New Africa* (London: Pall Mail Press, 1967), 37.

10. W. E. Abraham, *The Mind of Africa* (London: Weidenfeld and Nicholson, 1967), 37.

11. *Orisa* is the generic name for gods.

12. N. A. Fadipe, *The Sociology of the Yoruba* (Ibadan: Ibadan University Press, 1970), 261.

13. Henry O. Taylor, *The Medieval Mind,* 4th ed. (Cambridge, Mass.: Harvard University Press, 1959), vol. 1, 170–71.

14. Beetham, 88.

15. O'dea, *The Sociology of Religion,* 74.

16. Beetham, 24.

17. Henry Chadwick, *The Early Church* (Middlesex: Penguin Books, 1967), 29.

9

God and Mammon: Responses in English Christianity

JOHN ST. JOHN

Religion connects with social reality by means of various and often conflicting matrices of ethical values. These are not necessarily the same as, or even extrapolations from, the moral systems prescribed by virtually all faiths or the individual (e.g., the Judeo-Christian Ten Commandments or the Right Living of Buddhism). It is not as simple as that. When it comes to social ethics—to groups of people, to social classes, let alone nations and races—a different set of considerations and processes seems to operate; this is also true of the normally honest individual's relationship with society (e.g., the subtle, usually hypocritical difference between "legal avoidance" and "evasion" of personal taxation). In the words of Paul Tillich: "Any attempt to identify the problems of personal ethics and social ethics (as does legalistic pacifism, for example) ignores the reality of power in the social realm, and so confuses the organizational centredness of an historical group with the personal centredness of a person . . . [it] requires the development of a philosophy of power."[1]

Although this essay is limited to a consideration of social rather than personal ethics, inevitably the two are intertwined. I am also limiting myself in the main to the ethical development and values of Christianity in Western Europe, particularly in Britain—although even this one small nation covers such an immense slice of complex experience as to make it all but impossible to avoid oversimplification. Furthermore, I shall for the most part narrow the focus to Christianity's attitude to money, to the taking of interest and profits, to wealth and poverty, to what may be termed "commerce"—although, again, the penumbra of other social and personal ethical attitudes will always be present. As Britain was the cradle of the industrial revolution, its history provides certain insights into the shifts and conflicts between various sets of coherent ethical attitudes and responsibilities, all within the confines of a single faith that springs from the same divine inspiration, as recorded in an agreed text, the Bible.

My data are inevitably selective, but are intended to be representative, as well as illuminating, and not atypical. I have arranged these data under broad categories whose contents may overlap, but which do provide a framework within which to depict four contrasting varieties of religious response. In compiling the first category, I have leaned shamelessly on the work of R. H. Tawney (1880–1962), professor of economic history, University of London.

The Reflection and Justification of Contemporary Socioeconomic Structures

In *On the Seven Deadly Sins,* John Wycliffe (c. 1320–84) declared that anyone who makes money out of an upswing in the market must by definition be wicked—how otherwise could he have been poor one day and rich the next? In the medieval church the taking of "pure" interest—at a fixed rate in return for a loan without risk to the lender—was denounced unanimously as avarice or usury. It was in order for a man to seek a livelihood considered reasonable for his station in life, but to seek more was quite wrong. Payment "may properly be demanded by the craftsmen who make the goods, or by the merchants who transport them, for both labour in their vocation and serve the common need. The unpardonable sin is that of the speculator or the middleman, who snatches private gain by the exploitation of public necessities."[2] Profits could in certain circumstances be treated as a particular case of wages, provided the gains were not in excess of what society considered to be reasonable remuneration for the trader's labor; on the other hand, as Aquinas argued, if the trader is motivated merely by his own pecuniary gain without any respect for the public interest, he is guilty of converting a means into an end and his occupation "is justly condemned, since, regarded in itself, it serves the lust of gain."[3]

Medieval society was held together by elaborate balances of obligations. There were great differences in wealth and status, but on the whole everyone knew his station, knew where he fitted in; feudal landowners, merchants, traders, artisans, peasants, laborers—and of course the ecclesiastical establishments, including the influential monasteries and convents. It was the church that laid down all-embracing standards for human institutions and conduct. Its economic ethic reflected the realities of medieval agriculture, indus-

106

try and trade. Its teaching and those of the Schoolmen expounded the belief that the existing social edifice and its economic rules reflected an underlying moral purpose. Self-interest was subordinate to the achievement of salvation. The usurer's conduct was in conflict with both human and divine law. He ran the risk of being refused confession, absolution, and Christian burial. The church's doctrine of money, interest, and commerce dominated the lawmakers and the courts, secular as well as ecclesiastic.

As in all societies, practice by no means always matched precept. The fiat against usury was seldom enforced in connection with the financial transactions of the king, the big feudal barons, or even the bishops and abbots. The papacy itself usually overlooked the immorality of the great European banking houses on which it relied, even helping them to collect their debts from others by threat of excommunication. Despite, however, frequent departures from the accepted code of commercial ethics at all levels, despite the growth of a European system of trade and banking houses that operated essentially according to a very different (and historically premature) code, "the most fundamental difference between mediaeval and modern economic thought consists, indeed, in the fact that, whereas the latter normally refers to economic expediency, however it may be interpreted, for the justification of any particular action, policy, or system of organization, the former starts from the position that there is a moral authority to which considerations of economic expediency must be subordinated."[4]

How is it that the church and the outwardly Christian society of Britain—also, by and large, of Western Europe—instead of looking upon the receipt of pure interest and anything approaching a dividend or debenture interest, let alone naked usury, as a serious sin, were able to change to the present situation in which the church (or most of it) and the bulk of Western society considers all forms of "making your money work for you" or what the tax collector calls "unearned income" as not only legitimate but also respectable, even praiseworthy? Does religion admit it was once wrong?

To seek the answers, even in terms of Britain alone, requires an analysis of political, economic, and religious history over some five centuries. It was a period that embraced the Reformation and the break with Rome (completed in 1534); the Civil War and the beheading of a king (1649); the Industrial Revolution; the discovery and colonization of America and about one-fifth of the earth's land surface; and much else. It would be simplistic and, for the most part, grossly inaccurate to equate the volte-face in moral outlook with the rise of Protestantism in its several forms, but there are certainly links and it can at least be ventured that the conflict between economic interests—between the semifeudal, mercantilist past and the thrusting, new-style capitalism—were often played out in religious language and in disputes over theological doctrines, ecclesiastic courts, monastic power and properties, and even ritual. Even so, religion and the economy were seldom in step, with the latter forging ahead and the former both refusing, for long periods, to recognize the need to catch up and at the same time acting as an intermittently effective social brake whose application at best did something to mitigate the most rampant expressions of the new type of exploitation.

Luther, the first giant architect of Protestantism, denounced the traffic in interest in even stronger terms than the orthodox economists. "The devil invented it, and the Pope, by giving his sanction to it, has done untold evil throughout the world."[5] In England under Elizabeth I (reigned 1558–1603) there was a growth of capitalistic enterprise and foreign trade, of speculation and a money market. The new commercial classes allied themselves most strongly with Puritanism, and it was Calvin, their seminal inspiration, who first "accepted the main institutions of a commercial civilization, and supplied a creed to the classes which were to dominate the future."[6] Although this new, permissive attitude toward interest rates was hedged with qualifications, Calvin assumes "credit to be a normal and inevitable incident in the life of society . . . [he] argues that the payment of interest for capital is as reasonable as the payment of rent for land, and throws on the conscience of the individual the obligation of seeing that it does not exceed the amount dictated by natural justice. . . . On such a view all extortion is to be avoided by Christians. But capital and credit are indispensable; the financier is not a pariah, but a useful member of society."[7]

In its earlier stages, alongside the commercial permissiveness, went a constraining social policy. Although there were still plenty of remnants of what in effect were outdated moral teachings on commerce, essentially the way had been opened to the development over the next two hundred years of full-blown, virtually unrestricted capitalism, the system in which private enterprise is energized primariy by the search for profits. In the decades following the restoration of the monarchy (1660), economic individualism in a variety of guises steadily took over from stricter forms of Puritanism. Religion, at least in some of its more influential manifestations, provided the justification, the sanctification, that an economy based increasingly on money for its own sake needed. It now "insisted, in short, that money-making, if not free from spiritual dangers, was not a danger and nothing else, but that it could be, and ought to be, carried on for the greater glory of God[8] . . . [economic] enterprise itself is the discharge of a duty inspired by God."[9] The Calvinist Doctrine of the Elect provided the reassurance that success in commerce is the outward sign of divine approval.

The fusion of commerce and religious ideals now opened the gates in the eighteenth century to free enterprise and in the nineteenth century to the full flowering of a laissez-faire economy and of the "Protestant work ethic." The new emphasis in religion, its less attractive, sanctimonious attitudes notwithstanding, released the outburst of financial and industrial energy that was to make possible modern industrial society. The nonconformist virtues of upright and sober living, of devotion to hard work, a high sense of personal duty, were of value to the businessman in the next world as well as in this one.

The new spirit of individualism and liberty for the commercial entrepreneur received further justification from the equally new skills of "political arithmetic" or economics. As the Christian moralists replaced the condemnation of usury with the condonation of profit making, they in fact abdicated a large section of their territory. Their usurpers were "scientists" who had no concern with right or wrong, but only with impersonal forces and laws of commerce. With the eventual arrival of Adam Smith and Ricardo, objectivity proscribed the hampering quiddities of religious commercial ethics. Business now really was business.

It would require much deeper research and analysis to provide a complete answer to the question posed earlier as to how it is that Western Christianity managed to reverse its attitude toward the morality of moneymaking. Two variations of the same question automatically follow. Was the church's moral teaching allowed to slither toward the transposition of evil into good or did it adapt itself gracefully and legitimately to suit the requirements of an ever-changing industrial/commercial economy? Did it express the passive reflection of those changes or did it mold them according to its own principles?

The answer to each question probably lies between the two extremes, although it will vary from decade to decade, from place to place. The church's teaching has both mirrored and helped shape the socioeconomic structures in which it operates, but it is also very skilled—one might say *too* skilled—at adapting its teaching to provide the morality required of it to lubricate the economic wheels. It is difficult to avoid the conclusion that most of what has passed for moral guidance has been to justify and buttress the establishment and to indoctrinate the have-nots rather than the haves. On the other hand, adaptation is not necessarily sinful nor need it mean "chickening out." Cannibalism is presumably considered to be perfectly moral in a cannibalistic society, although anthropologists have discovered that in any society there are taboos on various types of conduct. The church's role has likewise been to establish taboos and sets of values that enable the society of the day to function with reasonable smoothness.

Despite its behavioral norm of justifying and underpinning the prevailing establishment, the church has, as already mentioned, tended frequently to oppose it, not so much because it hoped to change its morality as because the church clung to the morality of an earlier period; its prophetic witness, embedded in the Scriptures, put it at odds with capitalist forms of exploitation. Eventually it had, however, to come to terms with the fundamental changes in the economy that occurred in the seventeenth century. Similarly, in the twentieth century its clergy, with a few exceptions, failed at first to recognize the forces of social reform that emerged with the large industrial trade unions and the political expression of the working classes in the young Labour Party. In Britain today all the Christian faiths, and in particular the Church of England, still have to be on guard against a complacent social antiquarianism, which has a musty odor reminiscent of her thousands of almost empty, ancient buildings.

The Alleviation of Suffering and Poverty

The search for biblical texts with which either to attack or condone moneymaking is unsatisfactory. Denunciation of usury, particularly in the case of the poor and either in money or kind, can be discovered in Exodus 22:25, Deuteronomy 23:19–20, and Leviticus 25:36–7, as well as in several of the prophets and psalms (15:5). The few occasions when Jesus touches on it can easily be misinterpreted: thus, the expulsion of the money changers from the Temple (Mark 11:15) can be seen either as an attack on profit making or merely as removing an inappropriate activity from a holy place; even "You cannot serve God and mammon" (Luke 16:13), coming soon after the, to my mind, ambiguous parable of the unjust steward, has to be set against the parable of the talents (Matt. 25:14–30), in which the servant who had buried his talent seems to have been admonished severely and cast into the outer darkness because he did not invest the money at the bank at interest.

Conditions two thousand years ago in that tiny, remote province of the Roman Empire were in any case so different from those of our own day that it is surely impossible to draw useful parallels with contemporary values. As with so many of the parables and sayings of Jesus, these examples can be taken at more than one level and the important meaning may be transcendental. But when it came to the poor, Jesus was unequivocal. He was on their side. The small-town carpenter was one of them. He was also against the rich. It was Lazarus, not Dives, who was "carried by angels to Abraham's bosom" (Luke 16:22). "If you would be perfect, go, sell what you possess and give to the poor, and you will have treasure in heaven . . ." (Matt. 19:21). It was "easier for a camel to go through the eye of a needle than for a rich man to enter the kingdom of God" (Matt. 19:24). Whether or not needle refers to a narrow gateway in Jerusalem, the message is ambiguous.

Down the centuries the Christian churches have taken this teaching very seriously. They have been pioneers in succoring the poor by means of alms, clothing, food, and accommodation—just as they have been pioneers in education and nursing the sick. On the other hand, their attitude toward poverty has changed dramatically, in parallel, it can be maintained, to changes in economic practices and beliefs. In medieval times the relief of the poor was one of the obligations built into society's structure. For those who possessed property, the refusal of alms to obvious cases of need was a mortal sin; many of the monasteries and nunneries were highly organized sources of relief. Quite apart from practical charity, poverty in itself was envisaged by many to be a virtue. The cult of saintly poverty reached its medieval climax with Saint Francis, although his followers were persecuted by the immensely wealthy papacy under John XXII.

There was of course no shortage of other rich prelates, but by and large the medieval church's acceptance of and obligation to the poor were unquestioned. With the ascendance of the Protestants, religious attitudes began to alter. The Puritans, for example, looked

upon poverty not as a misfortune deserving pity, but as the result of moral failing. This of course was the obverse to the belief that riches were the outward sign of the upright life, of God's blessing. Increasingly, poverty was considered the result not of any economic cause, but of individual idleness. Society owed the poor nothing. Vagrants, including their children, could no longer expect automatic charity and, if unlucky, were caught by savage parliamentary acts that offered them a choice between harsh compulsory labor and a whipping. As Tawney comments wryly, "A society which reverences the attainment of riches as the supreme felicity will naturally be disposed to regard the poor as damned in the next world, if only to justify itself for making their life a hell in this."[10]

This attitude toward the poor continued through the eighteenth century and most of the nineteenth, softened only by help for the "deserving" as opposed to the "undeserving" poor. With the concentration of working people in the hastily built slums of Britain's new industrial towns of the Midlands and the north, poverty and squalor were matched by the horror of grossly long working days in factories and child slavery in mines and workshops. The condition of the poor did lead eventually to a profusion of charities of all kinds, before and during Victoria's long reign (1837–1901), in which the churches played the dominant part. But many of the old Puritan attitudes still prevailed, particularly in the influential movement within the Church of England known as Evangelicalism (founded in the 1780s), which laid heavy emphasis on man's sinfulness. Good works were necessary, but only faith could bring salvation.

It would be unjust not to credit the Evangelicals with their active concern for the disadvantaged groups such as the insane, and with their rigorous campaigns against slavery and the slave trade, against the employment of child chimney sweeps, and in favor of other reforms. Different religious groups and individuals also did devoted work: for example, the Ragged Schools movement, strongly linked with Sunday schools; the YMCA; the homes for children started by Dr. Barnado, who believed he was "under the direct leading of God in the work that he did for waifs and that without God he would never have done it. It cannot be doubted that the Christian drive of the Victorians included a drive to save and to better the poor and the sick. Christianity was integral to the ideals and the work of countless reformers."[11]

Without a Christian outlook and the widespread fashion of churchgoing, especially among the upper and middle classes, the extensive charitable work of the Victorians and of later generations would undoubtedly have been greatly diminished. It brought benefits to the well-to-do as well as to the poor. In addition to easing your conscience, the extent and nature of your charitable activities was a symbol of status and a sound investment in salvation. It also helped to dampen discontent in a century of social turbulence that had seen the Chartist agitation, the 1848 insurrections, and the horror of the Paris Commune (1871). In a laissez-faire economy the dispensing of charity was not, however, without its critics, because it interfered with the workings of a free market in labor, which, ideally, should go where it was needed, whereas charity was thought to keep the poor in areas where earnings were depressed. Worse, it sapped a man's will to improve his lot by his own efforts (see Samuel Smiles's best-seller *Self Help,* published in 1859 and directed particularly at the working man.)

Charity was no doubt often abused. The parochial clergy, particularly in the slum districts of large cities, were pestered by claims for help, many of them bogus. This led, under the influence of the Evangelicals, to the reinforcement of the conclusion that indiscriminate relief must at all costs be avoided; it should be reserved for the "deserving," thrifty poor. The "undeserving" should be left to the mercies of the deliberately harsh and inadequate Poor Law. To enforce such principles, the Charity Organization Society was founded and this led to the better coordination of the profusion of charitable bodies and to the investigation of individual cases. Although churchmen and religious lay workers played the leading part in this and other forms of systemization of charitable work, "the activities which developed from this newly gained knowledge and experience were in fact stages in the development of the collectivist State . . . systematic philanthropy was necessarily a step away from a system based on the ordinary personal service, which anyone can render, towards the creation of a scientifically organized State whose services could only be staffed by professionals."[12] Gradually and erratically, charitable services were being taken over by public, often local, authorities.

During the twentieth century much charitable work in Britain has been turned into social work; instituted largely after World War II, the so-called "welfare state" was originally designed to provide "cradle to grave" social services, including a universal medical service, as a *right,* subject only to relatively light inquiries into present circumstances. A great part of religion's social dimension has therefore been diminished and secularized. Nevertheless, with the poor and suffering there is certain always to be scope for Christianity's social dimension. Its belief that the other person matters, its central doctrine of love, should insure that this responsibility is not forgotten, although it may take new forms.

It was crystallized in the orotund words of Bishop Frank Weston, addressing an Anglo-Catholic Congress (1923): "You cannot worship Jesus in the Tabernacle if you do not pity Jesus in the slum. . . . It is folly, it is madness, to suppose that you can worship Jesus in the Sacraments and Jesus on the Throne of Glory when you are sweating Him in the bodies and souls of His children. . . . Go out and look for Jesus in the ragged, in the naked, and in the oppressed and sweated, in those who have lost hope, in those who are struggling to make good. Look for Jesus. And when you see Him, gird yourselves with his towel and try to wash His feet."[13]

Intercession and Concentration on the Individual Soul Rather than on Social Reality

The most obvious response of a Christian to the social dimension is through intercessory prayer. This is equally the case with a Christian who devotes all his energies to succoring the poor and distressed or to advocating radical measures to replace existing socioeconomic structures, as it is with the Christian who believes that no response other than prayer is called for. Those who hold the view that social reform and/or political activity of any kind are no concern of religion (whether or not they involve themselves in charitable work) can find quotations in the New Testament that appear to support them: "My kingship is not of this world" (John 18:36); "Then render to Caesar the things that are Caesar's, and to God the things that are God's" (Luke 20:25).

Some schools of theology have attached little importance to the social commitments of the church, if they have not rejected the need for them altogether. Today, as formerly, in many churches the stress is on the salvation of the soul rather than on social or political involvement, on individual (particularly sexual) morality rather than on social morals and justice. As Paul Tillich puts it: "It is regrettable that Christianity has often concealed its unwillingness to do justice, or to fight for it, by setting off instead of battling for the removal of social injustice."[14] It can be argued that this approach and extreme religious prudery are associated with authoritarian, right-wing politics. Radically minded Christians are certainly critical of it, declaring that "prayer and contemplation, in established religion, become purely private practices within a social order which they never question nor threaten. That order is simply a neutral backcloth for the practice of religion. Religion has become privatized, a phenomenon which some Christians actually welcome. Not only that, the private religions have become a multi-million dollar industry. They are part of capitalism's success story—religions as commodities, religions which in no way threaten or disturb social stability."[15]

Meditation, Christian or otherwise, which in recent years has attracted so many, might be thought an obvious target for this kind of criticism and, indeed, this may often be justified because naive meditation can lead to a denial of social reality; on the other hand, meditation, like prayer, can also lead to the reinforcement of the inner strength needed to cope with it, whether by means of charitable work or sociopolitical involvement. Those closed religious orders that eschew good works fall into a special category and can generate insights and spiritual power with which to energize religious social commitment.

A more vulnerable target is offered by those sentimental forms of pietism that cling to the gentle, comforting, reassuring aspects of the doctrine of Christian love and that would find the message in Saint John of the Cross's *The Dark Night of the Soul* totally alien. Spirituality, if it is not to be bogus, needs to be tempered by suffering, by encounter with the raw harshness of reality, with evil. But even the positive by-products of suffering can be twisted. Resignation of one's soul into the hands of God has always been a central and valid concept of Christianity, but, in the past especially, this too has been only too easily interpreted as a justification for ignoring social realities; for urging people to put up with poor wages and slum housing in this life so that they will merit rewards in the next one.

Of course, prayer and seeking a relationship with a personal God provide Christianity with its essence. There have always, however, been voices that have warned of the danger of allowing this central concern to lead to forgetfulness about others. Love of God and love of one's brothers and sisters, they say, should be inseparable. The fourteenth-century mystic John Ruysbroeck warned that "we find nowadays many silly men who would be so interior and so detached, that they will not be active or helpful in any way of which their neighbours are in need. Know, such men are neither hidden friends nor yet true servants of God but are wholly false and disloyal . . ."[16] In 1916 the sponsors of a National Mission of Repentance and Hope in Britain proclaimed that "there is a real difference between a converted nation and a nation of converted individuals. All the citizens of a nation might be individually converted, and yet the public life be conducted on principles other than Christian." Maurice Reckitt, after quoting this, comments: "the social order was in the intention of God a spiritual reality and an essential sphere of grace, with purposes which required to be understood and laws which needed to be obeyed. And since this was so, social righteousness could never be assumed to arise automatically out of the consecrated intentions of individuals."[17] It was another Anglican priest, Geoffrey Studdert Kennedy, who wrote: "Nobody worries about Christ so long as He can be kept shut up in churches; He is quite safe there, but there is always trouble if you try to let Him out."[18]

The Advocacy of Social Reform and Change

The church in Britain has never possessed the characteristics of a seamless garment. The widespread peasant uprisings in the fourteenth century, for example, were supported by the poorer parish priests and, in particular, by John Ball, who preached in favor of a primitive communism with a strong Christian character. This was also the time of John Wycliffe and the Lollards, who produced the first complete English translation of the Bible (1382), who attacked the rich upper echelons of the clergy and declared that in all society the right to wealth and authority should depend on the righteousness of the individual. From the sixteenth century onward the Protestant noncomformists showed a remarkable tendency to generate breakaway sects, which led to the proliferation into Baptists, Presbyterians, Quakers, Congregationalists, Unitarians, Methodists—so that it was said by an eighteenth-century Frenchman that "England has ninety religions but only one sauce!" Although these divisions were primarily religious, they frequently cloaked conflicts over social questions and differences in class status: thus the revolts of the Levellers and the Diggers against the dominant Presbyterians during Cromwell's Commonwealth had a religious as well as a political/class flavor; likewise the Primitive Methodists, who in 1810 broke away from the increasingly conservative main body, were identified with the humbler, working-class membership.

But for the most part the churches, as we have seen, have remained closely identified with the establishment of which they, and in particular the Church of England, have always formed an integral part. The gibe that the "Anglican church is the Tory (right-wing) party on its knees" has until very recently been essentially true. As the state church with the monarch at its head, with a bench of bishops in the House of Lords, and its huge network of parish churches and "livings," it has always been privileged. Until World War I many of its clergy were themselves wealthy, if not always quite on a par with the squire.

However devoted were many of its ministers, however valuable their service, it was inescapably a rich man's Church. It was endowed with great wealth, much of which had come into the personal possession of those who had held high office in it, and in the middle of the [nineteenth] century from time to time the large estates left by those who had been its bishops were noted in the press. Its priests tended to be recruited from one class in society, and to have been prepared for their work by an education which in normal circumstances was out of the reach of a poor man . . . this necessarily cut the Church off from a large section of society . . .[19]

In the large towns especially, the Anglican church, in comparison with many of the nonconformist chapels, was out of touch with the majority of the population.

Despite this separation there were, as already noted, quite a few professing Christians with power and influence who were concerned about the widespread poverty and degradation. The moral force of Christianity found itself at times in collision with an industrial and commercial system buttressed by the iron laws of political economy, which "forbade the exercise of wealth as the only desirable, indeed the only possible objective for corporate human endeavor."[20] Nevertheless, Victorian Britain, outwardly at any rate, continued as a Christian, God-fearing land. The later decades of the nineteenth century saw the emergence of what has been called the nonconformist conscience. "Its existence helped to condition public attitudes to moral issues, such as temperance, or prostitution, or Sunday observance, or Bulgarian massacres, or concentration camps in South Africa, or oppression in the Congo. It brought the strong conscience of the middle classes to bear upon national questions, sometimes in an emotional way, but seldom in a way which politicians could afford to disregard."[21]

Writers as different as Dickens, Ruskin, and Carlyle exposed and attacked the Victorian social order, including the churches. Their denunciations antagonized many of the senior clergy, but there were others who agreed. These included the Christian Socialists organized in groups such as the Guild of Saint Matthew and the Christian Socialist Union. Led by the Reverend F. D. Maurice and the writers Charles Kingsley and Thomas Hughes, they hoped for the peaceful replacement of the capitalist system by industrial cooperatives. Their movement remained very small, but they did present a coherent challenge to the worst economic practices and exploitation. Moreover, its influence endured and undoubtedly led to the early stages of British socialism taking on a Christian rather than a Marxist character.

Following the Great Depression of 1929–31, the churches could no longer be counted on as unquestioning defenders of economic orthodoxy or of the established social structure. Archbishop William Temple (of York and Canterbury) exemplified, despite great opposition in his own ranks, the church's deepening social conscience. For years he was actively concerned with issues such as chronic unemployment or the need for penal reform and abolition of the death penalty. Because of the doctrine of the Incarnation, he described Christianity as being the most materialistic of all religions. Always he took his stand on Christian principles, believing passionately that the church as the agent of God's purpose possessed a right and a duty to "interfere" in social and industrial problems.

In more recent times, in all the British churches, including the Evangelical wing, the stress on social/institutional/corporate sin has been more firmly established. In the main they have continued to reflect the broad stream of mild social reform, though individual clergy have adopted more radical responses. To a large extent this has echoed policies framed originally by secular groups and parties. On two problems in particular both the churches themselves and their adherents seem to have discovered an unfamiliar militancy; first, in the fight against apartheid legislation in South Africa (the Anglican communion remains a strong influence in most Commonwealth, ex-colonial countries) and against racial discrimination at home; second, in the campaigns for nuclear disarmament.

Theologically and liturgically, the Anglican church is extraordinarily tolerant. But one wonders how many of its incumbents and congregations would agree with the Reverend Kenneth Leech, one of its more openly radical priests, when he wrote recently that "the subversive character of Christian spirituality derives from the subversive character of Christ himself. . . . He was a threat to the established order of his day, to the *status quo* in Church and state, to established religion. The Kingdom of God dislocated the stable order and it does so still."[22]

The Alliance of the Supranatural with the Secular

It has been indicated that religion has steadily been edged out of the domains of commercial morality by economics, and of the relief of poverty and spiritual misfortune by social work sponsored by the state or local authorities. Similarly, other domains of religion have, in varying degrees, been surrendered to psychiatry and psychotherapy, to evolutionary biology, to astronomy and cosmology, to academic sociology and philosophy. The secularization of all departments of life has accelerated.

It can scarcely be denied that the purely or predominantly secular domains have stupendous achievements to their credit. The nonreligious do not find it difficult to argue that it has been precisely the liberation from antiquated religious concepts and restrictions that has made many of the advances possible. Theists can of course reply that society, to the extent that its institutions work for mankind's benefit, is merely "living off the fat" of religious morality, that secular individuals are, without realizing it, performing Christ's work. The argument soon becomes sterile, particularly when it is realized that the secular/religious division is usually blurred; scientists, economists, social workers, doctors, even psychiatrists may as individuals hold religious beliefs. In any case, there seem to be far more agnostics (including "religious agnostics") than there are atheists in all their purity. There are even Christians who declare that their religion is, in the best sense of the word, materialist.

Once one turns to society's ethical failures, and in particular to global-scale failures that threaten to annihilate us, purely secular ethics—or, if it is preferred, humanist ethics—appear to be far less adequate. Without embarking on an investigation of Kant's theory of practical reason or of whether there exist in man and also in society innate moral insights, it is difficult to avoid the conclusion that sociopolitical action by itself is failing. Communist societies have their own moral, social codes and they can be very rigid and strict, but without supranatural reinforcement morality is only too apt to be swallowed up by expediency. Any means can be justified to serve an end. The ends themselves, however praiseworthy at first, are soon fouled by the means. La Rochefoucauld remarked that "hypocrisy is homage paid by vice to virtue." Statesmen in nominally Christian societies are noted for their hypocrisy; in non-religious cultures they do not need to bother.

No one, I am sure, would suggest that the churches consistently propose correct or acceptable ethical formulas, or that their adherents faithfully abide by their teaching. Quite apart from what seems to be their built-in tendency to be identified with the secular establishment, religious beliefs in themselves seem nowadays to be in danger of being secularized. The churches are too ready to settle for what are no more than sanctified forms of humanism. "Today many contemporary priesthoods have turned to secularized value systems in a search for popularity and credibility. The switch to rationalism cannot generate the charisma that accrues only to those whose inner practices give strength to the heart rather than to the thinking mind. . . . In the modern West the extensive secularization of religion has largely destroyed the relation between individual spirituality and the systems of belief to which it used to belong."[23]

The adulteration, in particular of its unique essence, by a series of defensive withdrawals in the face of the successes—and even the failures—of secularism needs to be resisted. Leszek Kolakowski, an exiled professor of the history of philosophy from Warsaw, has written recently: "A religious worship reduced to its secular utility and oblivious of its original function can survive for a time, no doubt, yet sooner or later its emptiness is bound to be exposed, the irrelevance of its form to its content will become apparent, its ambiguous life sustained by credit from a non-existent bank will come to end and the forgotten links with the Sacred will be resumed in another place, by other forms of religiosity."[24]

Perhaps the correct conclusion is that religion should never cease making its special arational or supranatural prophetic contribution to society, and yet at the same time it should endeavor to increase its influence in, rather than regain control of, the secular domains that regulate society.

NOTES

1. Paul Tillich, *Morality and Beyond* (London: Routledge and Kegan Paul, 1964), 45.

2. Richard H. Tawney, *Religion and the Rise of Capitalism,* (London: Pelican Books, 1938), 48, Holland Memorial lecture, 1922.

3. Ibid., 47.

4. Ibid., 52.

5. Ibid., 104.

6. Ibid., 103.

7. Ibid., 116.

8. Ibid., 238.

9. Ibid., 245.

10. Ibid., 265.

11. Owen Chadwick, "The Established Church under Attack," *The Victorian Crisis of Faith* (London: SPCK, 1970), 91.

12. G. Kitson Clark, *Churchmen and the Condition of England, 1832–1885* (London: Methuen, 1971), 274.

13. *Anglo-Catholic Congress Report,* 185–86.

14. Paul Tillich, 39.

15. Kenneth Leech, 50–51.

16. John Ruysbroeck, *The Sparkling Stone,* vii, quoted in *Ruysbroeck* by Evelyn Underhill (London: Bell, 1915), 117.

17. Maurice B. Reckitt, *Maurice to Temple: A Century of the Social Movement in the Church of England* (London: Faber, 1947), 160.

18. Geoffrey Studdert Kennedy, *The Word and the Work* (London: Longmans Green, 1925). 66.

19. G. Kitson Clark, 320.

20. Ibid., 290.

21. Owen Chadwick, 95.

22. Kenneth Leech, 51.

23. John H. Crook, *The Evolution of Human Consciousness* (Oxford: Clarendon, 1980), 359.

24. Leszek Kolakowski, *Religion* (London: Fontana, 1982), 235–36.

10

The Discourse of Liberation Theology in Perspective
GUSTAVO BENAVIDES

... da selbst der *kritische* Theologe *Theologe* bleibt. Karl Marx, "Zur Kritik der Nationalökonomie"

The publication in 1971 of Gustavo Gutiérrez's *Teología de la liberación,*[1] constituted a major event in the discourse of Christian theology. Gutiérrez's work, as well as the writings by Assmann, Segundo, Galilea, and other theologians,[2] have been considered the first significant contribution of Latin America to the interpretation of the Christian message.[3] The academic success of the theology of liberation means that the theological articulation of the Christian faith is no longer the private domain of European theologians; it means that Christianity—not just as faith or practice, but as theology, that is, as a second-degree elaboration, as "discourse"—has outgrown the relatively narrow frontiers of the Northern Hemisphere. After the publication of Gutiérrez's *Teología de la liberación,* the theological enterprise has, for better or worse, begun to be articulated from a new perspective determined by the specific economic and social characteristics of the so-called Third World.

From a strictly theological point of view, nothing could be more welcome than this expansion of the theological world. Now, from being a mission territory, the Third World has become a space in which the Word is spoken, this time with a theological accent. My aim in this essay is not, however, a celebratory one. This is not a religious essay, but rather an essay about religion: the distinction, often forgotten, is, in spite of theologians, a valid one. Therefore, I will not try to elaborate, theologically, on the theology of liberation, nor will I criticize it by proposing an alternative theology. The first task is already well under way, as the recent publications by Gutiérrez, Assmann, Boff, Dussel, Galilea, Segundo, and others show. As for the other, a theological critique would presuppose a series of assumptions that I am unable to make.

Instead, my purpose in this essay is to place the discourse of the theology of liberation, particularly the work of Gustavo Gutiérrez, in a perspective that may help to clarify its role within contemporary Catholicism. In this context, it should be emphasized that Christian theology is not being taken as an autonomous corpus of beliefs—the response to God's primordial manifestation in history. Rather, Christian theology will be considered a reflection on the system of values that constitutes the core of a given culture;[4] a system of values that depends on, and reinforces, the structure of a society in a dialectical way.[5] Thus, Christian theology acts as a "superstructural" element, that is, as an "ideology," whereas Christianity—or the idea of Christendom—acts as one of the key components of the very structure of any society that considers itself "Christian." The same can be said, *mutatis mutandis,* of Islamic or Buddhist theologies (insofar as Buddhism may be said to have a "theology").

The theology of liberation must be seen, then, as sharing with other theologies the uneasy position of being an ideological construction that must nevertheless claim historical autonomy. In the case of theology of liberation, the situation is particularly complex, since Gutiérrez stresses both the historical foundations of his enterprise and, because of its being *theo*logical, its autonomy. In the opening lines of the first chapter of *Teología de la liberación,* he writes that theological reflection arises (*surges*) spontaneously in the believer, that is, in those who have received the gift of God's Word.[6] Later on, theological reflection is defined as a "critical reflection" (*reflexión crítica*) that "by definition does not want to be a mere Christian justification *a posteriori.*"[7] However, in a book entitled *Teología desde el reverso de la historia,* Gutiérrez writes:

. . . theological reflection is bound to historical processes, it is part of historical blocks [*bloques históricos*] without which it cannot be understood. Theology, like all thought, must be placed in a historical context. Theologies do not follow one another as a chain of thoughts in the air; they are answers—and can and must also be questions—to vast historical processes. Theological discourse is an effort by concrete persons who believe and think their faith in definite conditions; who produce actions and interpretations which play a role in social confrontations. The theologian does not find himself in a historical limbo; his reflection is placed in, arises from, its material foundations; he speaks from a specific situation.[8]

The fundamental ambiguity of Gutiérrez's position is due to the impossible task he has set for himself: to maintain the transhistorical foundation of his faith, while at the same time trying to situate that faith in the concreteness of contemporary Latin America. Theological reflection, like any ideological discourse, is, as Gutiérrez recognizes, bound to social processes, and it is only within these social contexts that theological reflection is to be understood. Inasmuch as this is the case, there are limits that even the most radical theology must respect, if this theology is to be considered "orthodox." No theology, however radical, is free to question the structural values of a society without losing its legitimacy in the process. When a particularly heterodox system is produced by a social group, the new ideology—or rather "utopia" in Mannheim's sense[9]—faces several alternatives. If the new system is perceived as being too extreme, its members may face physical annihilation (consider, for instance, the fate suffered by Mazdak and his followers),[10] or may be forced to commit collective suicide (as in the case of the followers of Jim Jones in Jonestown). Another alternative is the "domestication" of the new heresy, its accommodation into the prevalent ideology. In this case, the originally "dysfunctional"[11] teachings are manipulated in such a way that they can be integrated into the ongoing discourse (the assimilation of Buddha into the cycle of the *avatāras* of Visnu is just one example of the remarkable ability of Hinduism to assimilate and neutralize extraneous ideologies).[12] A third alternative left to orthodoxy is the "spiritualization" of the new movement. In this event, the socially unacceptable—and socially concrete—proposals of the new group are diluted and projected onto a spiritual realm where they are no longer dangerous. Thus, for example, millenarian movements[13] become interiorized, spiritual, mystical.[14]

The alternatives mentioned above certainly do not exhaust the options left to the orthodox forces or to the heterodox ones. One may also consider situations in which the members of a heterodox movement engage in "antinomian" practices, while at the same time maintaining (or not) a public façade of irreproachable orthodoxy.[15] Finally, one must consider the possibility of a more radical solution: the breaking away of the new group, the establishment of a political structure that legitimizes, and is legitimized by, the new ideology. It is in this context that we have to examine the alternatives left to the theology of liberation, as well as, in general, to those groups within the Catholic church that have adopted a radical position in regard to the economic conditions prevalent in Latin America. The first of the options mentioned above—physical annihilation—was exercised against the Colombian priest Camilo Torres after he had joined a guerrilla group.[16] More recently, in El Salvador, and elsewhere in Latin America, priests have been murdered by right-wing groups, usually with the support of the government. The domestication of the theology of liberation—in this case, its "spiritualization"—is already well under way, as the attempts by Alfonso López Trujillo, Galat, and Kloppenburg show.[17] López Trujillo, for example, attacks the theologians of liberation for assuming a Marxist model, including the notion of class struggle, and proposes instead, as a paradigm for social reconciliation, the spiritual reconciliation in Christ of Jews and gentiles.[18] In similar terms, Kloppenburg stresses the need for contemplation, which he finds lacking in the socially and politically oriented writings of Gutiérrez.[19] The more radical solution, that is, the establishment of a new society, appears as the only option left to the new theologians. The difficulties involved in such an enterprise, however, would almost certainly lead to the demise of those thus engaged.

It would seem, then, that the entire discourse of the theology of liberation will either have to become more radical, and sever itself from the authority of the established Catholic hierarchy, or it will have to accommodate itself as a more or less tolerated radical ("dysfunctional") wing within the theological establishment. This last solution would imply not only a change in the thought of the theology of liberation, but also a rearrangement of the position of the church. In considering these options, it is first necessary to examine what is taken to be, on the one hand, the "content," the "message" of the theology of liberation, and, on the other, the type of reasoning, the particular language and vocabulary, employed by Gutiérrez in his *Teología de la liberación*. In doing this we are not presupposing the existence of pure theological content as opposed to style or form of thinking. On the contrary, it is by becoming aware of the inseparability of form and content in theological, as well as in other, more extreme forms of discourse (such as the mystical),[20] that we are able to grasp the intricate connection between goals and means—in this case, the goals and means of the theology of liberation. An artificial distinction between form and content is as insidious as the parallel distinction between the realm of the political and that of the religious (or the artistic) and must be considered an ideological construction whose aim is the fragmentation and depolitization of social life. Regarding, then, the "content" of the theology of liberation, it should be kept in mind that the following exposition is not intended to be regarded as independent from the subsequent discussion of the "language" of liberation theology.

As developed in the work of Gutiérrez, the theology of liberation is a radical interpretation of the Christian revelation, one that does not accept the traditional distinction between sacred and profane realism, between sacred and profane histories.[21] For Gutiérrez, salvation is not to be regarded as an otherworldly affair, nor as a purely spiritual process, but as an integral one, comprising the spiritual, social, and political aspects of life. Theology, then, is not considered a self-contained discipline, but rather a critical reflection that takes into account the social and economic conditions that had made this act of reflection itself possible.[22] In the Latin American context, theology, as historical praxis, has to be aware of the situation of underdevelopment and dependence in which the continent lives. In his book *Teología de la liberación,* Gutiérrez deals extensively with the problem of economic development, criticizing those theories that propose mere "developmental" solutions (*desarrollismo*), instead of a structural change in the economic system.[23] The discussion of economic problems, which may appear quite out of place in a theological work, is fundamental because the integral view of man proposed by the theology of liberation considers that salvation is not something "beyond the world" (*ultramundano*); salvation, on the contrary—"communion of men with God, and communion of men with one another"—is something that takes place, in a real and concrete form, already in this world. In consequence, sin is no longer viewed merely as an obstacle for an otherworldly salvation, but, insofar as sin is a break with God, it is regarded as a historical reality, as a break of the communion among men.[24] The crucial Christian concepts of creation and salvation are interpreted by Gutiérrez as being almost indistinguishable: "The creation is presented in the Bible not as a stage previous to salvation, but as inserted in the salvific process." Furthermore, the act of creation is seen as tied—"almost to the point of identity"—to the liberation of Israel from slavery in Egypt,[25] a liberation that is a "political act," and "the beginnings of the construction of a just and fraternal society."[26] Finally, the God of Israel is the God of history, of political liberation, a view that makes the distinction between religious and political liberation untenable.

In response to the examples adduced by Gutiérrez, it must be said that the use of historical events, such as the history of the Israelites or the death of Jesus (or his possible connections with the Zealots), as paradigms for legitimizing concrete historical options centuries later is, despite any claims to the contrary, a procedure that de-concretizes the current political and economic situations. When, in the chapter entitled "Liberation and Salvation," Gutiérrez writes that "the liberation from Egypt is a political act," and states further that "the early chapters of Exodus describe the situation of oppression in which the Jewish people lived in Egypt,"[27] he is undoubtedly right; similarly, one can agree with the statement, cited earlier, about the liberation from Egypt being not only a political act, but also—ideally—the beginnings of a just and fraternal society. However, when Gutiérrez uses these events as transhistorical models for the interpretation of contemporary revolutionary movements in Latin America, he deprives the modern situations of their historical urgency. This "sacralization" of social struggle may be theologically necessary in order to counteract the conservative religious legitimation of unjust social structures. The mechanism of religious legitimation, characteristic of "archaic" cultures—romanticized by Eliade,[28] and studied in depth by Topitsch[29]—is reversed by Gutiérrez, who now proposes a religious legitimation of social change. In doing so, Gutiérrez is, nevertheless, still imprisoned by mythical thought—by a revolutionary *illud tempus* that may prove to be the undoing of any concrete application of the theology of liberation.

And yet, in the context in which Gutiérrez's theological enterprise is carried out, it would seem impossible not to make use of this mythical reasoning. In a universe lived, or conceived, religiously, certain modes of thought seem to inevitably take over and impose themselves. In this sense, it is perhaps unfair—as well as naive—to ask theologians to give up being theologians. On the other hand, it is also possible that the only way to successfully carry out political change of a radical type, and to maintain it, is through the skillful use—or manipulation—of the symbolic universe shared by the members of a culture. After all, if a society legitimizes itself through a religious ideology, the only avenue left to those who want to change that society is the utilization of the utopian counterpart of the prevalent ideology.[30] However, it should be kept in mind that there is a limit beyond which symbols, or ideologies, may not be manipulated; in other words, it is not always clear whether it is we who are using the symbols for our own purposes, or whether the ideology constituted by those symbols manages to perpetuate itself by allowing a certain degree of change—of illusory change—in its own discourse. Another danger consists in what could be called a case of *l'apprenti sorcier:* a utopian movement that, having acquired "functional autonomy," becomes independent from logical constraints and ends up by destroying itself.

As an example of the self-perpetuation of typically religious modes of discourse, we can examine Gutiérrez's understanding of "God's freedom" and "God's love for the poor." According to Gutiérrez, God's preference for the poor is not due to the goodness of the poor, but rather, this preference is grounded simply in the poor's poverty. Free choice, which does not take into account "the moral and personal dispositions of the poor,"[31] reveals, according to Gutiérrez, the gratuitousness (*gratuidad*) of God's love. In an interview published in 1980, he says, "A God who loves the poor because the poor deserve it, is a perfectly comprehensible God. However, to accept that God loves the poor simply because they are in a situation of oppression and exploitation, shocks us, and reveals to us the absolute gratuitousness of God's love, beyond any anthropomorphism."[32] Such a way of reasoning, admirable as it is in its commitment, can be understood as an "empty formula" in Topitsch's sense,[33] and can be easily reversed. Thus, a conservative theologian (from the *Opus Dei,* for example) may argue that God's absolute freedom allows him to gratuitously love the rich, not only without regard for the rich's goodness or evilness, but even because of the rich's evilness. As we can see, arguments involving "God's absolute freedom" or "God's absolute love" or those stressing the incognoscibility of God, are empty statements that can be interpreted to account for any state of affairs whatsoever. The history of Christianity, and indeed of all religions, is full of paradoxical and tautological statements, one of whose functions seems to be the validation of any possible factual or logical state of affairs. To say that God's love is absolutely gratuitous is to abandon the realm of meaningful discourse and to reach the limits of the process of communication: the meaningless poles of tautology and contradiction.[34] As a paradox, God becomes a *coincidentia oppositorum*—that in which good and evil, poor and rich, exploiter and exploited, master and slave, are reconciled.[35] As a tautology, God's love is a case of love for love's sake: a limitless and, therefore, meaningless love.[36] In any case, tautologies and contradictions, fascinating as they are from a logical—or "metaphysical"—point of view, are, because of their logical promiscuity, immensely vulnerable to ideological manipulation.

I am aware that Gustavo Gutiérrez would vehemently dispute the conclusions arrived at above, and I should therefore stress that I am not by any means questioning Father Gutiérrez's social commitment and religious convictions (which for him are indeed inseparable). My purpose in this essay is not to raise doubts about the personal convictions of those engaged in the elaboration of a theology of liberation, but to point out the difficulties and dangers involved in interpreting theologically problems as grave and urgent as poverty, exploitation, economic and cultural dependence, violence, and liberation. No matter how deeply felt one's personal convictions may be, it is always possible that in spite of oneself, one's choice of discourse (in case "choice" is possible at all) may determine to a great extent the efficacy of the actions brought about by those convictions.

In the case of the theology of liberation—while acknowledging the inevitability of having to use religious categories in the context of societies that are part of Christendom—the very fact of its being a theology, a discourse about "God," may prove to be the cause of its eventual spiritualization, domestication, and ultimate assimilation by the church. Therefore, the political interpretation of the Bible undertaken by the theology of liberation must be itself interpreted politically. We cannot but agree with Fredric Jameson when he writes that the political perspective is not a supplementary method, but rather "the absolute horizon of all reading and all interpretation,"[37] that is, in the context of the history of the Catholic church in Latin America.[38]

In this context, then, the theology of liberation may be seen as the continuation of the denunciatory efforts of Bartolomé de las Casas, the sixteenth-century Spanish missionary who plays such an important role as one of Gutiérrez's spiritual ancestors (another important one is the Peruvian Marxist Jose Carlos Mariátegui),[39] as well as of the millenarian atmosphere, which was an important component of the discovery and conquest of America.[40] The continuation of las Casas's missionary spirit is apparent in one of Gutiérrez's works, in which he mentions that las Casas sees the crucified Christ as being crucified again in each exploited Indian.[41] However, las Casas's theological perception—or theological interpretation—of the exploitation brought about by the system of *encomiendas* gives the impression of being less a humanistic than a theological act and can be seen as the theological response to Juan Ginés de Sepúlveda's theological legitimation of the political regime imposed by the newly arrived Christians. Eventually, the denunciations of las Casas were assimilated—and neutralized—by the church, whose function had to encompass both the legitimation of the social order and the "humanization" of the ongoing process of conquest. Four centuries later, the movement known as theology of liberation seems to be fulfilling the same basic role: in the larger perspective of Latin American history—from the Spanish conquest to the current situation of hopeless underdevelopment—the radical social awareness which these theologians have forced on socially unconcerned Christians, as well as on the hierarchy, could be seen as an effort, from within the church, to prepare the ground—the ideological, the political ground—for an eventual accommodation between the church and any possible development in Latin America. The fact that a large percentage of the total Catholic population of the world lives both as Catholic and as underdeveloped makes it imperative that the church—if it is to survive at all—try to account, theologically, for any coming radical social changes. This certainly does not mean that the movement known as liberation theology is the only response that the church is prepared to offer to new political developments[42]; on the contrary, it means that the theology of liberation is but one attempt to articulate in theological terms a social, economic, and ultimately political view arising from a world that regards itself as "Christian," with the ultimate—and quite understandable—aim of securing the survival of Christianity, that is, the survival of the church.

NOTES

1. Gustavo Gutiérrez, *Teología de la Liberación* (Lima: Centro de Estudios y Publicaciones (CEP), 1971). There is an English translation, *Theology of Liberation* (Maryknoll, N.Y.: Orbis, 1973); all translations are my own.

2. For a general background see Roberto Oliveros, *Liberación y Teología, Génesis y Crecimiento de una Reflexión* (Lima: CEP, 1980); Equipo Seladoc, *Panorama de la Teología Latinoamericana,* (Salamanca, Ediciones Sígueme, 1975) (includes articles by Boff, Gutiérrez, Míquez, Dusseel, Comblin, Assmann, etc.); Juan Luis Segundo, *Liberation of Theology* (Maryknoll, N.Y.: Orbis, 1976); Arturo

The Discourse of Liberation Theology in Perspective

Blatezky, *Sprache des Glaubens in Lateinamerika. Eine Studie zu Selbstverständnis und Methode der "Theologie der Befreiung"* (Frankfurt: Peter Lang, 1978).

3. See *Challenge of Liberation Theology: A First World Response,* ed. Brian Mahan and L. D. Richesin (Maryknoll, N.Y.: Orbis, 1981); Jose Míguez Bonino, *Revolutionary Theology Comes of Age* (London: SPCK, 1975); Robert McAfee Brown, *Theology in a New Key* (Philadelphia: Westminster, 1978); Robert McAfee Brown, *Gustavo Gutiérrez* (Atlanta: John Knox, 1981).

4. Cf. Clifford Geertz, "Religion as a Cultural System," *Anthropological Approaches to the Study of Religion,* ed. Michael Banton (London: Tavistock, 1966), 1–46; Jacques Waardenburg, "The Language of Religion and the Study of Religions as Sign Systems, *Science of Religion, Studies in Methodology,* ed. Lauri Honko (The Hague: Mouton, 1979), 441–57.

5. On the relationship between "structure" and "superstructure" see Marvin Harris, *Cultural Materialism* (New York: Random House, 1979), 70–75; Fredric Jameson, *The Political Unconscious* (Ithaca, N.Y.: Cornell University Press, 1981), 17–102; Raymond Williams, *Marxism and Literature* (Oxford: Oxford University Press, 1977), 55–71 (on ideology); 75–114 (on base and superstructure, determination, and hegemony).

6. Gutiérrez, *Teología de la Liberación,* 15.

7. Ibid., 179–80.

8. Gutiérrez, *Teología Desde el Reverso de la Historia,* 1st ed. (Lima: CEP, 1977); reprint, *La Fuerza Histórica de los Pobres* (Lima: CEP, 1979) 303–94, see esp. 390. The same fundamental ambiguity regarding the position of Christianity—and Christian theology—in an ideologically determined world can be found in Juan Luis Segundo, *Liberation of Theology,* p. 86; Segundo writes: "It must be admitted that the more we divest our minds of ideological trappings, the more we will free the message of Jesus from its ideological wrappings and get closer to its deeper, perduring truth." This statement, whose truth is far from self-evident (to a Buddhist or a Muslim, for example), is merely a repetition of the old doctrine about the soul being Christian by nature; on the other hand, Segundo writes on p. 122: "Faith, then, is not a universal, atemporal, pithy body of content summing up divine revelation once the latter has been divested of ideologies. On the contrary, it is maturity by way of ideologies, the possibility of fully and conscientiously carrying out the ideological task on which the real-life liberation of human beings depends." In other words, Christianity, like any other religion, is an ideology. The contradiction underlying the positions of Gutiérrez and Segundo could be resolved only if the theologians of liberation were prepared to consider Christianity as a provisional set of values, which because of the specific historical situation of Latin America (and only of Latin America), appears as capable of serving as a vehicle for radical social change. But even if they were to do so, it would still be difficult to imagine how it would be possible to provide a theological foundation for the liberation of the 'non-Christian' parts of the underdeveloped world, since this foundation is constituted by the mythologies of the Old and New Testaments. It would seem, then, that the theology of liberation is concerned only with providing religious legitimacy to move-

ments advocating radical social change in Christian societies, with the ulti-mate—and quite understandable—aim of securing the survival of Christianity.

9. Karl Mannheim, *Ideology and Utopia* (New York: Harcourt, n.d.); the German edition, *Ideologie und Utopie,* was published in 1929; the revised English translation was first published in 1936.

10. On Mazdak see Otakar Klíma, *Mazdak. Geschichte einer sozialen Bewegung im sassanidischen Persien* (Prague: Ceskoslovenské Akademie Ved, 1957); Geo Widengren, *Die Religionen Irans* (Stuttgart: Kohlhammer, 1965), 308–10.

11. On the dysfunctional aspect of religion see Robert Merton, *Social Theory and Social Structure* (New York: Free Press, 1968), 82ff.

12. Cf. Jan Gonda, *Viṣṇuism and Śivaism* (London: Athlone Press, 1970), 122.

13. Cf. Mannheim, *Ideology and Utopia,* 237ff.; see also *Millenial Dreams in Action,* ed. Sylvia Thrupp (New York: Schocken, 1970).

14. This does not necessarily mean that mystical movements, or "mysticism" in general, are inherently passive or reactionary. See *The Mystical and Political Dimension of the Christian Faith,* ed., Claude Geffré and Gustavo Gutiérrez (New York: Herder and Herder, 1974); Matthew Fox, O. P., "Meister Eckhart and Karl Marx: The Mystic as Political Theologian," *Understanding Mysticism,* ed. Richard Woods, O. P. (New York: Doubleday, 1980) 541–63; Herbert Grundmann, "Die geschichtlichen Grundlagen der deutschen Mystik," *Deutsche Vierteljahrsschrift für Literaturwissenschaft und Geistesgeschichte* 12 (1934): 400–29, reprinted in *Altdeutsche und Altniederländische Mystik,* ed. Kurt Ruh (Darmstadt, Wissenschaftliche Buchgesellschaft, 1964), 72–99.

15. A classical example of antinomianism can be found in the movement founded by Sabbatai Sevi; see Gershom Scholem, *Sabbatai Sevi, The Mystical Messiah* (Princeton, N.J.: Princeton University Press, 1973); on the more extreme antinomianism of the Frankist movement see Scholem, "La métamorphose du messianisme hérétique des Sabbatiens en nihilisme religieux au 18 siecle," in *Heresies et Societes dans l'Europe Pre-industrielle* (Paris: Mouton, 1968), 381–93 (and the discussion on 394—95); Scholem, "Der Nihilismus als religioses Phanomen," *Eranos* 43, 1974, 1–50.

16. The writings of Camilo Torres are available in English translation in *Revolutionary Priest, The Complete Writings and Messages of Camilo Torres,* ed. John Gervassi (New York: Random House, 1971); on the Colombian political situation at the time see Daniel Levine, *Religion and Politics in Latin America. The Catholic Church in Venezuela and Colombia* (Princeton, N.J.: Princeton University Press, 1981), 41ff.

17. cf. Oliveros, *Liberación y Teología,* 306ff.

18. Oliveros, 327–28; on López Trujillo see also Levine, *Religion and Politics,* 182.

19. Oliveros, 330.

20. The distinction between "form" and "content," or rather, between "experi-ence" and "interpretation" can be found, for example, in Ninian Smart, "Interpretation and Mystical Experience," *Religious Studies* 1 (1965): 75–87; see, however, Bruce Garside, "Language and the Interpretation of Mystical Experience," *International Journal for Philosophy of Religion* 3 (1972): 93–102;

and the articles contained in *Mysticism and Philosophical Analysis,* ed. Steven T. Katz (New York: Oxford University Press, 1978).

21. Cf. Gutiérrez, *Teología de la Liberación,* 186, 189ff.

22. Ibid., 28.

23. Cf. Gutiérrez, *Teología de la Liberación,* 35ff.

24. Ibid., 187ff.

25. Ibid., 191–94.

26. Ibid., 196.

27. Ibid., 194.

28. See, among other works, Mircea Eliade, *Traité d'histoire des Religions,* (Paris: Payot, 1970), first published in 1949; there is an English translation, *Patterns in Comparative Religion; Le sacré et le profane* (Paris, Gallimard, 1965), with an English translation, *The Sacred and the Profane; The Quest. History and Meaning in Religion,* (Chicago: University of Chicago Press, 1969). On Eliade's ideological position see Furio Jesi, *Cultura di Destra* (Milano: Garzanti, 1979), 38–50 and *Il Mito* (Milano: ISEDI, 1973), 66–69.

29. See Ernst Topitsch, *Vom Ursprung und Ende der Metaphysik* (Vienna: Springer, 1958).

30. On the dialectical interaction between ideology and utopia see Jameson, *The Political Unconscious,* 281–99, esp. 285, where Jameson deals with the utopian aspects of religion and Marxism; on this subject see also Jameson, *Marxism and Form* (Princeton, N.J.: Princeton University Press, 1971), 116–59 (on Ernst Bloch), esp. 117–18 and 157–58. For "gnostic" and neoplatonic elements in Marxism see Ernst Topitsch, "Marxismus und Gnosis," and "Entfremdung und Ideologie. Zur Entmythologisierung des Marxismus," in Topitsch, *Sozialphilosophie zwischen Ideologie und Wissenschaft* (Neuwied: Luchterhand, 1971) 3d ed., 261–327; Leszek Kolakowski, *Main Currents of Marxism* (Oxford: Oxford University Press, 1978), vol. 1, 9–80.

31. Luis Peirano, "Entrevista con Gustavo Gutiérrez," *Qué Hacer* (March, 1980), 110–11; see also Gutiérrez, *La Fuerza Historica de los Pobres* (Lima: CEP, 1979), 260ff. Gutiérrez discusses this problem in the context of the "Puebla Document."

32. Peirano, "Entrevista," 110–11.

33. Cf. Topitsch, *Vom Ursprung und Ende der Metaphysik,* 204–05 and passim: Topitsch, ed., "Uber Leerformel. Zur Pragmatik des Sprachgebrauches in Philosophie und politischer Theorie," *Probleme der Wissenschaftstheorie. Festchrift für Victor Kraft,* ed. E. Topitsch (Vienna: Springer, 1960), 233–64; Gert Degenkolbe, "Über logische Struktur und gesellschaftliche Funktionen von Leerformeln," *Kölner Zeitschrift für Soziologie und Sozialphilosophie,* 17 (1965), 327–38.

34. In Wittgenstein's sense; see *Tractatus logico-philosophicus* 4.46, 4.461, 4.4611, 4.462, 4.463, 4.464, 4.465, 4.466, 5.142, 5.143.

35. The concept of "coincidentia oppositorum" plays an important role in the philosophy of Nicholas of Cusa (see n. 36). For a phenomenology of religion

with the notion of "coincidentia" at its core, see Vicente Hernández Catalá, *La Expresión de lo Divino en las Religiones no Cristianas* (Madrid: B.A.C., 1972). The ideological uses to which the idea of an ultimate reconciliation of opposites lends itself are obvious; these dangers are usually not examined in the "phenomenological" studies of religion or mysticism current today.

36. See, although in a different context, the preliminary observations found in Gustavo Benavides, "Tautology as Philosophy in Nicolaus Cusanus and Nāgārjuna," *Buddhist and Western Philosophy,* ed. Nathan Katz (Delhi: Sterling, 1981), 30–53.

37. Cf. Jameson, *The Political Unconscious,* 17.

38. See J. Lloyd Mecham, *Church and State in Latin America* (Chapel Hill: University of North Carolina Press, 1966), rev. ed.; Hans-Jürgen Prien, *Die Geschichte des Christentums in Lateinamerika* (Göttingen: Vandenhoeck & Ruprecht, 1978).

39. On Mariategui, see Alberto Flores-Galindo, *La Agonía de Mariátegui* (Lima: DESCO, 1981). John Baines, *Revolution in Peru: Mariategui and the Myth* (Tuscaloosa, Ala.: University of Alabama Press, 1972).

40. Cf. Marjorie Reeves, *Joachim of Fiore and the Prophetic Future* (New York: Harper & Row, 1977), 126–35, esp. 128–29, where Reeves discusses Columbus's *Libro de las Profecías;* Prien, *Die Geschichte des Christentums in Lateinamerika,* 143ff.

41. Cf. Gutiérrez, *La Fuerza Histórica de los Pobres,* 361, 370–71.

42. Recently, for example, the conservative *Opus Dei*—whose influence among the middle and upper classes should not be underestimated—has been granted special status by the pope; this promotion is part of the anti-liberal policies pursued by the Vatican, and of a general ideological position not very different from that of the Reagan administration; on these issues see the recent publications by Ana María Ezcurra: *La Ofensiva Neoconservadora. Iglesias de USA y Lucha Ideológica Hacia América Latina* (Madrid: IEPALA, 1982); *Agresión Ideológica Contra la Revolución Sandinista* (Mexico: Nuevomar, 1983). English translation: *Ideological Aggression Against the Sandinista Revolution* (New York: New York CIRCUS Publications, 1984); *El Vaticano y la Administración Reagan* (Mexico: Nuevomar, 1984). In the different political context of the United States, we are witnessing a similar phenomenon: on the one hand, there is the hesitant, contradictory involvement of the Catholic hierarchy in the antinuclear movement and, on the other hand, the development among Catholic publicists such as Michael Novak of a "theology of the corporation" and of a theological legitimation of nuclear deterrence. See Michael Novak, *Toward a Theology of the Corporation* (Washington, D.C.: American Enterprise Institute, 1981), 37–42, esp. 40 ("Birth and Mortality," a rather peculiar theological darwinism); Michael Novak and John W. Cooper, eds., *The Corporation, A Theological Inquiry* (Washington, D.C.: AEI, 1981), 203–24, esp. 209–10. On the issue of a "just" nuclear war see Michael Novak, *Moral Clarity in the Nuclear Age* (Nashville, Tenn.: Thomas Nelson, 1983) with a foreword by Billy Graham and an introduction by William F. Buckley, Jr.; in this frightening little book, Novak uses as epigraphs Isaiah 2:4 (swords into plowshares), Joel 3:10 (plowshares into swords), Psalm 144 ("Blessed be the Lord, my rock, who trains my hands for war"); see also p. 90 where he laments the loss of "noble military causes."

11

Types of Religious Liberation: An Implicit Critique of Modern Politics

NINIAN SMART

Introduction

Much of contemporary life is taken up with the twin pursuits of freedom and happiness. The religious traditions of the world also in their own ways are concerned with these goals. But they provide a perspective from which to criticize secular aspirations for them. For what, in the ultimate analysis—or should we say "in the light of the ultimate"—is happiness? And in what consists true freedom? Thus for the Christian, Christ's freedom is something that goes beyond a merely commonsense absence of restraints; for the Buddhist true welfare or happiness (sukha) is in part consequent upon the recognition of the illfare and unhappiness that otherwise characterizes all sentient life. However, though the main religious traditions converge at certain points, there are also not inconsiderable differences. In the first part of this essay I wish to lay forth some of the chief varieties of belief in liberation or salvation; in the second part I will reflect briefly on them and consider how far they can be seen as complementary.

Types of Liberation

Since the main religions have a conception of the ultimate as somehow transcending "this world," however that may be analyzed, it is natural that liberation or freedom should be seen as becoming close to or realizing one's unity with, or attaining, the ultimate and thereby throwing off the restraints of this world. Liberation thus is seen as something transcendent itself or closely tied to what is transcendent. There is therefore, ineluctably, an otherworldly element in liberation. But as we shall see, this need not mean that we should not see salvation or liberation as having an important this-worldly component.

135

To flesh out my point: consider the following ways of seeing the state of salvation. It is the final departure of the soul (jiva), in the Jain tradition, from the karmic round of rebirth and its lodging motionless and omniscient at the summit of the universe. It is likewise, in Sāmkhya and Yoga, a state of isolation and absence of pain beyond the round of rebirth. In Theravāda Buddhism, there is no soul, but somehow in the disappearance of individuality there is attained the state of nibbāna in which and from which there cannot be any more rebirth. In Advaita Vedānta, liberation involves realization of one's essential identity with Brahman and the cessation of the karmic round. In theistic Vedānta on the other hand, through transcendence of the round of reincarnation (a common factor in the mainstream Indian traditions), salvation is pictured as everlasting life in heaven close to God. Incidentally, heavens are, of course, present in the Buddhist and other nontheistic traditions, but are thought of as places of nonpermanent residence, and since permanence is often seen as the mark of true and ultimate value, such heavens turn out to be no more than pleasant consequences of virtue, not ultimate goals to be striven for. Theoretically, this is the way it is seen in Pure Land Buddhism, that great efflorescence of Buddhist bhakti: but since in the Pure Land so many fervent spiritual hopes are centered, the goal of final nirvana beyond even the Pure Land itself fades—so that phenomenologically this variety of Buddhism approximates the Hindu theisms as much as the nontheistic schools. So far we come across two main motifs with variations: disappearance from rebirth into a static, blissful (or at least pain-free) state; and ascent to a permanent heavenly state close to God. The Advaita variant is in a sense intermediate: one is God, the Divine Being, and as such is liberated, save that you typically do not know it. In the first case, this-worldly individuality is lost. In Samkhya and Yoga and Jainism, liberated souls are "base," "nude," unclothed in bodily and psychological modes. In Buddhism, there is no real question of personality surviving since nirvana is delineated with a whole battery of appropriate negations. In Advaita, too, the worldly individual disappears, since the true self, which is discovered existentially to be divine, is not mine or yours, but unindividually universal. Similar remarks can be made about those Māhayāna developments where the Buddha nature, as a kind of quasi-self, is spoken of. It is ultimately empty (sūnya) and suchness, and in no way is embedded as a swarm of individual Buddha natures in different living beings.

It is useful here to make a distinction. In Sāmkhya and Dvaita Vedanta, for instance, there are many individual souls. But in Sāmkhya they are "standardized" so to speak—they are individuals but without individuality. Liberation means continuing individuation, but there, as they say, "once you've seen one you've seen them all." On the other hand, there is a Dvaita, a sense of individual uniqueness, and this is also the usual interpretation of the Christian doctrine of the resurrection of the body. So it may be useful to distinguish between a pluralism of individuals or souls on the one hand and the notion of the individuality or uniqueness of each soul on the other. For short I will call the first the doctrine of *numerous* individuals or souls and the second the doctrine of *personal* individuals or souls.

In the major Western traditions of Christianity, Judaism, and Islam, reincarnation of course had not had much prominence, so the whole nexus of ideas surrounding karma, samsāra, and liberation does not apply. Rather, notions of heaven predominate (and hell, etc.) Also the concept of the resurrection of the body has entered into mainstream Western theism. This latter notion has as part of its cash value the notion that what is sacred is the whole personality, as embodied. Perhaps for most purposes this is the whole of its cash value, since both traditionally and today the resurrection of the body has often been seen as mysterious, as involving God's creating new bodies perhaps not of earthly stuff. So by consequence the difference between this idea and that of a personal soul becomes diminished. The problem of the soul idea is its abstractness and lack of clear relation to personhood; the problem of the resurrection idea is its overconcreteness and propensity to degenerate into speculations about material reconstitution, for example, of ashes.

So far we can perceive various patterns of belief concerning liberation. First, there is the doctrine of numerous individuals who have transcended the round of rebirth. Second, there is the doctrine of liberated personal souls somehow related to God. Third, there is realization of unity with the ultimate in which both the idea of numerous souls and that of personal souls disappears (Advaita and Sūnyavada in Mahāyāna Buddhism).

We should also mention the conception of ancestors. Though not primarily a notion of salvation or liberation, it does have a role in our thinking about an afterlife. Ancestors typically are important in extending the community; the latter is seen not merely as constituted by the living, but extends to those who have passed into the invisible world, but an invisible world still close to us. Thus the cult of ancestors—giving them offerings, say—is just an extension of the veneration given to the old and the wise. It reminds us that sometimes freedom or liberation or salvation can also be viewed as a collective matter. This can be so in a narrower or a wider way.

More narrowly the focus may be primarily on a given people, such as Israel. The people may look forward to "last things" in which God will, perhaps through some charismatic leader or messiah, restore the people and settle them in peace forever. Secular ideologies such as nationalism and Marxism can echo this concept. Indeed, it is worth noting that in modern times "freedom" very often is thought of in terms of a collective national or social liberation. (But freedom also has to do with individual rights, and collective and individual liberties can collide.)

The broader way in which a collectivity of liberation may be conceived is universalism—that is, the doctrine that all eventually will be saved and that since no one can be finally happy while others suffer, individual and collective bliss becomes notionally simultaneous. This idea occurs in some Christian theologies and in the bodhisattva ideal in Mahāyāna Buddhism. For the bodhisattva puts off his own liberation until all are liberated.

We may observe that only one type of liberation is strongly personalistic. Neither nontheistic systems that hold that there are numerous individuals or souls nor those that believe in a monistic unity of all souls conceive of liberation as personal. It is by contrast characteristic of Dvaita in the Hindu tradition and theisms that emphasize heavenly liberation after some kind of judgment and reconstitution of the individual that have a place for salvation of the person. Yet of course it is a paradox: for though I may thus be guaranteed my ego, yet that self now is seen as truly happy when dependent on God. As it is said, "whose service is perfect freedom."

So you can, it seems, have perfect happiness as a person in a state of dependence or perfect freedom if you are prepared to give up your individuality. Happy slavery or unconscious freedom—is this the choice?

But the contrast between the nonpersonal and personal (which are also theistic ideas) is not as strong as it at first seems. For the nonpersonal systems also hold to the concept of the person who is "living liberated" or jīvanmukta. Such a one has attained assurance of release while alive and indeed is already liberated. His body and mind of course continue to operate, but there will be no rebirth when death arrives. As the usual image has it, he is like a potter's wheel continuing to spin after the potter has taken his hand off.

This notion of living liberation or jivanmukta means that we have the idea of an individual who will indeed lose his particularity at death (becoming either unutterable as in Buddhism or a standard soul as elsewhere in nontheistic Indian traditions); but on the other hand he is objectively a person. So he is a liberated person, or saint. I stress personhood twice here to drive home the point that here we have a living model of personal liberation, which does not in principle differ ontologically from that of the saved person beyond the grave in the theistic traditions—except only there is no relationship to God. But there is relationship to others in the community here and now. Also, of course, in theistic traditions there is sometimes the idea of living salvation, as when the believer has assurance that he is saved, because of some direct experience of God's grace, for example.

So far we have looked at ideas of liberation and salvation without asking the question "from what?" Here there is, of course, a variety of beliefs to consider. It is typical, however, of the Indian tradition that the most typical answer is at one level duhkha or illfare, suffering, pain (different translations are common but the first of these is what I favor). Deeper down we find that illfare arises in the last resort from ignorance, lack of insight. But monism does not see the problem simply in these terms because the doctrine itself implies that the multiple world of appearances is an illusion. So ontologically the world we transcend is unreal. Elsewhere it is real, but unsatisfactory. In gnosticism there was often the more radical idea that the world is evil. But it is only possible really to think of the world in this way if there is an evil creator of it (demiurge); for evil is an attribute that applys to the effects of an evil actor. Otherwise the world can be painful or illusory. On the whole, modern religious traditions have moved far from the concept of an evil God or even of a Satan. On the other hand, if there is but one God then the evil in the world is his responsibility unless you ascribe it to some primeval catastrophe, and this is where the Christian doctrine of the Fall comes in, and with it the idea that it is sin we need saving from, not ignorance.

Sin has come to have two components: one is that of alienation or estrangement or, in more traditional terms, unholiness in the sense of falling short of the holiness of God; and the other is moral evil and disobedience toward God. If we are to put matters positively, then the aim of those who would wish to be liberated from sin would be gaining holiness and communion with God on the one hand, and moral goodness on the other. But the very essence of a religion of the holy is a sense of duality between God and worshiper—that is, ontological difference—even when the sense of alienation is overcome. So salvation is not seen as merging or actually becoming God, but rather as being in the closest possible relationship to God. It is this sense of relationship, even in the life beyond, that no doubt accounts for the personalism of theistic salvation. Conversely, because liberation in the nontheistic traditions means isolation or unutterability, it is in *this* world, where relationships still exist, that we have the liberated person.

The holy or numinous character of God means that liberation can, strictly speaking, only come through his agency. For as the one God he possesses ultimately all the holiness there is—nothing beside him is holy. (If in Hindu devotional religion there seem to be gods and goddesses besides the Lord, they are, in the end, parts of him, refractions so to speak—which is why we may call such a system of myth and cult refracted theism.) Holiness flows from God, thus the ·idea of grace and of the transfer of merit. Even if we do things that are not admirable and are out of accord with his will, he can forgive us and count them as nothing. In such a way, though being good is in a sense a means to salvation, it is ultimately not so—for only grace is a means thereto. The moral endeavor is swallowed up in a wider and deeper sense of meaning.

On the other hand, in nontheistic systems, where there is scarcely any call to think of grace (except where bhakti and devotional religion begins to make itself felt, as with the growth of the bodhisattva ideal), moral action becomes an important ingredient in the path to liberation. It becomes much more directly a means of salvation.

But it is morality still in a context, and this supplies three motifs that typically affect the way goodness is considered. These are karma, tapas, and dhyāna—or in English, reincarnational effects, austerity, and contemplation. Belief in rebirth means that morality often becomes a mode—*the* mode sometimes—of acquiring merit and so of gaining a better life next time. Such a life may be in a heaven, but even here the worm of impermanence and potential suffering persists, for no heaven can provide ultimate freedom. So karma theory stretches the effects of moral striving. As for asceticism, in the Indian tradition especially there are deep impulses toward self-mortification as a means of neutralizing the effects of deeds, and we have as the ultimate symbol of this the great nude Jaina statues where creepers growing up the legs of a saint show how impervious he is to the environment, how indifferent to worldly things. Self-starvation becomes the perfect death. To the ascetic outlook belongs a view of the world not so much as illusion, as painful, or as sinful, but as entangling. Freedom must mean cutting off all those impulses that get you more deeply entangled.

But it is contemplation that possesses the greatest present-day interest. For it is characteristic of the Yoga traditions of India, of which Buddhism is in many ways the greatest, that they see the acquisition of a special type of higher consciousness as being the key to liberation. This higher consciousness is empty and pure, and yet it also brings knowledge. For the world seen now *sub specie eternitatis* has a different look, and the analysis that is part of the context of self-training is perceived existentially. So the world view of the yogi thus has confirmation in higher experience, and liberation also involves some kind of jñāne or viveká or prajña—in Greek, gnosis, a kind of what I call for fun "gnowing."

Such contemplative mysticism is not, of course, absent from theistic traditions, but there it has a different context and significance. For one thing, higher consciousness is seen as union with but not identity with the ultimate; and it is itself considered a product of grace. Moreover, since mysticism is not the predominant form of life in theism, where worship and sacraments are more pervasive, it has less centrality as a means of liberation than in the nontheistic religions.

We have seen some polarities and contrasts. Thus there is the sense of personal, heavenly salvation versus nonpersonal liberation in nirvana. There is individual versus collective liberation. There is liberation from sin and from ignorance and entanglement. There is the world as real and the world as illusion. There is grace as means of salvation versus austerity, morality, and contemplation. I wish now to reflect about some of these typical patterns in the more secular context that is becoming so pervasive in today's world.

Reflections on Traditional Concepts and Their Contemporary Relevance

Contemporary Western culture is dominated by utilitarianism, namely the doctrine that social policy should be aimed at maximizing happiness and minimizing suffering. We are descendants of Adam Smith and John Stuart Mill. There is much to commend in modern economics, and in social democracy there is an attempt to adjust and curtain the workings of "the market" in order to alleviate the suffering of the poor and needy. At the same time the most vital political force in modern times is nationalism, and this has sometimes run contrary to the individualism inherent in utilitarianism. Moreover, Marxism, with its collectivist thinking—especially as vulgarly understood by the ruling classes of Marxist countries—reinforces nationalism in practice, for it has proved a potent instrument of liberation from colonial and neocolonial bonds, which have largely been to the old capitalist nations of the north.

These reflections might seem far removed from the varieties of salvation I have been analyzing in this essay. But this is not so, for a number of reasons. First, the individualist ethos of liberal capitalism creates two problems, one of what may be called *external* identity, and the other of *internal* identity. As social persons we find identity in belonging to a group. For each person there may be an overlapping set of groups, but the most important is what may be called, in a somewhat Tillichian phrase, "the group of ultimate concern." In a nationalist era it is often the nation that functions thus, as that which demands if necessary your life in its service, and a large slice of your earnings and expenditure as a toll. Betrayal of the nation attracts the deepest opprobrium, as treason. But though national and ethnic identity may be built into the individual through his upbringing it need not be overriding. Its ultimacy may be questioned.

This is so in both theistic and nontheistic religion. Although one may be sympathetic to struggles for liberation (by Basques, Zimbabweans, Palestinians, etc.), the universal religions cannot see this political liberation as ultimate, for there is a higher community, of Christians or Muslims or Buddhists. Even where a faith is tied to a particular ethnic group (as appears to be the case with Judaism, except that the *ethnie* is both a matter of descent and of religious affiliation so that the religion defines the *ethnie* and not conversely), it may have a universal meaning, so that the group is a "light to the Gentiles" or an example to other nations. This means that though the group may be ultimate, its wider life is seen in a universal context.

Moreover, as well as widening our gaze horizontally to all humans as the ultimate group or even all living beings, the religions also expand it vertically, to the transcendent. And this becomes relevant to the problem of individual internal identity. It is by worship, in the case of theistic faiths, that you connect yourself to the transcendent, and by self-discipline and inner contemplation that you can aim for a "living liberation" as the ultimate ideal. This of course is relevant to the utilitarian program. For in both cases religions offer something beyond the usual this-worldly ideas of happiness or of suffering. Higher welfare need not of course be world negating, but they are what can be called world deepening and world transforming. They deepen the world, as in Buddhism, by inviting us to "see through" common sense. They can deepen it in theistic religions by creating a vision of the world as everywhere, even in its darkness, manifesting the Divine Being.

In all this, traditional religion becomes a critic of modern secular ideologies. It criticizes the flat happiness of materialist individualism; it criticizes the flat collectivism of Marxism; and it criticizes the narrowness of nationalism.

Yet the spirit of our secular age is pervasive. After all, how many people can believe, without effort or special commitment, in life after death or in rebirth? There is not much point in criticizing the ideologies of our time if it is from a radically foreign point of view. In certain important respects the old images of heaven and judgment and rebirth have to be taken now as regulative pictures. Let me briefly explain my meaning here.

One of the central problems, perhaps *the* central problem of philosophical theology, is how we conceive the junctures between the transcendent (whether God or nirvana or Brahman) and this world. I can understand the experience of realizing one's essential identity with Brahman; but how does this experience cause rebirth, a this-worldly phenomenon, to cease? I can understand how God supports and pervades the whole cosmos; but the manner of his becoming Christ eludes clear understanding. Again, how is it that there is a liberation, nirvana, and yet nirvana has no cause? In a sense, all questions of survival are such "juncture" questions: for if I survive only as a bull in the Argentine or as any kind of this-worldly being, how is that ultimate salvation? It is mere prolongation of life. So the images of redemption and the liberated state can hardly be clearly explicated. Rather, they help to point us to the ground of any hope and freedom, and that is the existence, as being or state, of that blessed transcendence to which the religions in varying directions point. In essence, then, the religions provide criticism of the secular because they have a transcendental outreach. This in turn means in human terms that a deeper experience of the world is found than in flat utilitarianism. Such depth experience helps us to see the world transformed.

This makes a difference to the significance of liberation theology, as distinguished from secular ideologies of liberation. The essential reason for seeing the material bases of human poverty and exploitation is that exploitation itself is an attack on human dignity, and that dignity is guaranteed by the divine spark or Buddha nature in each one of us. The worth of men and women relates not to class or ethnic group, but to their relation to the beyond and indeed reflection of what is transcendent.

The ideas of individual "disappearance" into the state beyond (in the style of Buddhism and other Yoga traditions) and of communion with God are complementary, for they point to two sides of religion and human life—a side that is full of images, worship, and outer cosmic vision, and a side that is empty of images, is contemplative, and seeks an inner light. We cannot know what liberation in the beyond is like, but we can here and now see its incarnated representatives. Thus the concept of liberation or redemption provides for transformed persons, who themselves are critics in their lives of the flatness and cruelty around us that follow from human nature and sometimes callous ideologies.

This is not to say Mill and Marx have not contributed to our world, but only when we see that material change and prosperity is essentially related to dignity do we see it in perspective. As I have said, the theories of salvation in the religions provide a deeper such perspective, even if we cannot say much about heaven or nirvana.

Part Four

RELIGION AND SOCIETY: SOME FUTURE DIRECTIONS

12

Freedom and Responsibility in a Secular World: A Christian View
HELMUT FRITZSCHE

The ideas of freedom and responsibility are fundamental to modern Western civilization and culture. This is especially the case in relation to humanity born in Europe, with its deep background in Christianity. We are accustomed to regarding human progress by the measures of personal, social, political, and spiritual liberty and responsibility. And I think it is right to do so. Freedom is one of the deepest values of humanity. But liberty without a deep sense of human responsibility is only another word for arbitrariness, despotism, or chaos.

At present we are faced with a deep crisis in relation to the ideas of freedom and responsibility. What does personal freedom mean for people in poverty or who are unemployed? Or for those torn by anxiety or oppressed? What does freedom mean for the wealthy who enjoy a high material living standard yet lack spiritual resources? What does responsibility mean for people without an adequate education? Facing the problems of our world—the anxiety of a threatening third world war, the arms race, oppression, and exploitation—the words *freedom* and *responsibility* run the danger of becoming a veil that more covers the lack of freedom than leads men to further liberation from actual oppression.

What does it really mean to be free, to be the artisans of our own destiny? What about personal and social self-determination? What are the connections between freedom and responsibility? What is the meaning of the liberation of peoples? Humanity's future depends on answers to these questions. It would be presumptuous to assume that Christianity and the other religions in the world could solve the problems of freedom and responsibility by themselves. But in the present dialogue of religions, cultures, and world views (weltanschauungen), especially in the struggle of ideas, lies an important claim on Christianity, because modern freedom and responsibility are ideas with a deep Christian background.

The modern ideas of liberty and responsibility—anticipated both in Greek humanism and the Christian announcement of salvation—were formed in the European Enlightenment and are therefore a product of secularization. Christianity and other religions should not try to roll back this process of secularization. On the contrary, they should seek to fulfill it. In the secularization process the human consciousness of freedom attains a new stage: man takes hold of the reins of his own destiny. In the process of secularization man has begun to enter maturity.

There is a close dialectical relationship between secularization and Christianity. Christian faith is one of the most important roots of the modern world's technical, industrial, and political power: these constitute, as it were, a commentary on the famous words of the Bible: ". . . be fruitful and multiply, and fill the earth and subdue it" (Gen. 1:28). On the other hand, the modern secularized world is a claim to humanity becoming as responsible as we should be before God.

In order to meet the present ambiguities in our understandings of freedom and responsibility, we must first understand the development of these ideas in the Bible and the history of Christianity. Against this background I will develop my own position. In the main, I will argue that freedom and responsibility are the central themes of a new experience of God in our age, one characterized by the ambiguities of humanity, power, and civilization in the age of progress.

The idea of freedom, especially the close connection between freedom and responsibility, is central to the Bible. In the Old Testament, prophets and priests are convinced that Yahweh has liberated his people from slavery in Egypt and will guide them to a freer life in an intimate community with God himself and without pressure from enemies, war, and miseries (Jer. 2). They were also convinced that catastrophes in history, like the deportation to Babylon, were God's punishment for sin. Prophets and priests emphasized that above all honors God gives to his people is the holy obligation to obey the high moral demands exemplified in the Ten Commandments. In the Old Testament freedom and responsibility are linked together and history is the point where human responsibility and God's grace or punishment meet each other.

In the New Testament the nexus of freedom and responsibility is even more important. Early Christianity worshiped Jesus Christ as God's son, who was crucified for human sin. His resurrection was

148

understood as a victory over human failure and the beginning of a
new age: men and women returning to God and grateful for God's
salvation were thus free to love everybody. This new quality of
freedom and responsibility is grounded in the power of Holy Spirit,
which makes believers free from egoism and worldly anxiety and
gives the believer a new attitude of trust and charity like that seen in
Jesus Christ. Both the spirit of freedom and the awareness of
responsibility are thus understood as gifts from God that transform
the human heart.

An important stage in the historical development of the Christian
understanding of freedom and responsibility was achieved in Martin Luther and especially his work *Christian Liberty*. Here we read
the famous words: "The Christian is a free lord over everything and
subject to no-one" and "A Christian is a servant of everything and
subject to everyone." In this twofold formula, Luther emphasized
that the true Christian attitude is grounded in faith since the one
who believes in God's grace and doesn't trust in his own efforts is
really free from egoism and anxiety and subservience. On the other
hand, the believer lives responsible before God, free to serve the
needs of all men in an attitude of charity.

Unlike the sixteenth century, we in Europe—and I think in
America too—are now living in a secularized world. The central
factor that characterizes a secular society is the separation between
the state, social organizations, and education on the one hand, and
religion, spirituality, and the churches on the other hand. For the
secular mind, the world, its laws, its coming into being, and its
prospects are viewed in wholly worldly terms without acknowledging God as creator and preserver. This scientific and humanistic
view of the world is all-embracing. Modern man seeks the causes
for our situation and its remedy in nature and history; he rejects the
notion of transcendent causes beyond the realms of nature and
history.

These convictions of human autonomy constitute a new stage in
the awareness of human freedom and responsibility. Religion thus
becomes a private matter. Everything in personal, social, and historical life, especially progress toward a more free and just society and
the overcoming of human suffering, misfortune, hunger, war, and
anxiety, depends on human activities or their failures.

Nevertheless, there is a deep continuity between the modern
secular world and the spirit of Christianity. It was faith in God as
creator and preserver of the world that gave wings to the discovery

of the laws of nature and human responsibility for using them. Faith in God as creator and in the world as God's creation was the spiritual background for the idea of the perfectability of the world. And faith in Jesus Christ as Lord and brother of all men was the most important spiritual background for the awareness that human needs entail the moral claim to help address and overcome those needs. In every needy and suffering person one meets Jesus himself according to his words in Matthew 25:40: "Truly, I say to you, as you did it to one of the least of these my brethren, you did it to me."

The secularized mentality and the awareness of human responsibility for this world are two sides of the same matter. Here, however, we encounter the ambiguity of progress in dominating nature and the continuation of human evolution. Facing the future of mankind we encounter two possibilities: the destruction of the earth and the demolition of humanity; and the building up of a peaceful, just, and wealthy world for everybody and all peoples. In this situation Christianity and all religions are called upon by the secular world to make a significant contribution to understanding freedom and responsibility. Indeed, it isn't only the secular world, but God as creator, preserver, and savior who claims a new and deeper awareness of human responsibility for the fate of our earth.

The basic theological contribution that Christianity can offer to our time addresses itself to the ambiguity of human progress. The call to progress is a claim of God. But the challenge to Christianity in the secular modern world is to find a way to articulate a new experience with God. That new experience with God is centered in the practice of a partnership between God and humanity that acknowledges a greater degree of human responsibility for this world. In Christian terms I would say that it is necessary to become more and more aware of the fact that God disclosed himself in the *unmighty* Jesus as a sign that he will entrust his creation and himself into the hands of men and women.

Against this background, then, I will outline the contribution I envisage Christianity might give to understanding and promoting freedom and responsibility in the secular world. For this purpose I distinguish four aspects or levels of the Christian understanding and practice of freedom and responsibility.

First, basic to a Christian understanding of freedom and responsibility is the religious conviction that freedom arises from the communion of man with God. Thus freedom is not man's possession, but a gift from God. Freedom is not an object you can point to, but a relationship between God and human beings. Freedom is a historical gift from God that allows us to seek liberation for humanity.

In this view liberty is internal, a religious and spiritual freedom within, which depends on God and the impact of God's salvation in Jesus Christ. The practice of internal freedom is that which gives us every day a new liberation from anxiety and other kinds of worldly care. Internal freedom is a fountain for a more and more enhanced sense of responsibility before God. The Christian God is a personal one and to be with him in faith is the Christian's internal liberty.

The second level of freedom and responsibility embraces the political sphere. Here freedom means achieving a just human society. Such a society enables human beings to acquire ever increasing degrees of self-determination and self-fulfillment. The political basis for the idea of a more just and human society, both establishing and stimulating freedom, is the realization of human rights. These rights were formulated in the United Nations' General Declaration on Human Rights, December 10, 1948, the International Convention on Civil Rights, December 16, 1966, and the International Convention on Economic, Social and Cultural Rights, December 16, 1966. These human rights respect every person's individuality within the universal community of humankind. The individual's civil, economic, social, and cultural rights are not, and should not be, separated.

The modern world should be viewed as one interdependent social process toward a more just society. But there are very different stages of development in particular regions of the world today. Social progress is not only to be regarded as the development to a higher level of material well-being. In addition we must see that development means social justice, growing participation in education, cultural goods, and social planning and decision making. All these things belong together. The development of the productive forces of scientific and technological advances plays an important part in the process but must be accompanied by social progress as well.

In the political sphere, freedom is neither a possession nor a historical condition, but a development in a permanent process of liberation from oppression and alienation. The struggle for sociopolitical liberation and the realization of human rights has to be different in the diverse regions of the world. For example, in most countries of the Third World, elimination of the alienating conditions of life and the abolition of the social roots of poverty are the main goals. But the solution of these problems must be linked with the efforts to create a more just system of international trade. In the industrialized, market-economy societies, unemployment, despite the high level of the means of production and labor-saving innovations in technology in industrial production, is a basic problem that must be addressed. In my own socialist country, we must further develop the economic base and the social achievements thus far attained in order to attain a humane society.

It would be impossible to deal with all aspects of sociopolitical freedom and liberation. We are interested in discerning and holding together the different levels of reality, especially those of Christian faith and political activity. According to the Bible, the ultimate root of the poverty and injustice in which men live is sin. Sin is man's selfish turning in upon himself, a breach of the relationship with God. Salvation is God's own matter. The promised coming of Christ's kingdom must not be confused with the building up of a just society in the earthly realm. The establishment of a more just human society is an endeavor that exists in its own rights. It is based on a rational analysis of reality and is carried out through the means of social and political power. The political sphere has its own proper integrity. We have to respect the autonomy of the temporal sphere. But from a Christian standpoint it is also true that social development cannot be separated from the coming of Christ's kingdom, which promises liberation from alienation to all people. Social structures are not sinful in themselves. Social structures arise in connection with the development of the forces of production and many social and cultural factors. Social structures may become sinful if they favor selfishness. Then the time has come for changing such structures. Indeed, it may be a sin not to change what favors injustice. But new social structures must be based on political reason.

These few remarks regarding the internal and the political view of our problem lead to the next level in the meaning of liberation: the cooperation of God and man in history.

The third dimension of freedom is the historical dimension. Hegel, the first philosopher to offer an all-embracing view of human development, argues that the history of the world is the progressive unfolding of freedom. The historical process thus appears as the genesis of consciousness and as the gradual liberation of man.

It was a mistake of Hegel and many influenced by him—for

example, Teilhard de Chardin in our century, and Schleiermacher almost two centuries ago—to assume that the human process of liberation was only the triumphal procession of civilization to freedom based on the development of science, technology, culture, philosophy, and religion. Indeed, we have seen the two World Wars, Auschwitz, and the continuing conflict of the last years. We now know that it is possible that we may end all civilized life in a nuclear catastrophe. The majority of humankind is living in alienating poverty. The progress of technology jeopardizes the natural base of our life and exploits the necessary resources for the future of humankind. Nevertheless it is true that man has become the very subject of history in a world ever more interdependent.

The emergence of human responsibility for life includes a deep and dangerous ambiguity. The notion of humankind as the subject of history is more a challenge to create a new consciousness of all humanity's growing responsibility than it is a triumphal statement of fact. History is a challenge to create a man who will conquer selfishness and be willing to live according to the natural zeal for love and friendship with others. It is primarily a challenge to make peace. History is also a challenge to conquer those social and political conditions that favor selfishness and create poverty. Accordingly, the social sciences must develop a deep awareness of human responsibility for the future in an unjust world.

Regarding the reality of history, we maintain that although there is no easy identification of the history of God's salvation and human history, there is a close relationship between the temporal process and the growth of Christ's kingdom. But progress and the growth of the kingdom are not to be identified. The points that the Christian view adds to secular considerations of history are *sin* and *salvation*. We cannot deny the role of sin in the historical development of humanity. But we also believe in the impact of the salvific spirit of the triune God who accomplishes his work not without but through man.

The point of convergence between the Christian view and secular historical philosophies is the *new man:* man becoming free from all alienation and free for self-determination. For Christians, the new man must be in the likeness of Christ. We must not disregard the deep ambiguity of all human progress based on human efforts. To attack the root causes of ambiguity in human development and to transform social structures that favor selfishness—these are the historical missions of humankind in our day. The mission of Christians in our time is to serve the building up of the earthly city motivated by hope in the coming of the kingdom. After two thousand years of Christian proclamation and worship in Europe and in many parts of the world, we have no reason for a Christian haughtiness. It is true that Christendom has created a deep awareness of freedom and liberation. To accept God's grace in keeping his promise of salvation means that Christians and churches must serve the process of liberation by working together with others, Christians and non-Christians, in building up an earthly city characterized by more solidarity, justice, freedom, and peace.

The fourth dimension of freedom concerns the utopian dimension. The fullness of liberation, communion with God and with all humanity, is a goal that takes us beyond human history. Christians also hope for a new creation. Man must dream of a new life in a better future, but he has to know he is dreaming and he has to work in order to bring the dream into the reality of human history.

The utopian dimension is, on the one hand, a liberating call to hope. Now the world of peace is still a utopia, but we need utopianism in order to transcend the present situation and move toward a spiritual liberation, to that real world of peace we all demand to live in. Perhaps dreaming of a better future was one of the roots of the development of an awareness of freedom. Spiritually, becoming free is based on transcending the given present situation.

On the other hand, utopian views tend to a dangerous radicalism against a necessary historical realism. Martin Luther's realistic thinking in his time probably contributed more to social consciousness and progress toward a more just society than Thomas Muentzer's dream of God's kingdom. The rejection of exploitation that concerned Thomas Muentzer is indeed found in the Bible. For example, Leviticus 25:23 emphasizes that God is the only owner of the land given to his people. But you cannot directly transfer biblical viewpoints into social reality. Utopias can only be realized in accordance with the development of the means of production and other social and cultural conditions. Thus we have to maintain the dialectic between the utopian aspect and political reality. Nevertheless, as Moltmann observes, utopias make us free to hope in the future.

Furthermore, utopia is indeed a horizon of faith. But this must be distinguished from personal faith, which we discussed earlier. God is close to man in faith and spirituality at every point of history. In the moment of faith, man is in eternity. This idea of mysticism, emphasized by Schleiermacher, may not be confused with hope for historical progress based on God's salvation. But both are branches of the one faith in God's salvation by Christ.

All four levels or dimensions of freedom discussed here have the same goal: liberation from misery and enslavement. But they have different contents. To become free from emptiness, to conquer the alienation from oneself by faith and Christian spirituality is not the same as liberation from social injustice and alienation from man's enslavement to poverty and economic misery. But he who becomes free from selfishness by faith also becomes free for charity and hope, which motivates one to be engaged in social life. Historical progress aims at an ever increasing liberation of man. But history is never the simple fullness of God's promise to man to become his unalienated partner in a renewal of creation. He who hopes for God's promise will be a utopian, but he will also be a realist who knows the difference between the present time under the conditions of sin and the future of a renewed creation.

These four levels of freedom embrace all branches of humanity and all peoples. But they also respect the different dimensions of each level. God is closer to man in faith than he is to men and women in social history. And finally God's promise concerns all peoples, Christians and non-Christians. All men and religions are challenged to social progress, but there are different ways to more justice and more peace and freedom in the different parts of the world according to the different stages of development.

Nevertheless, Christianity and all religions are called upon to make their contribution to our understanding of freedom and responsibility. In conclusion, then, I would like to summarize what are, in my view, the ten principles that should inform Christians as they act in a secularized world.

Christian Freedom Is God's Freedom for All People.

Christian freedom involves faith, hope, spirituality, and service. It is based on the liberation that is a gift of God in Christ to all peoples. There is only one freedom for all human beings. Christians do not have a special freedom for themselves, but they do have a special theological understanding of freedom and are called to witness to God's freedom for humanity and to serve human freedom in imitation of Christ.

Christian Freedom in Its Unique Universality Is Singular.

Freedom in the Christian view embraces creation and salvation, social and individual life, and eternal and temporal reality. It is both otherworldly and intrahistorical. Freedom is always more than is realized in a given moment in time. Freedom remains, ultimately, of God. Churches and religions bear witness to God's liberation, which is greater than all human experiences of liberation.

Although, in my view, all religions and philosophies contain elements of truth concerning freedom, the singularity of freedom as understood by Christians is the basis for Christians to cooperate with others on all levels. But the Christian witness to freedom is inauthentic if it fails to confess our many failures in the history of Christianity to serve freedom.

One Aspect of Christian Freedom Is Inward Religious Disengagement from the World.

To be free from the world is to be free from the attitude of alienation from God, neighbor, and oneself. Faith in God's grace means to love God more than the world, which liberates the Christian from the attitude of stress in relation to the restlessness and troubles of this life. Inward disengagement from the world is necessary because the world is a *corpus mixtum,* God's good created nature and man's sin are mixed together. Disengagement from the world is not the way of salvation, but a good inward discipline for an engaged style of living. Here I agree with Frederick Sontag: "The transformation that Christianity seeks to induce in us is one that does not remove its believers from the world but transforms them in the world."

Christian Freedom Creates a Deep Spirituality that Unites Temporality and Eternity in Human Experience.

Christians affirm the impact of the spiritual presence of the triune God. We use the term spirituality to indicate the dominion of the Holy Spirit, which guides individuals and communities to the way to become servants in the creation of the new man. At the very root of our personal and community religious life lies the gift of the triune God's self-communication. Far from being a call to passivity, this gift demands a vital, vigilant attitude. The practice of spir-

156

ituality does not eliminate tension and conflict, but sees in them the beginning of liberation from selfishness to service of God. Central to spirituality are the traditional practices of sacramental communion with Christ and his forgiveness, living brotherhood in a community, individual and common prayer, and the spiritual practice of meditation and contemplation. These are old branches of Christianity that are now being recovered under the impact of the East. Spirituality leads not only to service, but also to the emergence of the new man. Nevertheless, spirituality remains an experience of eternal life under the conditions of an earthly existence.

Christian Freedom Obliges Us to Solidarity with Other Religions insofar as They Take a Share in the Process of Liberation.

Given the scandalous involvement of Christian missions in the imperialistic policies of European states in the last centuries, Christians have no right to require conversion as the presupposition for solidarity. Although we believe in Christ, the light for all men, we meet other religions in dialogue presupposing the work of the spirit of the triune God in other religions. We join other religions in all efforts for liberation on both the religious and nonreligious levels of reality.

Christian Freedom Obliges Christians and Churches to Solidarity with All Efforts for a More Just Human Society.

The coming of the kingdom and liberating historical events are not identical, but liberation from sin embraces the social, political, and cultural spheres. Social exploitation, social misery, and political oppression are the reasons Christians must join the efforts to create a more just society.

Christian Freedom Stands Opposed to Socioreligious Messianism.

Jesus was not a zealot. He did not identify the social or political struggle with the coming of God's kingdom. His struggle for more love and justice was a universal one. All identifications of nationalism and religious faith are to be overcome for the sake of God's freedom for all men.

157

Christian Freedom Challenges Christians to Seek the Fulfillment of Secularization by Service to Liberation.

In the Christian view the very root of secularization is God's gift. God promises and grants that human beings may become the subjects of their own destiny. The proper realization of this self-determination is freedom in service to the liberation of humanity from all subjective and objective selfishness, haughtiness, and servility. Given the ambiguities in all human efforts and works, the separation of church and state is the better social basis for the free life of religions. The acknowledgment of the autonomy of social and political life was a spiritual liberation for Christians and churches in most European countries. But Christians must resist the temptation to retreat into an antiworldly, introspective attitude.

Christian Freedom Motivates Christians to Transcend the Given Situation in Hope for the Renewal of Creation.

Christian hope embraced the new being and intrahistorical new beginnings because Christian faith trusts in the permanent creation of new structured conditions for human beings sharing in God's own history.

Christian Freedom Requires Christians, Churches, Religions, and All Men to Seek Peace and to Create a World Where Nobody Need Fear.

God's own history, a history in which we all share, has reached a point where the self-destruction of humankind by a nuclear war has become a real possibility. It is a new stage in human history. God leaves his self-fulfillment in the hands of human beings. To destroy human existence is to offend God's existence. Since God has become man, humanity and human beings are God's living temple.

To stop the development and production of new systems of nuclear weapons, to stop the arms race by arms control, to support new serious negotiations concerning disarmament are some of the most important actual demands of Christian freedom today.

REFERENCES

Barth, Karl. *Das Geschenk der Freiheit*. Zollikon-Zurich: Evangelischer Verlag AG, 1953.

Fritzsche, Helmut. *Freiheit und Verantwortung in Liebe und Ehe*. Berlin: Evangelische Verlagsanstalt, 1983.

Gutiérrez, Gustavo. *A Theology of Liberation*. New York: Orbis Books, 1980.

Kasemann, Ernst. *Der Ruf der Freiheit*. Tübingen: J. C. B. Mohr, 1968.

Moltmann, Jürgen. "Die Revolution der Freiheit." In *Perspektiven der Theologie*. Munich: Kaiser Verlag, 1968.

Sontag, Frederick. *Love Beyond Pain*. New York: Paulist Press, 1977.

Tillich, Paul. *Systematic Theology*. vol. 3. Chicago: University of Chicago Press, 1963.

13

God, Humanity, and Nature: The Dialectics of Interaction

T. K. OOMMEN

It is necessary to note at the beginning of this essay the sense in which the notion of God is employed in this essay. If God is understood as a force or principle that moves, motivates, and guides man and as an entity on which man puts great reliance and hope, one can then speak of both a theistic and a nontheistic conceptualization of God. Whereas theism locates the ultimate spiritual reality "beyond man," nontheistic gods are located within man. Embedded in these notions are varieties of relationships between God and humanity, nature and God, humanity and nature. In what follows I propose to explore the implications of the conceptualizations of God for the future of man and society.

There is an amazing similarity in conceptualizations of God and society in the contemporary West. The essential feature of this conceptualization is dichotomization or polarization. Dichotomous constructions of human societies, starting with *gemeinschaft* and *gesellschaft,* have become commonplace in Western social sciences. Parallel to this are human efforts to model relationships to God, to gods, or to supernatural forces on the existing social relationships of society. Thus, religion is influenced by its social milieu. The attitude of respect man holds for the sacred becomes but an intensification of the kind of respect found in other social relationships. The point is well formulated by Ludwig Feuerbach: the conception of God is anthropological. "Religion is man's earliest . . . indirect form of self-knowledge . . . God is the highest subjectivity of man abstracted from himself."[1]

Conventional sociologists, in their attempt to conceptualize God-society relationships, attribute "functional specificity" to God: he has been disengaged from all aspects of life save the differentiated structure of religion, the this-worldly institutional interpenetration between God and society that persists in less "modern" societies of the East where God is not relegated to the religious realm, but rather presides over all aspects of life: economic, political, and cultural. This endows God with a holistic position in human life as against the compartmentalized position God has been assigned in modern Western societies. To experience God according to this conceptualization, man has to enter the realm of the sacred or holy; it is a charismatic experience. Thus, though God is retained in society and his presence in society is explicitly recognized, he has been "localized" in one of society's segments: the this-worldly institutional instrument, religion.

The Marxian perspective characterizes God as the creation of man, particularly the vested interests that want to maintain the status quo. These vested interests use God, it is argued, as an instrument to resist basic social changes, and religion, which is but the opium of the masses, is manipulated by the bourgeoisie to maintain the capitalist system, which suits its needs and interests. The Marxian approach explicitly acknowledges the primacy of man as the creator and relegates God to the position of a creature, contrary to theistic positions wherein God is the acknowledged creator and man God's creature. However, common to all the Western conceptualizations—social, scientific, and theological—is the dichotomization between God and society. It is my contention that unless we transcend this central tendency in Western thought—opposition and epistemological dualism—we cannot adequately perceive the interpenetration of the two. The basic problem here is the ill-conceived polarity between matter and spirit, knowledge and belief, sacred and secular, God and society. The logic here is one of reciprocal opposition. Hence it leads to one displacing the other, of what I call the zero-sum game. But the empirical reality forcefully points to the coexistence and intermeshing of these apparently (but not actually) inimical elements. Many may be tempted to dismiss this complex empirical reality as a transitional aberration in the long chain of social evolution. But we recognize it as a reality in itself with distinct properties. Although we do not deny that the evolutionary process and human innovation will inevitably influence man's conception of God, it is unlikely that gods will disappear, even theistic gods. Viewed thus, neither the current social scientific theories nor the theological conceptions of the West seem to be adequate to grapple with the "real, living God."

The polarization in conceptualization that we have referred to above is, however, characteristic only of modern Western man. To quote Frankfort et al: "The ancients, like the modern savages, saw man always as part of society, and society as imbedded in nature and dependent upon cosmic forces. For then nature and man did not stand in opposition and did not, therefore, have to be apprehended by different modes of cognition. . . . The fundamental differences between the attitudes of modern and ancient man as regards the surrounding world is this: for modern, scientific man the phenomenal world is primarily an 'It'; for ancient—and also for primitive—man it is a 'Thou'."[2]

Notwithstanding the fact that monotheistic religions, particularly Christianity, have contributed to dualistic conceptualizations in modern times, the biblical understanding of the relationship between God, humanity, and nature does not seem to support it. As the World Council of Churches' Conference on Faith, Science, and the Future put it:

In contrast to all dualistic or spiritualistic pictures of hope, humanity and the non-human creation thus remain intimately bound together in an open-ended history: the promise of fulfillment applies to the whole creation . . . human beings have . . . a duty towards the non-human creation: human beings who bear God's Spirit are the sign of the great promise of freedom for all creation.[3] . . . Humanity is temporally the last link in God's creation and, therefore, a part of nature not apart from it . . . what authority they possess, they possess within creation and not over it; further that authority is a gift of God and one for which men and women will be called to account by God.[4]

Man can be viewed as a maker (*homo faber*) and a cultivator, but the first is often overemphasized to the neglect of the second. However, "As God's creature, humanity is above all a receiver. In modern times, to the detriment of all creation, this dimension of our relation to God and nature has been hidden by the one-sided emphasis on *homo faber*. To counter this, it must be emphasized that even in making and cultivating, humanity is a receiver."[5]

This perspective seems to correct some of the distortions that have crept into the Christian understanding of the relationship between humanity and nature. But the relationship between God and humanity is still characterized by a dualistic conceptualization: God is the giver and man is the receiver. This has two implications for man: intellectual and moral. First, it denies, in effect, the creative talents of man; it inhibits his creative potentialities. If man's "creativity" is a gift of God, insofar as he is a mere receiver, he need not make the effort he is capable of. But God expects man to work hard and to put to use his ability to the fullest extent, lest what has been originally bestowed on him should be withdrawn (Matt. 25:14–30). To ensure man's authentic participation, his efforts should be explicitly recognized and of course rewarded. Second, to be eternally relegated to the position of a receiver is morally degrading. What imparts dignity is giving and contributing, not simply receiving and taking. The inadequate recognition given to man may frustrate him and may consequently render him aggressive, particularly when man tastes his power independent of God. It seems to me that this is precisely what happened during the last couple of centuries. Armed with the powers of science and technology, man arrogated himself to be God. Perhaps he was trying to "liberate" himself from the subservient position of a receiver.

It is this changed context that necessitates a new conceptualization of the God-humanity relationship from that of a giver-receiver to that of coworkers, partners, and participants. This should not be construed as an effort to claim, much less to establish, equality between God and man. I consider that an untenable proposition because equality is possible only between entities of similar qualities, which is clearly not the case here. My point is an endeavor to establish an authentic fellowship between God and man, which should be essentially participatory. Thus, man should impart a sense of self-responsibility. In turn, an authentic fellowship should be established between humanity and nature. Here again, the character of entities involved differs and hence the type of relationship would also be qualitatively different.

In the first part of this essay I tried to highlight the epistemological dualism characteristic of contemporary Western thought and how it fails to illumine our understanding of the interpenetration of God, humanity, and nature. It remains our task to investigate the substantive aspect of the issue, namely, the social forces at work that molded man's perception and understanding of the relationship between the three entities.

In the past, when man was constrained to live and work under the limitations of natural conditions, he viewed anything that surpassed his strength as mysterious. Perhaps the only option open to him was to subject himself to those forces that he could not control: to worship the multitude of objects—mountains, rivers, sun, etc.— all of which were deemed gods. This in turn has given rise to the belief that divinity infuses the natural world. To quote Toynbee, "In the pantheistic view, divinity is immanent in the universe and is transfused throughout the universe. In the monotheistic view, divinity is withdrawn from the universe and is made external to it; that is to say, divinity is made transcendent."[6]

The implications of this externalization of divinity from the universe for social transformation is far-reaching. As Ikeda puts it:

The difference between monotheism and pantheism is very telling in human civilization. Under conditions imposed by monotheistic faith, a great need to relate everything to an absolute being defines society and civilization and promotes the development of an all-pervasive uniformity. Because this makes the acceptance of alien elements difficult, when confronted with something foreign and new, a monotheistic society must undergo a win-or-lose, all-or-nothing transition. For this reason, changes in the historical current of the West have often been basic and far-reaching. In pantheistic societies, on the other hand, the value of alien ideas and things is recognized. The society is tolerant toward them; consequently, they can be introduced without the necessity of fundamental social alterations. No matter what new elements enter, the society remains basically unchanged.[7]

With the passage of time, man came to organize human society in large and efficiently constructed communities. At this stage, the worship of collective human power—primordial collectivities including nation-states—overshadowed the worship of natural forces. The gods who originally symbolized the nonhuman natural forces were now conscripted to serve as symbols of human institutions. But the implications of infusing human institutions with divinty, the sacralization of society, differed in different societies. For the followers of exclusive-minded monotheistic religions, the coexistence of more than one religion or language, in one society or nation-state is difficult to comprehend. On the other hand, in societies where polytheism or pantheism exist, religious or linguistic pluralism has been the normal state of affairs. This means not only the coexistence of religion and magic, science and religion, nationalism and communalism, without much conflict and tension, but also the central tendency in these societies has been one of coexistence and reconciliation.

Man's ability to coerce and exploit nature was limited so long as he used only animate energy. But with the unlimited inanimate energy that he could generate through the application of science and technology, men thought they had the license to exploit nonhuman nature, which is but a gift to him by God. And Western man's tendency to exploit nature was not inhibited by the pantheistic belief that nonhuman nature is sacred and that it has a dignity, like man himself, which ought to be respected. Thus the modern West has substituted the post-Christian faith in science for its ancestral Christianity; it discarded theism but retained the misconstrued belief, derived from monotheism, that it has the right to exploit nonhuman nature. This selective retention of a distorted religious faith along with the power of science has serious implications for humanity's present and indeed future. If under the previous Christian dispensation Western man believed himself to be God's tenant divinely licensed to cultivate and nurture nature on the proviso that he worshiped God and acknowledged his proprietary rights, by the seventeenth century man cut off God's head and expropriated the universe. Drunk with the power he acquired through science and technology, Western man refused to remain as God's tenant on earth, but claimed that he was a free holder, an absolute owner. The religion of science, like nationalism, has now become a global phenomenon.

The next major development in human history was that of crystallization of secular ideologies. If capitalism was believed to be an explicit offshoot of Christianity, at least some of its sects and denominations,[8] communism is, in fact, a Christian heresy. But unlike previous heresies it has insisted on a particular Christian precept that the Christian establishment has neglected. To quote Toynbee: "The mythology of Communism is Jewish and Christian mythology translated into a non-theistic vocabulary. The unique and omnipotent god Yahweh has been translated into historical necessity; the chosen people have been translated into the Proletariat, which is predestined by historical necessity to triumph; the Millennium has been translated into the eventual fading away of the state. Communism has also inherited from Christianity the belief in a mission to convert all mankind."[9]

The new religions—science, nationalism, communism—as distinguished from old theistic religions—Christianity, Hinduism, Islam—vary in that the old ones strive to control human activity and suppress human greed. In their conceptualizations, man was a tool in the hands of God. The new gods are tools in the hands of man. The new gods seem to have given birth to, or at least have been explicitly used for, the fulfillment of that greed. However, all the gods, both theistic and nontheistic, share one thing: absolutization. The understanding and hope of the "believers" is that their gods, independently and unequivocally, hold the key to the ultimate solution of problems.

It seems to me that what we need is a new conceptualization about God: not a god who views man simply as his tool or a man who presumes to use the gods of his creation as his tools for his selfish advantages. What is feasible is a conceptualization in which God and man are viewed as partners. Further, we need to accept a system of laws universal to all forms of life. Such a system of laws should emphasize the harmony and unity of humanity with nonhuman nature also. From the current dichotomous constructions of the West we must move on to a trichotomy. The trinity involved here is God-man-nature, not necessarily in a hierarchical ordering, but in a mutually harmonious and nurturing relationship. It is incredible that modern Western thought did not attempt this task since the Trinitarian doctrine embedded in Christian theology "presents the relationships between God, humanity and nature as a differentiated unity."[10]

In the spiritual Trinity of Christianity, one, the son, had a human incarnation in Christ. This human incarnation of Christ facilitated the process of developing a concrete, historical, empathy-building relationship between God, humanity, and nature. This experientially crucial dimension, which is essentially a communication channel, a rapport-building enterprise between God, humanity, and nature, did not seem to have adequately registered in the cognitive map of Western Christian theology. In contrast, Eastern Christian theology has "taught 'union participation' not only between God and humanity in Christ but also between humanity and nature."[11] And this syncretism seems to be the inevitable corollary of the social milieu in which Christian faith is practiced, societies in which polytheistic and pantheistic religions have originated and coexist with monotheism.

I would like to point out here that the combination of modern scientific "progress" and a distortion of Judaic monotheism has been largely instrumental in the man-nature disengagement. At the core of modern scientific civilization lies the conception that man and nature are two oppositional entities and that for the sake of human progress it is necessary to conquer nature. The scientific method has been the chief instrument of realizing this conquest. The Judaic monotheistic belief that the spiritual presence in and behind the universe is a single, transcendent, humanlike God reinforced the further belief that nothing else in the universe is divine.

This God is not only the creator of man and nature, but is also endowed with the power and right to dispose of what he had created. And God placed the whole of his nonhuman creation at the disposal of his human creatures to use it for his benefit. God blessed man and said, in effect, "Have many children so that your descendants will live all over the earth and bring it under their *control*. I am putting you *in charge* of the fish, the birds, and all the wild animals" (Gen. 1:28–29). The convenient focusing of attention on one aspect of the story of creation has led to distortions. For example, according to Genesis 23:10, God has entrusted the land to his covenant people as a *loan:* it is not their possession. Further, every seventh year the land should be left fallow (the year for revitalization of the land) and every fifty years the land should be equitably redistributed (Lev. 25).

Before man developed the ability to control nature, nature's fury was believed to be capable of destroying man and his nonhuman environment. The story of the flood symbolizes the potentiality of natural forces to threaten mankind. But Noah's ark contained not only man, but representatives of nonhuman species. Yahweh comes to the rescue of man, as well as nonhuman creatures. In spite of this, on the one hand, man sees the relationship between himself and nature as an I-It relationship. On the other hand, believing himself to be closest to God of all creatures, he thinks it is natural that he subjugate all other species and put them into his service. Thus, once man developed the ability to control nature through science and technology, not only did he divest the natural environment of its former aura of divinity, but he even stripped God of his divinity. Indeed, modern Western man has no compunction about destroying the human environment.

It is important to remind ourselves here that the roots of this ideology were first formulated in Palestine as early as the ninth century B.C., but it was put into practice in Europe only after twenty-five centuries, that is in the seventeenth century A.D., when Western science emerged. Jesus taught that economic greed was incompatible with service to God. He averred: "You cannot serve both God and money" (Matt. 6:24). He advised the people: "Do not store up riches for yourselves here on earth, where moths and rust destroy, and robbers break in and steal" (Matt. 6:19). Jesus condemned the accumulation of capital, technology, and the glorification of economically remunerative work. It may be stressed here that Jesus lived in Palestine, when it was predominantly an agrarian society, wherein human living was in harmony with the nonhuman environment. Although accumulation of capital and conspicuous consumption were rare in his social environment, Jesus perceived and denounced the greed that is innate in human nature irrespective of time and place. Jesus glorified the nonmaterialistic attitude of birds and wild flowers and held this up as an example for human disciples to emulate. Yet distortions crept into the Christian conceptualization of the man-nature relationship, which combined with the advancement in science and technology to conspire against the harmony between man and his environment. This rendered the evolving and sustaining of an ecologically balanced and just society nearly impossible.

Recent thinking on this theme, however, has recognized the problematic involved. I cannot do better than quote a World Council of Churches document:

The cultural context has radically changed since biblical times. In the biblical period humanity was confronted with an overpowering nature. The command to rule the animals and to subdue the earth delivered people from fear and from the temptation to divinize or demonize nature, and encourage them to overcome suffering and to build culture. The power relations have since been reversed by science and technology. A desacralized nature is in the power of humanity which is now able to destroy its own species and perhaps even all life on the earth. Our own technological inventions and our social processes are threatening to get the upper hand to become as over-powering as nature once was. What needs to be emphasized today, therefore, is the *relatedness* between God and his creation rather than their *separateness*. The dignity of nature as creation needs to be bound up with our responsibility for the preservation of life.[12]

It is against this background that I plead for a new conceptualization about God. Notwithstanding all the spectacular achievements of man through science and technology, it is clear that he is infinitely inferior to the nonhuman natural world in several respects. At the same time, it is also certain that man's superiority is clearly discernible in several contexts. For future material development the Western monotheistic attitude is valuable. But for protecting the autonomy of all groups of people and for putting a stop to pollution and destruction of the natural environment, the Eastern approach is more viable. What is needed, then, is a religion, a conceptualization about God that can go beyond the differences of the East and West and bind the whole of humankind into a unified body. Such a religion will save the Occident from its present crisis and the Orient from its current hardships. [13]

The theological understanding and conceptualization about God, the gods, or the divine are invariably anchored in religious texts. The characteristic skepticism theologians have of scientific tools and empirical methods renders their analyses incomplete if one wants to understand God from the perspective of ordinary believers. In theological analysis we encounter only the abstract, universal, invisible, and transcendental God. In contrast, social scientists focus on the concrete, the local, the visible and the pragmatic God, which they can understand through scientific tools, often ignoring the fact that their subject matter in this context is not easily amenable to empirical analysis. Their effort is to understand God contextually, in terms of the social milieu in which it is located. If theologians strive for a top-down understanding of God, the social scientists insist on a bottom-up analysis. Although both these perspectives are valuable in themselves since they illuminate different aspects of reality, they are inadequate taken independently. The "universal gods" of theologians are not those experienced by people; the "specific gods" studied by social scientists are often vulgarizations of the sophisticated notion of God. And yet there is considerable interaction between the local and the universal gods; they mutually influence and, not infrequently, reinforce one another.

Even in a pluralistic society in which a diversity of gods are recognized and worshiped by the differing folk traditions, the elite tradition often recognizes only one God. On the other hand, notwithstanding the multiplicity of gods worshiped in the variety of folk traditions in a given society, there is invariably a tacit recognition of a sakti, a force or energy that is reckoned as ultimate reality. Therefore, the "disjuncture" between the monist God of the elite and the plurality of gods of the folk, is often a tension of form and not necessarily of substance. The significant question for us to investigate, however, is the basis of the differing conceptualizations of theologians and social scientists.

Broadly speaking, the two leading sources of conceptualizations about God are religious doctrines and societal characteristics. Ideally, we can postulate a continuum in each of these contexts, moving from unity and uniformity of religious doctrine to the multiplicity and diversity of religious doctrines. Similarly, we can arrange societies on a continuum from relative homogeneity to extreme heterogeneity. Variations in religious doctrines obtain not only among different religions that radically differ in their conceptualizations of God (monotheism, polytheism, pantheism), but even among different sects and denominations in the same religious tradition.

Similarly, the elements that contribute to societal heterogeneity are not only primordial identities—religion, languages, region, caste, tribe—but also variations in terms of sociopolitical ideologies—capitalism, socialism, communism, secularism—and the level of economic development and scientific and technological advancement. With this understanding, we can postulate four ideal-typical but empirically plausible societal situations that would influence conceptualization about God. These ideal types are shown in the following diagram:

Diagram 1: Sources and Nature of Conceptualization About God

Religious Doctrine(s)	Type of Society	Nature of Conceptualization About God
1. Homogeneous	Homogeneous	Consensual; single God
2. Homogeneous	Heterogeneous	Substance may be uniform but forms may vary
3. Heterogeneous	Homogeneous	Substance may vary, even if forms are uniform
4. Heterogeneous	Heterogeneous	Both substance and forms vary; plurality of Gods

The concrete societies of the contemporary world, with frayed edges and loose textures and constantly exposed to alien influences, afford only a few examples of type 1. Most of the societies in the world today would fall into either type 2 or 3. Indeed, there are a few cases of type 4, the classical one being that of India.

In all probability, protest against and rejection of old gods and accommodation of new gods will constantly take place, particularly in heterogeneous and complex societies. But whether or not this process will generate conflicts between gods who compete for loyalty from their existing or potential clients will depend on the overall ethos of the society, which in turn is largely conditioned by the nature of dominant religion of a given society. If the dominant religion is one that conceptualizes the sacred and the secular, the transcendental and the mundane in monistic and oppositional terms, the possibility of the coexistence of a multiplicity of conceptions about God is remote. On the other hand, if the dominant religion conceives the sacred and the secular, the divine and mundane, in terms of a continuum and as present in a variety of contexts, interpenetrating all aspects of life, the possibility is that differing conceptions of God will be accommodated with relative ease. Such a societal situation will not call for the displacement of one God by another, rather it would facilitate the coexistence of a multiplicity of gods. The process of redefiniton or reconceptualization of gods may take place either through the emergence of sectarianism or denominationalism within the same religion or through the acceptance of altogether new conceptions of God through the process of embracing new religions, either through conversion or by founding new ones.

Perhaps it is useful at this stage to briefly indicate how varieties of religious protests mold social conceptions of God. We may identify five such empirical possibilities as shown in Diagram 2.[14]

Diagram 2: Types of Protests and Social Conceptions of God

Style of Protest	Mechanisms of Articulation	Conceptions of God
1. Reform	Monasticism	Institutionally insulated
2. Retreatism	Mysticism	Individualized
3. Rebellion	Sectarian Secession	Oppositional
4. Innovation	Sectarian Secession	Communal insulation and oppositional
5. Revolution	Secession from one religion to another	New communal God, expansionist

It is not suggested here that all these styles of protest, mechanisms of articulation, and concomitant conceptions of gods will be found in any given society or at a given historical phase. What is, however, significant is that the styles and mechanisms of protest are likely to mold conceptions about the gods. If so, it is clear that for an adequate understanding of differing conceptions of God we should focus our attention simultaneously on the nature of religious doctrines and the historicity of our social milieu.

NOTES

1. Ludwig Feuerbach, *The Essence of Christianity,* trans. George Eliot (New York: Harper & Bros., 1957), 30.

2. Henri Frankfort, Mrs. H. Frankfort, J. A. Wilson, and T. Jacobsen, *Before Philosophy* (Middlesex: Penguin, 1949).

3. Paul Abrecht, ed., *Faith and Science in an Unjust World* (Geneva: World Council of Churches, 1980), 31; a report of the World Council of Churches' Conference on Faith, Science, and the Future, vol. 2, "Reports and Recommendations."

4. Ibid., 161.

5. Ibid., 34.

6. Arnold Toynbee and Daisaku Ikeda, *Choose Life: A Dialogue,* ed. R. L. Gage (London: Oxford University Press, 1976), 298.

7. Ibid., 297–98.

8. See Max Weber, *The Protestant Ethic and the Spirit of Capitalism* (Glencoe, Ill.: The Free Press, 1960).

9. Toynbee and Ikeda, 295.

10. Abrecht, 29.

11. Ibid., 29.

12. Ibid., 33.

13. Toynbee and Ikeda.

14. Compare Thomas F. O'dea, *The Sociology of Religion* (New Delhi: Prentice-Hall of India, 1969).

Toward a Grammar of the Spirit in Society: The Contribution of Rosenstock-Huessy

M. DARROL BRYANT

As we move into the planetary era in the history of humankind, it becomes increasingly imperative for the religions of humankind to disclose their respective contributions to our common but multiform social future. Unlike earlier ages, when the adherents of different faiths and the bearers of different traditions lived in relative isolation from one another, the believer increasingly today—and more so in the future—will live in the presence of other believers and the multiplicity of religious traditions. This emergent situation will place new demands on us all. As one who does not share the widespread conviction among Western intellectuals of a "religionless future," nor the belief that secularization means the end of religion, it seems crucial that the insights and wealth of our respective traditions be brought to bear on our common social horizon.[1] Thus one of the great questions that confronts us at the end of the second millennium of the Christian era is this: what contribution, if any, can faith make to our common, but multiform, social future?

Here my focus is on religion and society and the connection between the life of the spirit and society. Ever since the industrial revolution, there has been increased attention among Christian thinkers on the issue of the life of humankind in time, to social reality.[2] What does this shift from doctrine to society portend? In my view it reflects a growing awareness that we must find our way toward a viable social future in which we can discern anew the transforming presence of God amidst the seeming chaos of our multiform life in time. Moreover, it portends a quest—as every question does—for something still dimly glimpsed, but nonetheless passionately sought: social peace. For the Christian thinker, despite the seemingly endless debates among rival positions, God and the life of humankind *in time* are intimately and inextricably linked. Thus the life of the spirit may be discerned in the life of society.

But where do we turn in our efforts to understand the multiform relationships between the life of the spirit and society? Are there religiously inspired efforts that point us in fruitful directions? It seems to me that there are figures in our respective traditions who are addressing themselves to these issues, figures whose actions are luminous or whose perspectives are full of promise. I think here of the efforts of Gandhi earlier in this century and of the current actions of Dom Helder Camara in Brazil and Mother Theresa in India, or the intellectual creativity of Sri Aurobindo and Martin Buber. All of these persons act and speak in ways that transcend the boundaries, religious and otherwise, that often separate us from one another. At this stage of the emergent planetary discussion it strikes me as crucial that we strive to make the resources of our particular traditions better known to one another. To this end I will focus here on the work of the little-known Christian social thinker Eugen Rosenstock-Huessy (1888–1973).[3] His work has been immensely instructive to me and is, in my view, an example of a promising new direction from within the Christian tradition for those seeking to understand something of the connection between the life of the spirit and society.[4]

For Rosenstock-Huessy the events of our century disclosed the necessity for a grammar of society that could contribute to the creation of social peace. Unfortunately, in his view, the emergent social sciences had been bewitched by the methods of the natural sciences and the focus on the movement of objects in space. However, the social sciences required a new orientation, one that would focus on the *intergenerational life of humankind in time.*[5] Moreover, the tumult of our century requires new approaches that move beyond the reigning antitheses of modernity: subjective *or* objective, faith *or* science, materialist *or* idealist, determinist *or* indeterminist. But where does one turn to find a way beyond these reigning antitheses, a way that could lead to an encounter with the fullness of humankind's life in the spirit and in time?

For Rosenstock-Huessy, the inspiration for the project that was to occupy the whole of his life was drawn from the Christian faith. As he wrote in terms drawn from the Christian traditions, "Today we are living through the agonies of transition to the third epoch. We have yet to establish Man, the great singular of humanity, in one household, over the plurality of races, classes and age groups. This will be the center of struggle in the future. . . . The theme of future history will be not territorial or political but social: it will be the story of man's creation. The next thousand years may be expected, consequently, to concentrate on the third article, namely to wrestle with the task of revealing God in society."[6]

Faith as Orientation: Toward a Social Grammar

Rosenstock-Huessy was profoundly shaken by the events of the First World War. It meant, he believed, that one could not continue with "business as usual." Instead, we entered a new and more open situation where we had to relearn the dynamics of social life that lead to social peace. For Rosenstock-Huessy, the initial scent of the way beyond the dominant antitheses was to be found in faith that he understood in terms of *orientation*. Faith was not so much a set of doctrinal beliefs, but the way human life is oriented toward the future. In his words, "faith, properly speaking, is always belief in some future, a world to come."[7] Thus it is the power to move us beyond and ahead. It stands on the front line of the future as the antidote to decadence. This existential and temporal understanding of faith reveals Rosenstock-Huessy's dissent from those accounts of humankind's life in time that ground themselves in a belief in the autonomy of reason. It also points to a way ahead that acknowledges the spiritual foundations of social life.

When Rosenstock-Huessy grounds his grammar of humankind's life in time in faith it is not for the sake of placing his grammar beyond criticism, but rather to make explicit its own presuppositions. Moreover, the truth of an understanding of society is measured by its capacity to illuminate our lived experience in time, not by reference to a presumed standard of objectivity. On the other hand, Rosenstock-Huessy's approach to society not only stands over against conventional social theory, it also stands over against other explicitly Christian understandings of society in that it does not appeal to either doctrinal or ethical criteria for its justification. Rather, in speaking about the Christian faith, Rosenstock-Huessy argues that Christian dogma is "not an intellectual formula but a record and promise of life."[8] Thus, his path seeks to overcome the conflict between faith and science that has been so pervasive in the post-Enlightenment West.

The distinctive understanding of faith in relation to the creation of an adequate understanding of the life of society in time is reflected in Rosenstock-Huessy's discussion of the Christian creeds. As he writes, "Its three articles guarantee our trust in the unity of creation from the beginning (God the Father made all things in heaven and on earth), our liberty to die to our old selves (given us by God's Son, who implanted the Divine itself in human life by living as a man, and dying, yet rising again), and the inspiration of the Holy Spirit which enables us to commune with posterity and start fellowship here and now."[9] Here one can see the effort Rosenstock-Huessy is making to open Christian faith out to an account of the underlying spiritual dynamics that inform our life in society. He makes this even more explicit when he contends that

. . . the third article of the Creed is the specifically Christian one: from now on the Holy Spirit makes man a partner in his own creation. In the beginning God had said, "Let us make man in our image" (Genesis 1:26). In this light, the Church Fathers interpreted human history as a process of making Man like God. They called it "anthropurgy": as metallurgy refines metal from its ore, anthropurgy wins the true stuff of Man out of his coarse physical substance. Christ, in the center of history, enables us to participate consciously in this man-making process and to study its laws.[10]

Thus, although Rosenstock-Huessy's social grammar is inspired by Christian faith, his project is not a conventional religious one. For him the fundamental issue is not the knowing of God in himself, nor conformity to a received doctrinal tradition, nor the elaboration of abstract ethical norms, but rather it is to understand the life of humanity in time, the making and remaking of the human race. Hence the Christian faith opens out into the life of society in time, the world in which we daily find ourselves. It is here that the Spirit is present as our partner in our own making and remaking.

Faith, then, provided Rosenstock-Huessy with an orientation, not a solution, to the project that lay before him. The project was an understanding of the life of humankind in time, and the solution to that lay in a turning to the very processes and dynamics of social life, not in recourse to doctrine. In other words, it is the actual life of human beings in society that is the subject of social research and investigation. But that actual life is, in his view, one that is grounded in God, and humankind thus finds itself within a divine imperative—the making of humanity—and not as Enlightenment social theories argue, in relation to itself. Humanity is defined by response, not by autonomy. His rejection of the Enlightenment doctrine of "autonomy" as a modern conceit is parallel to his rejection of Christian approaches of the life of society grounded in ethics, or doctrine. Rosenstock-Huessy is seeking to articulate a grammar of social life that can disclose that the very processes of social life already bear witness to the life and presence of the spirit. Thus for Rosenstock-Huessy—unlike many others—the issue is not one of trying to overlay the processes of social life with a religious framework. Nor is he seeking to argue, as do many Latin American liberation theologians, for the identification of a certain stand of political development with the purposes of God. Instead, he is engaged in "the search for the omnipresence of God in the most contradictory patterns of human society."[11]

Rather than speaking of his project as "social theory," he prefers the term *social grammar*. The reason for this is that in a "grammar" we have performed a distinctive task, namely, the recognition and articulation of "multiformity within unity."[12] This is crucial since, in Rosenstock-Huessy's view, social thinkers have been too much burdened by the search for a single determinate cause in terms of which all social processes are understood. One sees this, for example, in Marxian theories, which make everything a reflection of economics. Instead, Rosenstock-Huessy argues for the necessity of basic terms that respect the multiform character of social life. Thus we need a grammar of social life that raises to the level of consciousness the very processes that are in fact taking place in our social exchange and interaction. Second, Rosenstock-Huessy described his work as a grammar because it is intimately linked to speech and language as central to all social processes. Speech is "the lifeblood of society,"[13] yet social thinkers tend to overlook this most obvious feature of our life together. As creatures of time, we are continually speaking to one another as we reason, pass laws, tell stories, sing, instruct our children, express our hurts, champion our causes, lament our failings. It is these manifold activities that Rosenstock-Huessy focuses on in his social grammar. In this social grammar, he writes, "a science is sought by which we may diagnose the power, vitality, unanimity and propriety of the lifeblood of society, of speech, language, literature . . . our method represents remedial linguistics, testing the powers of peace and war."[14] Moreover, he contends that "the grammatical method is the way in which man becomes conscious of his place in history (backward), world (outward), society (inward), and destiny (forward). The grammatical method is, then, an additional development of speech itself; for, speech having given man this direction and orientation about his place in the universe through the ages, what is needed today is an additional consciousness of this power of direction and orientation."[15] What is central to this social grammar—and implicit in the citation—is what Rosenstock-Huessy calls the "Cross of Reality." It is to this foundational insight and model that we now turn.

The Cross of Reality: The Crucible of the Creature

When we turn to the actual life of human beings, one of the fundamental features of creaturely life that discloses itself is that it is life lived in *space and time*. However, that space and time further discloses itself as multiform, not uniform. Thus Rosenstock-Huessy notes:

Now and here, we are living in a twofold time and a twofold space. As living beings, we are responsible for the conservation of the accomplishments of the past, the fulfillment of the future, the unanimity of the inner, the efficiency of the external front of life. In order to live, any organism must face backward, forward, inward and outward. . . . The now and here of all of us, means that we are living in a two fold space and a twofold time. And the term twofold is literally true. . . . Forward, backward, inward, outward lie the dynamic frontiers of life, capable of intensification, enlargement, expansion and exposed to shrinking and decay as well.[16]

These two axes of time and space, then, constitute the crucible of creaturely life, both personally and socially. Thus Rosenstock-Huessy came to argue that reality itself—not the abstract reality of physics, but the full-bodied reality of human life—is cruciform. Our existence is a perpetual suffering and wrestling with conflicting forces, paradoxes, contradictions within and without. By them we are stretched and torn in opposite directions, but through them comes renewal. And these opposing directions are summed up by four that define the great space and time axes of all men's life on earth, forming a Cross of Reality.[17]

This Cross of Reality, this crucible of creaturely life, can be presented schematically in the following diagram:

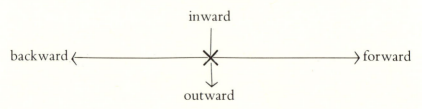

The creature and society live at the intersection of these four fronts of life. Here we live and die—and are renewed.

The Cross of Reality, as the *name* of our condition in time and space as creatures, is fundamental to Rosenstock-Huessy's social thinking. It is his denial of both reductionism and abstractionism. It serves to bring into focus those manifold forces that everyday assail our life and, at the same time, it clarifies the imperatives inherent in our situation. Moreover, wrote Rosenstock-Huessy, "since the four fronts differ in quality and direction they are *ultimate and irreducible dimensions of human existence,* but the mind with its imperious urge to relate and unify everything is tempted to over-simplify life and deny the Cross of Reality by reducing the four to one."[18] But it was this temptation that Rosenstock-Huessy resisted and the consequence is a grammar of the spirit infinitely richer than those that have dominated contemporary discussions. In the light of the Cross of Reality a major revolution in our social thinking is required.

This cruciform understanding of reality reveals, upon analysis, the spatial "conflict of inner and outer processes" and the temporal "conflict between responsibilities toward the past and the future."[19] These axes are not extrinsic to the creature, but pass through the very heart of our being. We are creatures of the cross. "Therefore," wrote Rosenstock-Huessy, "life is perpetual decision: when to continue the past and when to change, and where to draw the line between the inner circle we speak to and the outer objects we merely speak of and try to manipulate."[20] In the absence of a cruciform understanding of the reality of creaturely life, we tend to see only one or another front, one or another dimension of life. The consequence is a distortion of the situation of the creature, which then skews our thinking and our responses.

In our social life, the cruciform character of life results in a certain division of social labor. As Rosenstock-Huessy notes, "society compensates for our individual inadequacies by division of labor."[21] He continues:

Teaching, ceremony and ritual preserve our continuity with the past, and teachers, priests and lawyers serve on this front for all of us. We build up social unanimity by playing, singing, talking together, sharing our moods and aspirations and on this inner front poets, artists, and musicians are typical representatives. We win our living and protect our lives by learning to control natural forces and manipulating them for our ends in farming, industry and war; scientists, engineers, and soldiers typify the millions who fight for us on the outer front. Lastly, religious and political leaders, prophets and statesmen are responsible for initiating change and drawing society into its future.[22]

Thus, society itself takes on a certain cruciform reality in order to respond to the multiple claims upon its life. The virtue of Rosenstock-Huessy's insight here is that the division of labor is not just an economic phenomenon, but touches the very fabric of our life together in a society: the functions of different groups within society contribute to the welfare of the whole society. This perspective also contains a way of analyzing social distortion and social breakdown. For example, without the presence in society of those whose lives are given over to the fulfillment of the social task of nourishing social unanimity, the evil of inner disunity emerges. Contemporary society, "dominated for several centuries by natural science and its applications, suffers most of all from obsession with the outward front," and this obsession has "led to a distortion that threatens our future."[23] Hence, in Rosenstock-Huessy's view, "social health depends on preserving a delicate mobile balance between forward and backward, inward and outward."[24]

When the Cross of Reality is placed at the heart of one's social grammar the result is a multiform understanding of social life and the multiform character of speech. Against one-dimensional understandings of society and speaking, Rosenstock-Huessy asserts that "whenever we speak, we assert our being alive because we occupy a center from which the eye looks backward, forward, inward and outward. To speak, means to be placed in the center of the cross of reality."[25] However, we do not speak in a single mode, but rather in the mode appropriate to the front to which we are most attentive at a given moment. This results, says Rosenstock-Huessy, in a fourfold understanding of speech: projective (forward), subjective (inward), trajective (backward), and objective (outward).[26] Here again the creature finds himself called upon to differentiate his speaking so that it is appropriate to the dimension of our cruciform reality addressed. Moreover, the maintenance of these different modes of speech is at the heart of social well-being. In Rosenstock-Huessy's words:

Men reason, men pass laws, men tell stories, men sing. The external world is reasoned out, the future is ruled, the past is told, the unanimity of the inner circle is expressed in song. . . . The energies of social life are compressed into words. The circulation of articulated speech is the lifeblood of society. *Through speech, society sustains its time and space axes.* These time and space axes give direction and orientation to all members of society. Without articulated speech, man has neither direction nor orientation in time or space.[27]

Thus the Cross of Reality when correlated with a fourfold understanding of speech gives rise to a grammar of social analysis and points the way to social renewal. We are, in this sense, creatures of speech, or in Christian terms, the Word.

In making the point about the centrality of speech to social life, Rosenstock-Huessy turns to our actual life in time and space rather than to philosophical reflection upon speech as has become common in the contemporary interest in the philosophy of language. Contra the search of the early Wittgenstein for an ideal language, or the later Wittgenstein for the disease of ordinary speech, or Cassier's "symbol-making," or Heidegger's view of language as the "house of being," Rosenstock-Huessy turns his attention to speaking and listening as the key to social living and dying. Speech is the matrix of our life together.

Rosenstock-Huessy believed that the cruciform method he developed allowed for "the diagnosis of the complete soul" as well as the "healthy society."[28] Unlike the social thinkers who followed the lead of the natural sciences into a preoccupation with external space, Rosenstock-Huessy sought to turn our attention to the reality of human life on the cruciform of space and time. Here in the responses of human beings and societies to the imperatives that arise in the unfolding of events the fate of humankind is lost and won. Rather than searching for timeless abstractions, Rosenstock-Huessy sought to teach us the value of timing and timelessness. Rather than a philosophy of language, Rosenstock-Huessy sought to sharpen our ability to hear the spoken word since "all we can learn is to listen better and better," and heed the life-sustaining, renewing, and inspiring word we speak on the Cross of Reality.[29]

The Grammar of Social Life and Death

Earlier we indicated that Rosenstock-Huessy's social grammar acknowledges that the social thinker is a participant in, rather than an observer of, the social life of humankind. Thus the social thinker is compelled, as are other members of society, "to pass judgment on the trend of affairs in society. Is it decaying? Is it disintegrating? Is it going to last? Is it going to live?"[30] Thus, Rosenstock-Huessy claimed that "behind every one thinkable problem of our social sciences we can trace this major preoccupation of distinguishing between the living and the dead elements of the social pattern. The danger of death is the first cause of any knowledge about society."[31] Given Rosenstock-Huessy's cruciform analysis of the life of society, there emerges a set of characteristic social dangers and evils that face society on each front. Every society is faced with the perpetual problem of orchestrating the multiform imperatives of each front into a healthy whole in which each front is given its due. But this social peace is difficult to attain, indeed it is the perpetual challenge to every society.

"What is wrong with society?" asks Rosenstock-Huessy.[32] When we grasp the dynamics present within the Cross of Reality, then we can see that society is continually seeking to create inner unanimity, outer efficiency, respect for the past, and faith in the future. But each of these fronts of life is threatened by the evils of anarchy or the lack of inner unanimity or common aspiration, war or the inability to efficiently organize external space, revolution or being over-whelmed by the future and doing violence to the past for which we feel no sense of gratitude, and decadence or the inability of the older generation to inspire the new generation by giving it a heritage. These threats to social life on each front can be presented schematically as follows:

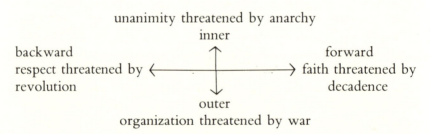

In terms of Rosenstock-Huessy's social grammar, the time axis involves the intergenerational life of society. Thus the issue is the capacity of the older generation to inspire the new generation such that there can be change without violence. At the same time, it is crucial that the past provide a heritage that does not stifle the need to let the new come into the life of society. Revolution is thus the result of the failure of peaceful intergenerational change such that the future is brought in with violence. On the other hand, the future may run roughshod over the past, including the "liquidation" of the past when there is no healthy respect for the achievements of past generations. Faith in the future and respect for the past require each other in order that the life of society in time can be sustained. Society finds itself continually confronted with the question of what from the past we need to let go of and what we need to conserve and what from the future we need to say yes to and what we need to resist.

Likewise, anarchy and war are "symptomatic of the evils of the order of society in space."[33] What Rosenstock-Huessy is pointing to here is the need to establish—or better create—a certain rhythm and connection between the inner life of the members of society and the outward organization of its space. When that inner unanimity breaks down, when everyone is preoccupied with "making his pile, grabbing more than his share"[34] then society cannot function as one body politic and rise to meet the challenges of organizing its life in space. Thus there is a reciprocal relationship between the inner and the outer just as there is between the future and the past.

Moreover, Rosenstock-Huessy notes that we "sustain the time and space axes of our civilization by speaking."[35] We, citizens and social thinkers alike, "take our place in the center of civilization, confronted as we are with its four aspects, its future, its past, its inner solidarity, its external struggle. And in this delicate and dangerous exposure to the four fronts of life, to the inner, the outer, the backward, and the forward front, our words must strike a balance; language distributes and organizes the universe, in every moment, anew. It is we who decide what belongs to the past and what shall be part of the future."[36]

Central to the process of articulating what is necessary to the achievement of social peace is the triumph over the social forms of death, the social evils that threaten social well-being. These triumphs over death are never, in his view, once-and-for-all events. Rather, they are daily events in our life in society. For Rosenstock-Huessy such a social grammar is rooted in the conviction that "God becomes known to us in all the powers that triumph over death."[37] Thus the survival of society is itself testimony of the presence of that divine spirit in our midst. "If," he wrote, "the Divine becomes known in our lives as the power of conquering death, it is something that can only happen to us in this or that particular moment of time; it is known as an *event,* never as an essence or a thing. And it can happen to us only in the midst of living."[38]

This dynamic and cruciform grammar of social life seeks, then, to heighten our awareness of the very processes of social life. It is a grammar grounded in the actual experience of human beings in society, though many of the basic insights are inspired by Christian faith. It is Christianity, in his view, that has seen most clearly the seemingly paradoxical relationship between death and life, namely, that "death" often precedes life. In the death and resurrection of Jesus Christ the great reversal takes place, but this is something we also know in our social and daily life. Often the way to the future involves our "dying" to old habits, enduring a great crisis, letting go of idols and in myriad ways seeing a new life emerge from suffering and spiritual "death." What is striking is the way that Rosenstock-Huessy wrests insights from faith that are illuminating for our life in society and time. For Rosenstock-Huessy the daily life of society depends on the *spiritual virtues* of faith and love, since it is finally these spiritual powers that are "stronger than death."[39] Thus our spiritual life and social well-being are ultimately linked to one another.

Death as a biological reality for the life of individuals and generations is also a central problem for society. Here the issue is the way to link intergenerational life within society so that society may achieve continuity despite death. Again we are confronted in this situation, argues Rosenstock-Huessy, by the centrality of the spirit to social life. What links generations together across the abyss of death is the spirit as loyalty to prior achievements, faith in those who come after us, and bonds of love that sustain us in the present. Through these spiritual powers we are threaded into intergenerational life. Rosenstock-Huessy remarks:

In society, in our historical community, we move as men born through the living Word into our times and places, into our future destiny. We have the singular privilege of contributing to the everlasting survival of acquired faculties which we embrace and to contribute to the everlasting relegation to hell of those acquired faculties which we wish to see extirpated. Thus, Creation is taking place under our very noses. And nobody can stay neutral in this spiritual war between bequeathing the good qualities to the future through faith or giving up from despair the task of weeding out the diabolical qualities.[40]

On our Cross of Reality we too take up the task of making and remaking society. It is this "life of the spirit" that constitutes the creation of "our true time, our full membership in history."[41]

Rosenstock-Huessy's attention to what he called "the full-bodied reality of human life" led him to a grammar of social life that was not predicated on the arbitrary distinction and separation of what we have come to call the "spiritual" and the "secular." Rather, his investigations led him to recognize the presence of the spirit in the daily life of human beings and society. The wholeness of life within our multiform reality cries out for a grammar of social life that accords with our lived experience on the Cross of Reality. In this effort to find a social grammar, Rosenstock-Huessy is, in my view, a pioneer of great importance.

Conclusion

At the outset of this essay, I pointed to the emergent necessity of opening the wealth of our respective religious traditions to our common, but multiform, future. Rosenstock-Huessy's social grammar is, in my view, one such pioneering effort in this direction. His work is, as we have seen, deeply indebted to the Christian faith from which he draws his inspiration and many of his basic terms. However, he certainly hoped, in doing that, not to create obstacles to grasping the grammar of social life he was attempting to articulate. Whether he was successful in this must be left to the judgment of others. But it needs also to be pointed out that Rosenstock-Huessy was aware—though this was not central to his own work—of the necessity of incorporating the inspiration of other traditions into the social grammar he was proposing. As he affirmed in *The Christian Future,* written in the late thirties and early forties, "Today Orient and Occident are shaken by a cataclysm which shows the insufficiency of both in isolation. A new penetration of the Cross is required which shall draw together the hearts of men in East and West by showing that each has some essential ingredient of life which the other needs."[42] He then went on to offer a cruciform analysis of "how Orient and Occident both have given us a pair of re-founders or re-directors of human nature—Buddha and Laotse, Abraham and Jesus—who together have created man's full freedom on all fronts of the Cross of Reality."[43] While he acknowledged the sketchy character of what he was attempting, it does point to the openness of his grammar. At the same time, the basically Christian sources of his inspiration and efforts must be acknowledged. At this point we are left more with a question than an answer: can we find our way to a grammar of social life that incorporates what Rosenstock-Huessy called "the oneness and interdependence of all mankind?"[44]

Although this question must remain open, it does seem to me that in the social grammar Rosenstock-Huessy articulates—and that I have here, albeit sketchily, outlined—is an important contribution to a dialogue and conversation that will only intensify in the future. The current and many-layered crises that societies both East and West, North and South, are undergoing make clear that the social boats that normally ferry each generation from birth to death are in danger of being swamped. As we move toward the end of this century we are all called to renewed efforts to rediscover and create anew patterns of life together that can sustain the future of humankind on the Cross of Reality—and that recognize the spiritual dynamics that make for social peace.

NOTES

1. Such views are not only widespread among intellectuals influenced by the Enlightenment view of religion as superstition, or the Marxian view of religion as an opiate, or the Freudian view of religion as illusion, but have also made considerable inroads among Christian theologians, particularly those known as the "secular theologians." Such views were especially popular in North American theological circles in the 1960s, but seem to have waned considerably more recently. For a collection of essays on this theme see *New Theology No. 5,* ed. M. Marty and Dean Peerman (New York: Macmillan, 1968).

2. Here I am thinking of the movements—for example, the Social Gospel movement in North America and the European and British movements for Religious Socialism—that arose in response to the industrial revolution. One aspect of this shift is the renewed interest among Christian thinkers in history. For a collection of readings on this topic see *God, History, and Historians, Modern Christian Views of History,* ed. C. T. McIntire (New York: Oxford University Press, 1977).

3. Since Rosenstock-Huessy is so little known and since his work is so intimately related to his own efforts to find his way through the agonies of our century, it may be helpful to briefly review his life. Eugen Rosenstock-Huessy was born into an emancipated, educated Jewish family in Berlin, Germany, in 1888. From an early age he revealed a fascination with languages and speech and even translated some Egyptian poetry into German for his sister's birthday when he was in his early teens. While still in his teens he entered the Christian church. He was a precocious student and completed doctoral studies at the University of Heidelberg in his early twenties. From 1912 to 1914—until the

outbreak of the war—he taught the history of law at Leipzig. The course of his life, however, was to be profoundly altered by the First World War. These events shook him, as they did many of his contemporaries, to the core. During the war he was an officer in the German army, serving at the front near Verdun. Later he was to call this period of his life a decisive turning point. For Rosenstock-Huessy, the meaning of the war was clear: the great institutions of European civilization—the church, the state, and the university—had failed in their task to preserve the peace. Consequently, after the war he turned down offers to work in these institutions and went instead to work in an automobile manufacturing plant. But already, in his correspondence with Franz Rosenzweig, a close friend who was to become a leading Jewish theologian, he had begun to outline a speech method that was to lie at the heart of his life and work over the next half century.

In 1914, Rosenstock-Huessy married a Swiss, Margrit Huessy, and following a Swiss custom added his wife's surname to his own. When their first and only child, Hans, was on his way, Rosenstock-Huessy returned to university life, becoming a professor of law at the University of Breslau. But his passions and efforts were still very much connected with issues associated with the Academy of Labor he had founded at Frankfurt. After the war and into the twenties he was associated with the Patmos circle—a group that included Franz Rosenzweig, Hans Eberhardt, and Martin Buber among others—and the journal *Die Creature,* which further developed his speech thinking and "grammatical method." When his Roman Catholic friend Joseph Wittig was excommunicated, he collaborated with Wittig in writing *Das Alter der Kirche.* And at the end of the twenties, he organized voluntary work service camps in Silesia that brought workers, farmers, and students together in an effort to recreate social relationships devastated by the war and its effects.

With great prescience, Rosenstock-Huessy anticipated and wrote about the emergence of a Hitler-like figure in German society. Thus, despite the fact that his great work, *Die Europaischen Revolutionen,* had been published in 1931 and did much to establish his reputation—it was later to be rewritten and published in the United States in 1938 as *Out of Revolution, Autobiography of Western Man*—he immediately resigned his post at Breslau when Hitler came to power. He then emigrated to the United States. After three years at Harvard, he joined the faculty at Dartmouth College, where he taught social philosophy until his retirement. While in the United States, Rosenstock-Huessy continued to write, publishing *The Christian Future, Or the Modern Mind Outrun* (1945), a much expanded *Soziologie* (1956–58), *Die Sprache De Menschengeschlechts* (1963), and *Speech and Reality* and *I Am an Impure Thinker* (1970). The last volume, *I Am an Impure Thinker,* well describes Rosenstock-Huessy, since he had no respect for the disciplinary boundaries that characterized intellectual life in the modern university. For Rosenstock-Huessy, it was the life of humankind in time that lay at the center of his attention, it was the sciences fixed on objectivity and space that needed to be challenged so that the temporal character of social life could emerge.

For two studies of Rosenstock-Huessy see Harold Stahmer, *"Speak That I May See Thee!" the Religious Significance of Language* (New York: Macmillan, 1968) and the more popular exposition of his thought in Clinton C. Gardner,

Letters to the Third Millennium (Norwich, Vt.: Argo Books, 1981). See also the unpublished doctoral dissertation by Bruce Boston, "'I Respond Although I Will Be Changed' The Life and Historical Thought of Eugen Rosenstock-Huessy" 1973, Princeton University, Princeton, N.J. The introduction to *The Christian Future, or Modern Mind Outrun* (New York: Harper & Row, 1966), reprint, by Harold Stahmer provides a fuller exposition of the leading events in Rosenstock-Huessy's life and an account of his work. The works of Rosenstock-Huessy cited in my account are available through Argo Books, Norwich, Vermont.

4. See my earlier analysis of *Out of Revolution: Autobiography of Western Man* entitled "Revolution and World Pluralism" in *The Ecumenist* 10, no. 3 (1972).

5. For Rosenstock-Huessy, the objective is but one of four modes of speech necessary to social life. See E. Rosenstock-Huessy, *Speech and Reality* (Norwich, Vt.: Argo, 1970), esp. 45–66. See also the important essay "Farewell to Descartes," in *Out of Revolution: Autobiography of Western Man* (Norwich, Vt.: Argo, 1969) reprint, 740–58.

6. Rosenstock-Huessy, *The Christian Future,* 115–16.

7. Ibid., 173.

8. Ibid., 98.

9. Ibid.

10. Ibid., 108.

11. Rosenstock-Huessy, *Speech and Reality,* 42.

12. Ibid., 9.

13. Ibid., 16.

14. Ibid., 17.

15. Ibid., 18.

16. Ibid., 17–18.

17. Rosenstock-Huessy, *The Christian Future,* 166.

18. Ibid., 169. It is important to stress the antireductionism of his position and at the same time to note that he seeks to give full voice to each of the four fronts of life. The temptation to reduce the four to one seems to be rooted in the tendency to oversimplify, but the real question is whether or not Rosenstock-Huessy's account of the four is adequate.

19. Rosenstock-Huessy, *Speech and Reality,* 54. His point here is that we often experience conflict between these two fronts, not that rhythm between them is impossible. The term rhythm is important here in order to emphasize the dynamic relationship between inner and outer.

20. Rosenstock-Huessy, *The Christian Future,* 168.

21. Ibid., 169.

22. Ibid.

23. Ibid., 170. Note that he speaks of an *obsession* with the outward front and thus his point is a certain distortion in modern civilization rather than a rejection of the dominant scientific methods as such.

24. Ibid., 168.

25. Rosenstock-Huessy, *Speech and Reality*, 52.

26. Ibid., 189. For a fuller discussion of these modes of speech see esp. 45–66 and 155–89.

27. Ibid., 16.

28. Rosenstock-Huessy, *The Christian Future*, 172.

29. Rosenstock-Huessy, *Out of Revolution*, 710.

30. Rosenstock-Huessy, *Speech and Reality*, 21.

31. Ibid., 21.

32. Ibid., 11.

33. Ibid., 15.

34. Ibid., 12.

35. Ibid., 19.

36. Ibid.

37. Rosenstock-Huessy, *The Christian Future*, 92. For a fuller discussion of this central theme see 92–131 and the material in *Speech and Reality*, 11ff.

38. Ibid., 94.

39. Rosenstock-Huessy, *I Am an Impure Thinker* (Norwich, Vt.: Argo, 1970), 69.

40. Ibid., 70–71.

41. Rosenstock-Huessy, *Biography-Biography* (New York: private printing, 1959), 24.

42. Rosenstock-Huessy, *The Christian Future*, 174. Every thinker develops his thought in relation to different sets of questions and issues. Rosenstock-Huessy's work was certainly centered in the Western tradition, and he once remarked that his work was devoted to refuting Nietzsche's claim that "God is dead."

43. Ibid., 174.

44. Ibid., 176.

Contributors

Gustavo Benavides Lecturer, Department of Religion, La Salle College, Philadelphia, Pennsylvania

M. Darrol Bryant Associate Professor of Religion and Culture, Renison College, University of Waterloo, Waterloo, Ontario, Canada

Siddhi Butr-Indr Head of the Department of Philosophy & Religion, Professor of Social Philosophy, Director of Graduate Studies in Philosophy, Chiang Mai University, Chiang Mai, Thailand

Padmasiri de Silva Chairman, Department of Philosophy, University of Peradeniya, Peradeniya, Sri Lanka

Helmut Fritzsche Dean of the Faculty for Theology, Wilhem-Pieck-Universitat, Rostock, East Germany

Rita H. Mataragnon Chairperson and Associate Professor, Department of Psychology, Ateneo de Manila University, Manila, Philippines; Population Council post-doctoral fellow in population psychology at the University of North Carolina, Chapel Hill, North Carolina

Acharya Karma Monlam Representative of His Holiness the Dalai Lama, India

Olusola A. Olukunle Lecturer, Department of Religious Studies, University of Ibadan, Ibadan, Nigeria

T. K. Oommen Centre for the Study of Social Systems, Jawaharlal Nehru University, New Delhi, India

Richard L. Rubenstein Robert O. Lawton Distinguished Professor of Religion, Florida State University, Tallahassee, Florida; President, The Washington Institute for Values in Public Policy, Washington, D.C.

Ninian Smart Professor of Religious Studies, University of California at Santa Barbara and University of Lancaster, United Kingdom

John St. John author and editorial consultant, London, United Kingdom

Geshe Lobsang Tsepal Lecturer, Namgyal Monastic Institution, Representative of His Holiness the Dalai Lama, India

Constantine N. Tsirpanlis Professor, Church History and Patristics, Unification Theological Seminary, Barrytown, New York

Manfred H. Vogel Professor, Department of Religion, Northwestern University, Evanston, Illinois

Index

Index

Hobbes, Thomas, 10
holiness, 139–40, 160
Holy Spirit, 84, 102, 149, 156, 176
Hopkins, Gerard Manley, 26
human rights, 151
Hughes, Thomas, 118
humanism, x, 66, 67, 82, 119, 120, 129, 148, 149
humanistic psychology, 34, 37
humanitarianism, 68–69, 71–72, 81
hyprocrisy, 120

id, 36–37
idealism, 174
ideologies, 67, 69, 70–71, 85, 123–24, 127–29, 144, 165, 167
Idowu, E.B., 93
Ikeda, Daisaku, 164
illusion, 70, 77, 139, 141
impartiality (upekkha), 77–78
Incarnation, 82, 84, 118
India, 23, 99, 100, 170, 174
individualism, 3–5, 24, 109, 142
individuality, 136–37, 138, 151
Indochina, 66
Industrial Revolution, 105, 107, 173
industrialised countries, 68, 95, 152
industrialization, 4, 23, 148
industry, 23, 106–7, 117, 152, 179
injustice, 47, 88, 89, 114, 153, 155
Inkeles, Alex, 19, 24
inspiration, 174, 176, 185
instincts, 33, 37, 38–40
intolerance, 100, 102–3
Iran, 94, 98, 100, 101, 103
Iraq, 101
Islam, 71, 98, 100, 101, 103, 123, 137, 165
Israel, 47, 54, 126–27, 138

Jainism, 23, 136
Jameson, Fredric, 129
Japan, 7, 12–14, 24, 95
Jews, 23, 45, 86, 88, 125
Jewish history, 45–46, 52–53, 126–27
jivanmukta, 138–39
John XXII, Pope, 111
John of the Cross, Saint, 115
Jones, Reverend Jim, 96, 124

Judaism, viii, ix, xii, 46–47, 49–52, 137, 142, 166–67
    social dimension of, 45–46
Judeo-Christian tradition, xi, 10, 105, 165
Jung, Carl, 34
justice, 47, 86, 127, 149, 150–52, 154, 157, 168

Kahl, J.A., 19
Kant, Immanuel, 119
karma, 61–62, 64, 77, 136, 137, 140
Kennedy, Geoffrey Studdert, 116
Khomeini, Ayatollah, 94, 101
Kingsley, Charles, 118
klesha (affliction), 61
Kloppenburg, Bonaventure, 125
Kolakowski, Leszek, 120

La Rochefoucauld, François Duc de, 120
laity, 7, 85, 86
language, 68, 93, 164, 170, 177, 179–81, 183
Lao Tzu, 185
Latin America, 21, 95, 96, 122–30, 177
Laurentius, Justinian, 88
leaders, 70, 71, 81, 138, 180
Leech, Reverend Kenneth, 119
Levin, David, 34, 37
liberalism, 67
liberation, x–xi, 135–39, 142–44, 147–50, 152–55, 157: see also, Freedom
liberation struggles, 87, 102, 127, 142, 144, 147, 151, 157
liberation theology, x, 122–30, 144, 177
liturgy, 84–85
Locke, John, 10
love, 40, 74, 82–83, 85, 86, 88, 89, 115, 128, 153, 157
loving-kindness (metta), 71, 73–75
Luther, Martin, 108, 149, 154
Lutheranism, xi, 150

MacIntyre, Alasdair, 30–31

Index

Index

Index

Index

Tsongkhapa, Acharya, 59, 65
Tsunenori, Yamamoto, 12
Turkey, 21

underdevelopment, 95, 126, 130
unemployment, 8–10, 118, 147
UNESCO, 70
Unification church, 100, 103
Unitarians, 116
United Nations (UNO), 70, 151
United States (USA), 5, 8–9, 103
universalism, 130, 150
urbanization, 6, 20, 24
usury, 106, 107, 109, 110
utilitarianism, 141–42, 143
utopia, 124, 127–28, 154–55

Vedanta, 136–37
violence, 70, 72, 73, 78
Visnu, 124

war, 70, 72–73, 78, 101, 147, 148, 149, 153, 179
    nuclear, 9, 69, 95, 119, 158
    WWI, 101, 153, 175
    WWII, 101, 113, 153
wealth, 10, 68, 72, 86, 87, 89, 96, 105, 106, 128, 147, 150
Weber, Max, 7, 23
Welfare State, 113
Western civilization, vii, ix, 4, 14, 149
    attitudes of, 23, 25, 34–35, 66, 147, 173
    colonialism, 67, 97, 99–101
    religion of, 38, 160–63, 166–69, 185
Weston, Bishop Frank, 114
wisdom, 58–60, 62, 65
Wittgenstein, Ludwig, 181
women, 21–22, 97
World Council of Churches, 162, 168
worship, 83, 99, 120, 141, 142, 144
Wycliffe, John, 106, 116

Yoga, 136, 141, 144
Yoruba religion, 93

Zealots, 127, 157